Dr. Cureton, 68, leading participants during the midday break at the Symposium held in his honor on April 25-26, 1969.

EXERCISE AND FITNESS – 1969

American ✓

Proceedings

of a

Symposium

honoring Dr. Thomas Kirk Cureton, Jr., "The Grand Old Man of Fitness," upon his retirement from the College of Physical Education, University of Illinois, Champaign-Urbana Campus, April 25-26, 1969.

Sponsored by
Department of Physical Education for Men
With the cooperation of
The Athletic Institute,
University of Illinois Foundation, and the
Division of University Extension

Edited by

B. DON FRANKS

Library of Congress

Catalog Card Number 75-109497

$6.00 per copy

The Athletic Institute   SBN 87670-804-1   Chicago, Ill.

FOREWORD

It has been an honor for the Department of Physical Education for Men to sponsor this Symposium on Physical Fitness honoring Professor Thomas K. Cureton, Jr. The University of Illinois firmly believes that its major functions encompass the three areas of teaching, research, and service. Looking back on Professor Cureton's twenty-eight years at the University of Illinois, and his forty-five years in the profession, there can be no doubt as to the significant contributions which he has made in each of these three areas considered to be a function of the University. The research papers which were presented at this Symposium mark a fitting tribute to Professor Cureton. The scientific value of these papers truly reflects the quality of teaching, research, and service that Professor Cureton has instilled in his former students. The Department of Physical Education for Men would like to acknowledge its appreciation to the participants in this Symposium. The research papers presented by the former students of Professor Cureton will contribute to the ever-growing body of knowledge in this field of study. We also extend our best wishes to Professor Cureton for continued success and good health in his retirement. We are confident that he will not be any less active, but will merely direct his efforts in new directions.

ROLLIN G. WRIGHT, Head
Department of Physical Education for Men

It has been a privilege for me during the past eight years to have been associated in various ways with Dr. Cureton and the physical fitness laboratory. Seldom do you find a man with such total dedication to a cause.

The College of Physical Education is grateful for the work he has done here in building the reputation of our research laboratory. Upon his retirement, we salute him as a dedicated exponent and world authority on fitness among humans.

KING J. McCRISTAL, Dean
College of Physical Education

The Athletic Institute deems it a privilege to participate in the symposium to honor Dr. Thomas K. Cureton, Jr. Dr. Cureton has been a driving force in the "fitness" movement in our country. Through his numerous research studies, his devoted graduate students, his own example, Dr. Cureton has done much to "spread the gospel" of fitness.

This symposium marks the retirement of Dr. Cureton from his academic career at the University of Illinois. However, Tom Cureton will never really be retired. His message will continue to work toward a truly "fit America."

The Athletic Institute thanks Dr. Thomas K. Cureton, Jr. for his numerous contributions to physical education. It was a pleasure to contribute our assistance in honoring a great leader.

FRANK B. JONES, President
The Athletic Institute

v

PREFACE

It seems proper to pay tribute to the immense contribution that T. K. Cureton has made to exercise science and related areas at the time of his "retirement" from the University of Illinois. It does not seem appropriate to speak of an "end of an era" because all who know him realize that this is just a brief pause in the *midst* of his career. Friends need not sigh in regret (nor opponents in relief) because this man, his ideas, his storehouse of knowledge, his vigorous debating style and his prolific writing remain with us. My prediction is: "you ain't seen nothin' yet."

B. DON FRANKS

Champaign

ACKNOWLEDGMENT

It would have been impossible to have had the Symposium in honor of Dr. Cureton without assistance from many sources, including:

1. The Graduate Department of Physical Education and Department of Physical Education for Men, under Dr. Earle Zeigler (1967-68) and Dr. Rollin Wright (1968-69) and their staff — Mrs. Naomi Vonesh, Mr. Tom Trimble, Mrs. Jane Powell, Mrs. Loralee LeBoeuf, Mrs. Dale Heigold, and Mrs. Doreene Knight — for unending support in many forms.

2. The College of Physical Education, under Dean McCristal who added just the right touch at the Banquet, for support and helpful suggestions.

3. The Physical Fitness Research Laboratory Staff — Mrs. Betty Frey, Mr. Chris Milesis, Mr. Maurice Jetté, Mr. Sandy Molnar, Miss Lori Schutt, Mrs. Mary Lee Jewett, Mrs. Bea Storey, and Miss Sue Bender — who helped in many ways.

4. Dr. Bradley Rothermel who assisted in gathering much of the necessary background information, and Dr. R. H. Pohndorf who coordinated the retirement dinner and made many helpful suggestions.

5. Dr. Marianna Trekell and Miss Sharon Plowman who taped the sessions.

6. The University of Illinois Foundation and its Executive Director, Mr. J. W. Skehen, who supported the Symposium with a grant.

7. The Athletic Institute, Dr. Frank Jones, President; and Cy Yttri, Publications Director, for undertaking the publication of these proceedings.

8. The Extension Division, especially Mr. Norm Johnson and Mrs. Carol Johnson, who handled the administrative details expertly helping us avoid many potential mistakes.

9. Finally, the men who presented the research papers and prepared them for publication, and the men and women who participated in various parts of the Symposium.

CONTENTS

viii

Exercise Programs in Preventive Medicine

April 24, 1969

(This meeting was called by Professor Cureton at the request of Dr. Figarola as consultation to discuss procedures of possible interest to the Marshall Space Center regarding protection of their administrative and scientific personnel from heart disease and other chronic ailments, to the extent that the exercise and "dynamic fitness" programs might apply. Professor Cureton had previously consulted at Huntsville, and offered a "positive health" program to the personnel in administration and research at the request of Dr. Wehrner von Braun. It was a follow-up meeting with the Chief of Preventive Medicine, Dr. Figarola and Dr. Robert Phillips, administrator. ed.)

PRESIDING:

Thomas K. Cureton, Jr., Ph.D., Director, University of Illinois Physical Fitness Research Laboratory

PARTICIPANTS:

Lloyd Arnold, National Secretary, Physical Education Division, Y.M.C.A., U.S.A.

Kirk Cureton, B.S., entering University of Illinois Medical School, Fall, 1969.

Tulio R. Figarola, M.D., Chief, Preventive Medicine, SysteMed Corporation, Medical Center, Marshall Space Flight Center, Huntsville, Ala.

B. Don Franks, Ph.D., Supervisor, University of Illinois Physical Fitness Research Laboratory

John Haberern, Editor, *Fitness for Living*.

William Haskell, Ph.D., Director of Program Development, President's Council on Physical Fitness and Sports

Maurice Jette, Assistant Professor, Department of Kinanthropology, University of Ottawa, Ottawa, Ontario, Canada

Fred A. Kummerow, Ph.D., Biochemist, Director, Burnside Research Laboratory, University of Illinois

Chris Milesis, Assistant Supervisor, University of Illinois Physical Fitness Research Laboratory

Curtis Mitchell, Free-lance writer

Sandor Molnar, Research Assistant, University of Illinois Physical Fitness Research Laboratory

Bob Payne, post coronary who participated in Cureton's fitness program

Dr. Robert Phillips, Administrator, Marshall Space Flight Center, Huntsville, Ala.

Richard H. Pohndorf, Ph.D., Director, Measurement and Evaluation Laboratory, University of Illinois

Michael J. Pollock, Ph.D., Director, Physical Fitness Research Laboratory, Wake Forest University, North Carolina

John W. Pollard, M.D., Cardiologist, Carle Clinic, Urbana, Illinois
Bradley L. Rothermel, Ph.D., Associate Professor, Physical Education, University of Illinois, Chicago Circle
Ben T. Williams, M.D., Pathologist, Mercy Hospital; Consultant to the University of Illinois Physical Fitness Research Laboratory

CURETON.

Most of the fitness work done during the last 25 years in the University of Illinois Adult Fitness Program and Physical Fitness Research Laboratory has been to increase the dynamic health of unfit (but non-pathological) middle-aged adults. An occasional "post-coronary" or other debilitated subject was in the program in cooperation with the work of local medical doctors.

All potential participants in the Adult Fitness Program are interviewed by the Physical Fitness Research Laboratory Director, given relevant material to read concerning the safety precautions to be included in fitness programs, have medical approval for participation and take a series of physical fitness tests before being admitted to the program.

All men are encouraged to work by themselves, without competing with others nor being led by enthusiastic young instructors, and to begin very gradually — to walk before they run. The lab. staff is available on the running areas for consultation during this time. After several months of progressively increasing time and amount of work done per work-out, the person may become a part of a training group or particular research study. Consultations are available by request at any time.

Although all persons are cautioned to begin at low levels and work up, persons who have had some type of cardiovascular disease are taken only after special request of their physician if there is staff available for individual treatment.

(See bibliography following "What I Have Learned" for more information on specific training programs, safety precautions, results of such training, etc.)

FIGAROLA.

We are planning a fitness program for some of our employees, many of whom have had some kind of cardiovascular disease; specifically, I have the following questions for patients who have had: (1) recent myocardial infarction; (2) evidence of coronary artery disease or angina pectoris; (3) arterial hypertension; (4) occasional arrhythmias such as supraventricular fibrillation; and (5) rheumatic heart and valvular involvement that do not present any symptoms of coronary artery disease or congestive failure:

1. When should a physical fitness program begin?
2. How much exercise to begin with?
3. What increments and when?
4. What guidelines should be used to evaluate their progress, increase or decrease the exercise, or stop a session on each case?

MITCHELL.

One of the most amazing things about Cureton's fitness program is that, although he has dealt with thousands of persons, there have been no known cardiac accidents caused by the program. From a nonscientific viewpoint, I have observed that his program differs from other fitness programs in the following respects: (1) deep breathing throughout the work-out; (2) long, gradual warm-up (15-20 minutes); and (3) longer duration of total work-out (45-60 minutes daily). I can't cite any evidence that these things *caused* the success of his programs; however, they do differentiate his fitness programs from many others.

HASKELL.

I would add a fourth aspect of Cureton's fitness program; namely, a tapering-off period at the end of the work-out. This gradual warm-down is an important aspect of the work-out and is sometimes ignored by people in fitness programs. The "taper-down" is strongly advocated in the Illinois program.

FRANKS.

Not only should the tapering-off be included in the work-out, but also in the physical stress tests that are used to evaluate the persons. Thus, after typically working at increasing work-loads until some predetermined criterion, the subject should taper-off at a reduced load before sitting down for the post-exercise observations, and should walk a bit after the observations are over.

MOLNAR.

Shkhvatsabaya reported a secondary shortening of the left ventricular ejection period after the termination of strenuous work, which was attributed to reduced venous return. The same has been found here by Wiley, Richter and myself. Wiley also found a secondary shortening after sub-maximal work in untrained men which was eliminated after five months of training. This research simply emphasizes the importance of the tapering-off period.

POHNDORF.

Yes, it is important to warm-down just as it is to warm-up. The type and purpose of the conditioning is another aspect to be considered.

PAYNE.

After discussing his personal history, he felt that it was helpful in the fitness program to have a qualified leader who would encourage him to slow down when trying to do too much in the beginning, and encourage him to do more as he was able to adapt to the work.

HASKELL.

In response to question number four raised by Dr. Figarola, although certain objective standards can be established and may be the basis for the program, increases, decreases, etc., there is no substitute for qualified leaders

3

who can give the men individual attention in their training. The physical education men usually work with the subjects.

POLLARD.

In responding to Dr. Figarola's questions in general, the person begins to move about very soon and his subjective feeling is the best guide as to how much and what increments. Concerning the different types of cases: (1) myocardial infarction, after six months or so of easy exercise in the home (with adjustment to increased activity), a very cautious, light fitness program can be started; (2) arterial hypertension, unless very extreme, the usual safeguards discussed here are sufficient; (3) angina pectoris, make sure that the person stops with any pain or discomfort (just before the pain is the best place to stop); and, (4) valvular involvement will probably cause some future trouble and my opinion is that this person should live moderately and not engage in a vigorous fitness program which might bring the trouble sooner. Some adapt well to exercise and some do not.

KUMMEROW.

The chemical aspects of arteriosclerosis were discussed. The main benefit of exercise in this respect seemed to be that it burns up certain foodstuffs before they can be changed into cholesterol.

CURETON.

The discussion has clarified many points. Supervised exercise takes on a greater and greater role, and needs to be studied carefully. The more important work is undoubtedly PREVENTIVE, to get at it before there is an infarct or blood clot. The habitual cardiovascular status is of great importance and needs to be cultivated from youth. Not enough emphasis has been put on this. We have great faith that those who ultimately develop CHD are those who allow the cardiovascular system to deteriorate prematurely, mainly through neglect of sufficient endurance exercise. After there is a CHD "depressed ST segment" it is almost too late. More attention should be paid to cardiovascular status all along before there is trouble. Larger numbers of adult men and women should be gotten into regular progressive fitness work. It takes time and supervision, and it is all treated too casually.

FIGAROLA.

Thank you.

Thomas Kirk Cureton, Jr.

CITATION FROM THE DEPARTMENT OF PHYSICAL EDUCATION FOR MEN

Saturday, April 26, 1969, 6:00 p.m., Retirement Dinner, Ramada Inn, Champaign, Illinois.

Announcement of establishment of Thomas Kirk Cureton Research Fund by Professor Richard H. Pohndorf.

CITATION FROM UNIVERSITY OF ILLINOIS

Saturday, April 26, 1969, 6:00 p.m., Retirement Dinner, Ramada Inn, Champaign, Illinois.

Presented by J. W. Peltason, Chancellor for Urbana-Champaign Campus. Citation reads:

To Thomas K. Cureton, Jr.

The Board of Trustees of the University of Illinois desires to record and formally express to you on the occasion of your retirement its appreciation of your many years of loyal and devoted service to the University. In giving you this token of its appreciation and esteem, the Board of Trustees extends to you its best wishes for many years of good health and happiness.

Signed:

The Board of Trustees of the University of Illinois
Earl Hughes
Secretary of the Board
David D. Henry
President of the University

CITATION FROM THE STATE OF ILLINOIS

Saturday, April 26, 1969, 6:00 p.m., Retirement Dinner, Ramada Inn, Champaign, Illinois.

Presented on behalf of the Governor by William Masica, Health and Fitness Director, Springfield, Illinois YMCA.

Citation reads:

STATE OF ILLINOIS
April 26, 1969

The State of Illinois recognizes Thomas K. Cureton, Jr., Ph.D., for his outstanding humanitarian service in the field of better health and fitness.

Signed:

Governor
Richard Ogilvie
Superintendent of Public Instruction
Ray Page

CITATION FROM THE PRESIDENT'S COUNCIL ON PHYSICAL FITNESS AND SPORTS

Saturday, April 26, 1969, 6:00 p.m., Retirement Dinner, Ramada Inn, Champaign, Illinois.

Presented by William Haskell, Director of Program Development, Washington, D.C.

CITATION FROM THE NATIONAL YMCA

Saturday, April 26, 1969, 6:00 p.m., Retirement Dinner, Ramada Inn, Champaign, Illinois.

Presented by Lloyd Arnold, National Physical Education Director for YMCA.

Plaque reads:

For Distinguished Service in YMCA Aquatics.

I have the privilege tonight to sit at this head table to represent the YMCA and the many friends that Dr. Cureton has in the YMCA.

In 1943 the YMCA Physical Directors Society of North America awarded the Robert-Gulick award to Dr. Cureton. This is the highest award this professional society can give to a member of the physical education profession.

Dr. Cureton joined the YMCA at the age of nine in Jacksonville. In addition, he was a member at Atlanta, Ga. and the Student Ass'n. at Yale. He was a member of the Springfield College Faculty from 1929 to 1941 where he did much to elevate standards of training and research in YMCA Physical Education.

The attendance of YMCA Physical Directors and laymen at this symposium gives ample evidence of the impact that Dr. Cureton has had on YMCA physical fitness programs. His workshops, fitness testing, counseling and guidance have become synonymous with physical fitness in most YMCA's across the country. His summer workshops have been the advanced training grounds for many "Y" physical directors.

Because this very special contribution to YMCA physical education is so much in evidence here tonight I would like to switch the theme and talk with you about another major area of programming where he demonstrated creative leadership for the YMCA.

In 1933 he published his first book on swimming. In 1937 he served as chairman of the First National YMCA Aquatic Conference at George Williams College in Chicago. He was also appointed chairman of the National YMCA Aquatic Committee and editor-in-chief of all materials developed in the above conference.

From 1938 to 1943 he edited:

1. *The New Aquatic Program*
2. *The YMCA Aquatic Tests*
3. *The YMCA Life Saving Syllabus and Tests*
4. *The Standards for Testing*

and including charts, worksheets, test-forms, and master charts and in addition many special articles on YMCA aquatic programs.

Since 1938 he served as Chairman of the National YMCA Aquatic Committee and as a member of the Physical Education Committee of the National Council of YMCA's.

Among other responsibilities he served as a member of the committee on the Association Profession, Chairman of the professional training committee for YMCA Physical Education. He served on swimming school faculties at Blue Ridge, Estes Park, and College Camp, and conducted hundreds of Aquatic Institutes in local YMCA's.

Born out of the ideas of a hundred creative minds in attendance at the first National YMCA Conference at Lake Geneva some 37 years ago, the National YMCA Aquatic Program has advanced through the past several decades to a position of unparalleled depth and comprehensiveness. Since the new aquatic materials began rolling from New York's Association Press in 1938, the name of T. K. Cureton, Jr., has soared to a position synonymous with Aquatic leadership at its finest. As Chairman of the National YMCA Aquatic Committee, "T.K.'s" moniker has appeared on millions of awards, certificates and materials; his ideas and research have been translated into the enduring, National Aquatic Program; his trumpet-like voice has spoken with unmistakable authority and conviction, while his prolific capacity for the written word has resulted in countless volumes and studies related to all aspects of swimming and diving. It was good for us that this dynamic personality has given to the "Y" his time, inventiveness and energy. We have all claimed him with a sense of pride, for in communities across the country our peers in allied organizations easily identify with this flamboyant and renowned personality, a physical educator of professional excellence.

Very recently the National YMCA Operating Council for Aquatics has developed and designed an award to be presented to selected individuals who have made outstanding contributions to the YMCA Aquatic Program over a long period of time.

It gives me a great deal of pleasure to announce that this award will be given for the first time tonight to the number one man in YMCA Aquatics, Dr. T. K. Cureton, Jr.

CITATION FROM AMERICAN DENTAL ASSOCIATION

Saturday, April 26, 1969, 6:00 p.m., Retirement Dinner, Ramada Inn, Champaign, Illinois.

Presented by Dr. F. J. O'Brian, Brockton, Massachusetts.

Citation reads:

Certificate of Recognition
The American Dental Association Awards to
Dr. Thomas Kirk Cureton, Jr.

This certificate of recognition for his extraordinary contribution to the dental community in the area of personal health maintenance — also for a significant contribution to better public understanding and appreciation of dental health.

Signed:

Hubert A. McGuirl, D.D.S.
President
Harold Hillenbrand, D.D.S.
Executive Secretary

CITATION FROM THE GEORGIA COUNCIL ON PHYSICAL FITNESS

Saturday, April 26, 1969, 6:00 p.m., Retirement Dinner, Ramada Inn, Champaign, Illinois.

Presented by Fred Allman, President of the American College of Sports Medicine.

Citation reads:

Award of Honor presented to Thomas K. Cureton, Ph.D. in recognition of his outstanding contribution in leadership, guidance, and promotion of physical fitness throughout the world.

Signed:

Governor's Council of Physical Fitness
State of Georgia
May 1, 1969

HONOR AWARD — AMERICAN COLLEGE OF SPORTS MEDICINE

Announced at dinner, awarded at Annual Meeting of the American College of Sports Medicine.

Citation reads:

American College of Sports Medicine Honor Award to Thomas K. Cureton, Ph.D.

A Charter Member of the American College of Sports Medicine, a prolific writer, an outstanding teacher and respected scientist, through interaction with multi-disciplines advocated that everyone's physical image could be improved by health and fitness. His sincerity, dedication, energy and zest for living will long be remembered.

Signed:

Fred L. Allman, Jr., M.D.
President
Donald E. Herrmann
Executive Secretary

INTRODUCTION FOR DR. CURETON

May I say how pleased I am to be introducing Dr. Cureton this evening to speak on the subject, "What I Have Learned." How does one introduce someone like this man? Obviously, the answer must be *"Briefly."* Our plan this evening is that Dr. Cureton will speak about 45 minutes. At that time all sorts of gongs and sirens will go off. Then we invite you to take part for a question-answer-discussion session.

Seeing so many of you here this evening is really a wonderful sight. I know that I speak for Professor Rollin Wright, our Department Head, and for Dean King McCristal, of our College, when I offer you a most sincere welcome. Think for just a moment how many others in various places on this continent and around the world are with us in spirit this weekend. For example, I have in my hand a greeting from Nick Strydom in South Africa, where he is Chief of the Applied Physiology Division in the Human Sciences Laboratory of the Chamber of Mines. He says, "How I wish I could be there to see all of my old colleagues once again."

Without going into detail, I plan to merely mention some words or concepts — and allow you to make the associations in your own mind. Yale; competitive swimming; aquatics; track; Springfield; Columbia Teachers College; books and then more books; articles and more articles; monographs and more monographs; Y.M.C.A.; testing of champion athletes; wartime fitness and aquatics; Staley; Illinois; master's theses; doctoral theses; Physical Fitness Research Laboratory; fitness clinics; President's Council; awards, more awards, and then still more awards; energy and talent pouring out in all directions; no end in sight.

What has this man learned? Ever so much more than he'll be able to tell us in 45 minutes tonight. From very close observation of him over a period of years quite recently, I would like to tell you five things that I think he has learned — but which he won't be able to say to you this evening:

1. That if you are willing to work twice as hard as the next fellow, you are going to get ahead in this world.

2. That if it weren't for administrators like McCristal, Wright, and Zeigler, he would have been able to get still more important work accomplished — and all the time we thought we were helping. . . .

3. That when people are concerned about ideas and putting them into practice for the welfare of other people in this world, they haven't much time to be concerned about pettiness, gossip, and other such trivia that can be very time-consuming.

4. That when students have a goal, and when they are truly willing to work and sacrifice to achieve their purpose, in the final analysis the outcomes are quite surprising and rewarding to the professor and student alike.

5. And that people really do — in the final analysis — appreciate a man's efforts when he is completely and absolutely dedicated to his work and those beliefs for which he stands.

Dr. Roy Moore's little poem is quite appropriate.

"John Donne tolled the bells,
Alfred Lord Tennyson crossed the bar,
Douglas MacArthur faded away,
But Dr. Cureton is still running by those tombstones."

Ladies and Gentlemen: It has been said that Dr. McCloy was Physical Education's Man of the First Half of the Twentieth Century. Tonight we are very proud to be able to present to you Physical Education's Man of the Second Third of This Same Century — Professor Thomas Kirk Cureton, Jr. He resides in Urbana, Illinois, but he belongs to the world.

                                        EARLE F. ZEIGLER
                                        April 25, 1969

"I Have Learned That . . ."*

by Thomas K. Cureton, Jr.

A. After 28 years at Illinois, and 45 years in the field of Health, Physical Education and Recreation, I have a few impressions which I have been asked to pass on for whatever they are worth. So, I have even written them down so that they might not disappear as the wind.

1. I am impressed with the worth of *physical activity* (1) as a great medium among children to learn many skills; (2) as a means of building stamina and fitness of various kinds, and for media of hard play and competition among young men and young women; and very much as a means of maintaining dynamic health and vigor after 25 years of age, when the normal tendency is to retire from most of it in favor of sedentary pursuits and the life of indulgence. This area is as interesting to me as it ever was on all of these levels, even though I confess to a fascination with new discoveries and clarifications in the 25-65 year age span of life, related to what we call the physical fitness of the middle-aged adult.

2. I have learned that sport has many specifics, and likewise, physical fitness and dynamic health also have many specifics in the way of exercises for various parts of the body, and for the major organic systems, the several kinds of endurance, the principal components of motor ability, the many types of physical work and efficiencies, the many tests and multitudinous interpretations that are all around us as we work in this field. We draw data and methods from many fields and we have much data and some methods which are our own — and the psychological aspects, the mechanical and kinesiological aspects, the physiological aspects, the sociological aspects, historical and administrative aspects are all needed. I have tried to be a scientist in my work but I have doubled too as a practitioner, never losing sight of the practical value of physical activity.

I have learned after excursions into physiology and psychology, into sports-medicine and anthropology, into educational administration and philosophy, ethnology and widespread travel and observation — that we have our own field to study, our own subjects, and we must deal with them in our own way — still being scientific (without M.D. degrees).

3. It has been possible to train Ph.D.'s in our own area who have carried the knowledge and methods of exercise and sports into various areas (and the list includes a few who earned only the M.S. with us):
Physical Fitness — Haskell with the President's Council, Bernauer, Bosco and others with NASA, Kasch, Sherman
Corrective Therapy — Bosco, Rasch, Van Huss, Kasch, Engerbretson

---

*Dr. Cureton's request that his paper not be edited was honored.

Applied Physiology — Michael, Rochelle, Royce, Morehouse, Heusner, Sterling, Hodgson, Golding, Liverman, D. K. Matthews, Landry, Ed Sloninger, H. Campney, D. Cundiff, Knowlton, Tipton, Weber, Banister, Mastropaolo, Strydom

Applied Psychology — Hubbard, McAdam, Popejoy, Kruzic, Espenschade, Franks, Gutin, Schmidt, Noble, Hayden, Meeland, Stoedefalk, Pollock

Directors of Educational Research in H.P.E. and R. — Massey, Doroschuk, J. Joseph, Elder, S. Brown, Eyler, G. Moore

Public Health — Montoye, Skinner, Haskell

State Education Supervisors — George Grover (N.Y.)

Heads (or Chairmen) of Depts. — Hunsicker, Popejoy, Orban, DuToit, Powell, A. O. Warner, Fordham, Kireilis, A. Seidler, Shea, Murphy, Roby, MacLeay

Applied Statistics — Hubbard, Franks, Adams, Rothermel, Montoye

Applied Biochemistry and Nutrition — Metivier, Riendieu, Gualtiere

Mechanics and Kinesiology — Ganslen, Pohndorf, Counsilman, Jay Bender, Baley, Wickens

Atmospheric Environment — Bynum

Exercise in Medicine — Barry, Skinner, Oscai, Herron, Bohm, Yuhasz, Tipton

A good many laboratories of applied exercise science are under these men. These and others have vied with those who have taken their degrees in other fields, such as:

> Psychology (Latham, Meeland)
> Ed. Research (Huffman, DeVries)
> Physiology (Robinson, Tipton, Dill, Karpovich, Buskirk, Knutgen)
> Medicine (Balke, Naughton, Boyer, Allman)
> Educ. Administration (A. C. Moore, Dave Field, Ed Shea, Edmund Shay, D. Warner)

A few have combined athletic work with their academic duties, such as: Counsilman, Meadowes, Dempsey, Karr, Kroll, Reuter, Kristufek.

Nearly all of these combine scientific work in exercise and sports with their work in physical education, an ideal which Dr. S. C. Staley has put forth for a good many years. The emphasis we have put on the scientific aspects of exercise and sports would not have been possible without the insight and interest of men like Seward Staley, Coleman Griffith, Dean Carmichael, and former President Stoddard, who helped us to get this upper-level training under way.

4. I know too that the scientific training given as a background has put into the leadership such coaches and teachers of swimming as Dr. James Counsilman, Charles Silvia, Bill Heusner, Tom Krizan, Dr. John Y. Squires, the memorable and original Fred Lanoue (inventor of drownproofing), Charles Kristufek, T. Yanagita (Japan head trainer), Bartolome'(Philippines), Carlisle (Australia), Van Rossen.

5. Although we have worked constantly at this problem — how to make the unfit college man take interest and develop his fitness — it is only par-

tially solved. The workbooks we wrote (for P.E.M. 60) probably were not as important as dynamic personal leadership of really interested instructors. Each student needs both a practical and a scientific education in this area of "Dynamic Health for the Entire Life." Some of us will actually lead and demonstrate this work, some will teach "Scientific Foundations of Physical Fitness" and "Scientific Analysis of Physical Education Activities" — and some will become Public Health Statistics workers, or Lecture-Demonstrator Salesmen — but most of us will teach graduate students and foster their life-time interest in applied physiological, psychological and anthropological aspects of this work — THE SCIENCE OF EXERCISE AND SPORTS. More and more the long-range health aspect has come into the picture but always modified by the need to understand the exercises at hand. I have learned that the work with adults is very important, that it is inadequately provided for in the present collegiate set-up, nor is it properly led and supervised in the community at large. Adults need to be educated to a higher level of understanding about physical activity and health, the many training programs, and need day-to-day guidance, especially in the begin-ning stages. The use of tests of physical fitness opens the way for such guid-ance but in society it is mainly DISEASE that captures the interest and the money, not progressive physical activity for DYNAMIC HEALTH.

6. I have learned that Physical Fitness does not stand alone. We divide ourselves into two camps: (1) Fitness of Sports Participation and (2) the larger area, Fitness for Life. In discussing the relative merits of these two with Prof. Paul Weiss, related to the AAAS Symposium in Dallas, 1968, "Sports and Its Participants," Dr. Weiss also came around to see the great meaning of the "Fitness for Life" part of this, and agreed that my part should emphasize the latter. In the end, he preferred this "Fitness for Life" part over the sports aspect for publication, although he also wanted some of the "sports fitness." This is very complicated and is related to each and every sport very specifically. Nevertheless, we should associate ourselves with sport, to the extent that it is possible, and foster those studies in which we can engage with the cooperation with coaches, or by using former coaches. In dealing with editors of *Life* and *Time,* and of *Britannica Encyclopedia,* they have shown a preference for the long-range view of fitness for life, rather than fitness for any one sport. But we must also work on "fitness for swimming," "fitness for gymnastics," "fitness for basketball," "fitness for track, etc.," "fitness for baseball," "fitness for soccer" — so Pohndorf, Fardy, Ganslen, Rothermel, Counsilman, Silvia, Dempsey, Meadows and others who have carried on the steady work on scientific principles in this area of appli-cation should be applauded.

7. WHAT IS WANTED OF US BY THE PUBLIC? — They want personable, smart coaches of high-grade character — but they want also physi-cal educators who can lead the public and their children to higher levels of fitness, who can tell and show the methods, and PRACTICE WHAT THEY PREACH. In one case, it has been impressive to them to see a man over

65 leading high school youth, and putting on strenuous demonstrations. It is what they all want — to be able to keep up physical ability, vigor, and to be relatively free from chronic ailment and debility. It is a horror for everyone to see themselves as helpless old people, racing toward financial ruin before 65, to be wards of the government in Medicare.

One job is to teach and inspire the students, but for those of us who can, some time must be devoted to inspiring and educating the public — the older and more informed we are, the better. Teach, research and SERV-ICE, is the way it is put at the University of Illinois. In the past 10 years I have learned that work with the adult public is important.

The written materials carry great power. We have spread our written materials across the land: papers, books, sheets and pamphlets, reaching hundreds of thousands. We have sold our thesis abstracts to hundreds of libraries and they are in most libraries and in the Library of Congress. Hundreds of Physical Fitness announcements have been broadcast in the cities, and newspaper articles by the thousands have appeared; the radios have broadcast our messages and there have been many TV appearances. The CBS has featured "Questions and Answers" for $2\frac{1}{2}$ hours at a time — following a positive statement — then responding to questions — so have Westinghouse TV and CBS, these in Boston, Chicago, Pittsburgh and several other cities. A Physical Fitness Clinic means usually a radio and a TV appearance, a press conference, a side-talk before a service club, meeting the ministers and public health and school officials, and some doctors and dentists in every city.

To win a Billy Graham, a Senator Proxmire, a Governor Kerner, a President Kennedy, a Vice-President Humphrey — and the like people of importance — will do us no harm. I was honored to stand in the Rose Garden and be complimented by President Johnson, as was Paul Hunsicker in 1965 in Washington. In 40 countries of the world I have made speeches, put on demonstrations, and met important people — talking about physical fitness, training methods in athletics and dynamic health. Perhaps I have learned something from all of these and have given a lot of time and energy to it.

8.   THE POWER OF LEADERSHIP IN PHYSICAL FITNESS — The public is hungry for available leadership in physical fitness. Effective speaking, visual presentations and good practical demonstrations are powerful means of educating the public. Part of my role has been to go to communities on week-ends to represent the work we are doing in Health, Physical Education and Recreation. There are several aspects of this which seem to have taken very well: (1) Demonstrations of Continuous Rhythmical Activity; (2) Demonstrations of the 18-Item Motor Test; (3) Demonstrations of the 8-Station Battery, 30 Adults Going Through in a Morning; (4) Land Drills and Water-Fitness Drills in the Pool; (5) Slides Showing the Evidence of Physiological Deterioration; (6) Slides Showing the Improvements Produced by Various Programs; (7) Slides Showing the Testing of a Sophisticated

Nature Going on in Our Laboratory of Physical Fitness; (9) Evidence of Improvement of Fitness in the Cardiovascular-Respiratory System; (10) Variations of Interval Training, Circuit Training, Steeplechases and Obstacle Courses. Much consultation work has been done — and much more is needed.

In my experience many important people have come into these demonstrations and lectures in PTA's, Y.M.C.A.'s, Churches, Schools, Athletic Clubs, Military Bases, Medical Schools, Dental Schools, Dental Clinics, Assemblies in the Name of the President's Council, Conventions of School Superintendents, State Legislatures, Conventions of Business Men (at one time the Commissioner of Public Health in Chicago, Dr. Sam Andelman, convened 300 of the very top business men at the Blackstone Hotel to listen to my speech and to see my slides; again, 1800 insurance men listened at the Hilton Hotel in Boston, members of the Million Dollar Round-Table; in Minneapolis 400 insurance agents were taught to "sell" physical fitness along with insurance; in Atlanta 1200 dentists listened and saw my demonstrations, as they have in New York, Chicago, San Francisco, Cincinnati, Dayton, Minneapolis, Toronto, Atlanta, London, Winnipeg, Vancouver, Montreal, Cleveland, Boston, Fort Worth, Dallas, Phoenix, Nashville, Birmingham, Seattle, Jacksonville, San Diego, Tucson, Houston, Knoxville, Miami, and in many other cities!

There is power in having at hand the facts about physical fitness in its role for preventing physiological aging. In the Cambridge Y.M.C.A. sat 700 at one dinner to listen and watch a demonstration. There is power in good visual materials. There is power in an articulate and colorful presentation using human cases. We have learned the value of working harder at this end of our job.

9. DEDICATION — Physical Education is avowedly dedicated to the education and training of youth, in schools, on playgrounds and in camps — but we must present our unique case for "Physical Fitness and Dynamic Health" before group after group in the public. This means we must have many experts among us to do this right. The need for wider biological and public health training is apparent.

The men of our field who have reached eminence, of my personal acquaintance, are Robert J. H. Kiphuth, Alonzo Stagg, William G. Anderson, James Huff McCurdy, George B. Affleck, Seward C. Staley, Dr. J. F. Williams, Dr. R. Tait McKenzie, all but two have been my own teachers, have all carried the message of "making man better, mentally and physically." This idea led to pioneering fitness efforts in this country, so sorely needed.

There are certain unique aspects about physical education: (a) aims to improve people, mentally and physically and spiritually; (b) toughens the physical and mental fibre; (c) teaches a balanced program of living — hard work alternated with enough rest and relaxation, with many contacts and relations with people; (d) works to improve the handicapped; (e) struggles to improve health and safety; (f) develops continuously the science of exercise and its applications; (g) correlatively works with doctors, psychologists, therapists and city officials to bring about effective programs and improvements in the mental and physical state of people. But our people need to know physical activity in and out. Increasingly hospitals and public health centers are drafting people from our field to work with the physical activity of a directed, graduated kind, under supervision.

I have learned that as one gets older, more and more people are known, especially if one comes into any limelight of national events; then it gets harder and harder to keep up with the mail, the incessant stream of visitors, the outside calls for lectures, writings, attendance at meetings. By working hard at "this public," one meets many kinds of people, and serves some very important people from time to time, and now a great many of these are among my acquaintances. High "good will" stock can come from this. I feel that this aspect has great value, and I hope that a continuing committee will help us use this great assortment of people to the future benefit of an expanded and improved physical fitness INSTITUTE program to improve the dissemination of our research materials.

What we have done with a small laboratory, and with the help of our friends in physiology, biochemistry, psychology, anthropology and other fields, especially in dentistry and medicine, is a recognizable gain in the knowledge and service offered in physical fitness work, but it is but a beginning to what it could be. We either go out to serve the people who want our services and demand them, or we bring them here to be tested and interviewed. We certainly have some services that they want. An Institute to "serve the people" could be developed here, with the good will that we have, with the continued support of Curtis Mitchell, Rev. Billy Graham, Ezra Levin, the local doctors and dentists, our friends in insurance, in business life, in medicine and in dentistry. It is an area of "Adult Health Education," working through tests and interviews, and a follow-up program, that wins people. Our technical, visual material is quite extensive, and our resources for work-outs, but we are woefully pinched for lockers, space for our graduate students, a gym floor for experimental programs (as Gym 302 in Huff) and generally we are too crowded in our offices and small laboratory to file and keep our materials in order. My own office has been so overrun, at least ten times the material is there that should be in an office of that size, and every file is crammed and bulging.

B. SPECIFIC AREAS OF PHYSICAL FITNESS RESEARCH PIONEERED AT THE UNIVERSITY OF ILLINOIS — SUMMARIZED

1. In the period 1941-50 the entire motor ability field of work with young men was investigated, factor analyzed and several improved tests were added:

First Laboratory for investigation of physical fitness, 1944.

14-Item Motor Ability Test and an equivalent form of 18-Items (without apparatus). At least 100,000 people have been through these tests (cf. *Jour. A.M.A.* 133:69-74, Sept. 11, 1943; also Life-Time book, *The Healthy Life*, 1966).

First comprehensive study of muscular endurance, *Endurance of Young Men,* 1945.

Workbooks published: *Physical Fitness Workbook,* 1942, 1944, 1947.

First Graduate Textbook on *Physical Fitness Appraisal and Guidance,* 1947.

First Sports Fitness School for Boys begun, 1949.

2. In the period 1948-53 a pioneering effort was made to measure Olympic and top-flight athletes. This resulted in the book, *Physical Fitness of Champion Athletes,* University of Illinois Press, 1951. This investigation included approximately 4000 athletes tested on many fitness tests.

3. A practical Physical Fitness Clinic was pioneered, operated in the afternoon from the Men's Old Gym, 1941-44 to which students deficient in various aspects of physical fitness could attend for conference, work-outs and tests — shifted in 1944 to Huff Gymnasium when the Physical Fitness Laboratory was built. Cureton drew the plans for this laboratory and ordered the equipment. It represented the first "Treadmill Station" in the Midwest.

4. *Warfare Aquatics and Basic Physical Fitness* service courses were pioneered in the World War II period, both resulting in nationally published books.

5. A cardiovascular testing station (laboratory) was developed in Huff Gym for the routine administration of cardiovascular-respiratory tests in 1944 and since more than 10,000 individuals have been tested, usually before and after various courses in physical education, or sports, and exercises. This led to publishing about 100 articles on cardiovascular fitness in normals, related to physical education courses. As many as 104 tests have been factor analyzed and incorporated into experimental programs.

6. Huff Gym became known the country over as a center for the investigation of "The Science of Sports" and to a certain extent it has continued to be that to this date and books by Cureton's students are known all over the world, such as, Counsilman's *Science of Swimming;* Ganslen's *Mechanics of the Pole Vault,* and material of Cureton's in Bunn's *Science of Athletics.* (The Program of the 135th Meeting, in Dallas, A.A. Advancement of Science featured in 1968 reports by Cureton and several of his students — and a book will appear edited by Professor Paul Weiss, of Yale University.)

7. The LOW GEAR, MIDDLE GEAR, HIGH GEAR progressive exercise system, featuring cardiovascular-respiratory exercise, and "Run for Your Life" actually began at Huff Gym, went on to the Cleveland and Cincinnati Y.M.C.A.'s, and then by many clinics and demonstrations by Cureton spread to military bases at Colorado Springs, Houston, Quantico, Va. and then all over the country with the aid of The President's Council and Life-Time publication *The Healthy Life.* Pollock and Kapilian earned Ph.D.'s in this area of work.

8. Physical fitness for dentists began by Dean Isaac Schour asking Cureton to lecture at the Dental College, and then at the Graduate Seminar at Bailey's Harbor, Wisconsin. This led to studying dentists at Palm Springs, at other Graduate Seminars, and many week-end Clinics over the whole

country; and to articles in dental journals and in *Preventive Dentistry* (1966).

9. Appearances at the Million Dollar Round Table in Boston, and on the General Manager's Program in Atlanta led to the adoption of physical fitness and dynamic health philosophy related to the sale of insurance — a DOUBLE-BARRELED PROGRAM of doing something for the man himself in the way of physical fitness advice, then also to sell him a policy to protect his estate and his family.

10. The *first* Research Methods in *Health and Physical Education* was originated at Illinois in Huff Gym, and it was a widely used book by other colleges and universities, in graduate physical education, now being in its second stage of revision.

11. The first studies related to reducing cholesterol and triglycerides by exercise began in Huff Gym under Professors Cureton and Staley's sponsorship, and with the aid of Dean Louis Howard and Dr. Fred Kummerow, the latter now director of the Burnsides Laboratory. Pohndorf, Golding, Metivier, Mrs. Hoyman completed Ph.D. theses — then the U.S. Public Health Service set up a joint study between the Heart Disease Control Unit in Washington and the U. of I. work under Dr. Cureton, and sent Dr. John Holloszy here for two years to help — and James Skinner completed his Ph.D. in this set-up, leading to major articles published in a Symposium Report, *Work and the Heart, American Journal of Cardiology,* December, 1964. Some of Cureton's work appeared in the First Symposium and International Conference on "Preventive Cardiology" the book edited by Dr. Wilhelm Raab. Barry, Rochelle, Montoye and others have contributed to this work.

12. The first work in physical education on multi-channel recording of brachial and carotid pulse waves, the electrocardiogram, and the ballistocardiogram and sound waves began at Illinois, in the Atmospheric Environment Lab began under Cureton's sponsorship. Many of his students have made studies in this area to clarify the relations between these important measurements in physical fitness (Eric Banister, Don Franks, Liverman, Wiley, Molnar and Sharon Plowman). Such measurements are basic in the area of studying effects of various stresses on the body. Cureton and Franks, and Cureton and Banister have published several scientific articles on this work. Others who earned Ph.D.s were David Cundiff and Professor Don Franks.

13. Pioneering studies came from the Sports-Fitness School, over 50 graduate theses in this area alone, and it was shown that various types of endurance programs were good for young boys, overcoming a long-held prejudice. A major monograph was published, *Improving the Physical Fitness of Youth,* 1965. Alan Barry assisted in this area and earned his Ph.D. in this work as did Cedric Dempsey.

14. A pioneering effort was launched under Cureton's sponsorship to determine if wheat germ oil was an effective aid to men and boys in stressful physical fitness programs. Many papers have been published in this area alone. A major monograph is nearing completion on this work, which will be published by C. C. Thomas and Co. in this next year. The area is a

controversial one. Cureton's work was challenged by Dr. P. V. Karpovich in 1964. The hearing in Springfield, Mass., resulted in Cureton's favor, and Dr. Cornell, expert statistician, testified that if he had planned the experiments he would have done them the same way that Cureton had done, matching parallel groups. Many thousands of athletes and older men, in fitness programs, have used the VioBin wheat germ oil, and all know of this work and follow it closely.

15. I feel that I have been a pioneer missionary for physical fitness in many European countries: England, France, Germany, Denmark and Finland, Italy, Belgium, Holland and also in five South American countries. Last summer I worked in Japan, Hong Kong and Korea. In 1956 I was a member of a Commission to study the Australian Olympic Games and presented papers at the World Congress on Physical Education in Melbourne.

16. A pioneering Symposium was held under the sponsorship of Dr. Staley, Dr. Cureton, Dr. Stafford and Dr. Laura Huelster in 1960 at Allerton Park. The report, edited with the help of Dr. Alan Barry, was published by The Athletic Institute in 1960.

17. The multi-variate approach to analyzing the contribution of tests to various types of performances has been applied to prediction of cholesterol, treadmill running time, all-out ergometer bicycle ride times, swimming times in various events, and Maximal Oxygen Intake. The stepwise multiple regression equation techniques have been applied to many problems, not before studied by such multi-variate methods. The use of Sewell Wright's "Path Coefficient" system to analyze the *net* percentage contribution of various causal factors to explain selected criteria has resulted in numerous publications by Cureton, and by Wayne Van Huss, William Adams, Herbert Weber and Annelis Hoyman in Ph.D. reports.

18. New tests have been devised, and several validated in an original way. Twenty years ago the heartometer machine was an unknown device. Many studies on it at the University of Illinois have been published, and 100 such studies recently were reviewed in Cureton's new book, *The Physiological Effects of Exercise Programs on Adults* (1969), Thomas.

19. *Physical Fitness and Dynamic Health,* published in 1965 (5th printing in 1967) is a pioneering effort to explain a scientifically backed system of *progressive* exercise to the public. The Canadian 5 BX, written by Wm. Orban, one of our graduates, was an abbreviated version of this system, which sold over 4,000,000 copies in the United States without a cent of Royalty. It was used by the Air Forces for a while, and lately the *Aerobics* program has followed the lines of researches by Lt. Col. Cooper and the "Run for Your Life" type program, previously written up by Curtis Mitchell and attributed to us.

20. The interest in physical fitness is certainly marked by our works and the leadership of many students, who have multiplied our own works 100 times. Several summaries appear in encyclopedias, *The World Book, Our Wonderful World* and most lately an up-to-date review will appear in *En-*

cyclopedia Britannica's pioneering type book, *Science and the Future,* to be published next year.

21. Many thousands of people know that we have improved the circulatory-respiratory fitness of a portion of the American public, thanks to our wonderful collaborators in the Y's all over the country. By going to the Y's and by having the physical directors come here for summer study, the results of our research have been put into practical application. Now, nearly all systems of exercise have been influenced by it, the "Continuous Rhythmical Work" and by getting the Calorie expenditure in exercise up to an average of 300 to 500 Calories per day.

PERSONS WHO HAVE RECEIVED
PH.D. UNDER T. K. CURETON

Adams, William C. (1964), University of California at Davis
Banister, Eric W. (1964), Simon Fraser University, British Columbia
Barry, Alan J. (1957), Division of Research, Lankanau Hospital,
   Philadelphia, Pa.
Bender, Jay (1951) Deceased
Bernauer, Edmund M. (1962), University of California at Davis
Bosco, James S. (1962), San Jose State College, California
Breen, James L. (1959), George Washington University, Washington, D.C.
Brown, Stanley R. (1957), The University of British Columbia, Canada
Corroll, Victor A. (1967), University of Manitoba, Canada
Cundiff, David E. (1966), University of Toledo
Dempsey, Cedric W. (1963), University of the Pacific
Doroschuk, Eugene V. (1962), La Commission Solaire Regionale Youville
   Montreal, P. Q., Canada
du Toit, Stephanus F. (1966), University College, Durban, Natal,
   South Africa
Fardy, Paul S. (1967), California State College at Fullerton, Calif.
Farhi, Aasher (1966), Vanderbilt University
Franks, B. Don (1967), University of Illinois
Ganslen, Richard V (1953), Texas Woman's University
Getchell, Leroy H. (1965), Ball State University, Indiana
Golding, Lawrence A. (1958), Kent State University, Ohio
Gualtiere, William S. (1967), Montefiore Hospital and Medical Center,
   New York
Haskell, William L. (1965), President's Council on Physical Fitness and
   Sports, Washington, D. C.
Hayden, Francis D. (1962), The Joseph P. Kennedy, Jr. Foundation,
   Washington, D. C.
Herron, Robert E. (1964), Baylor College of Medicine
Heusner, William W., Jr. (1955), Michigan State University
Holmes, Harold Z., Jr. (1969), University of Eastern Kentucky
Hoyman, Annelis (Mrs.) (1963), University of Illinois
Hubbard, A. W. (1950), University of Illinois
Hunsicker, Paul A. (1949), University of Michigan
Ingold, John (1969), Goshen College (Indiana)
Jette, Maurice J. (1969), University of Ottawa
Kapalian, Ralph H. (1969), Boston
Knowlton, Ronald G. (1961), Southern Illinois University
Landry, Fernand (1968), Universite Laval, Quebec, P. Q., Canada
Liverman, Robert D. (1965), Temple University, Pennsylvania
Massey, Benjamin H. (1950), University of Illinois
McAdam, Robert E. (1955), University of Minnesota

Métivier, Guy (1960), University of Ottawa, Canada
Michael, Ernest D., Jr. (1952), University of California at Santa Barbara
Molnar, Sandor (1969), University of Illinois
Montoye, Henry J. (1949), University of Michigan
Moore, George C. (1954), University of Arkansas
Moore, Roy D. (1967), North Carolina A. and T. University
Murphy, Harvey F. (1967), University of North Carolina at Charlotte
Noble, Bruce (1964), University of Pittsburgh, Pennsylvania
Orban, William A. R. (1957), University of Ottawa, Canada
Oscai, Lawrence B. (1967), Washington University, St. Louis
Phillips, Everett E., Jr. (1960), University of Florida
Pohndorf, Richard (1956), University of Illinois
Pollock, Michael L. (1967), Wake Forest University, North Carolina
Popejoy, Imogene (1967), Michigan State University
Powell, John (1964), University of Guelph, Ont., Canada
Ribisl, Paul M. (1967), Kent State University, Ohio
Rochelle, Rene H. (1953), University of California at Santa Barbara
Rothermel, Bradley (1965), University of Illinois at Chicago
Seidler, Armond (1953), University of New Mexico
Sherman, Michael A. (1967), University of Pittsburgh, Pennsylvania
Skinner, James S. (1963), Pennsylvania State University
Sloniger, Edward L. (1966), University of Indiana, Pennsylvania
Sterling, Leroy F. (1960), Central Michigan University
Strydom, N. B. (1959), Chamber of Mines of South Africa,
    Johannesburg, South Africa
Sward, Sidney B. (1967), Virginia State College
Tuma, James W. (1959), Office of the U. S. Naval Attache,
    APO San Francisco
Van Huss, Wayne D. (1953), Michigan State University
Weber, Herbert (1965), East Stroudsburg College, Pennsylvania
Wells, Harold P. (1958), Northern Illinois University
Wiley, Jack F. (1968), University of South Alabama
Wolf, J. Grove (1950), University of Wisconsin
Yuhasz, Michael S. (1962), University of Western Ontario, Canada
(Currently working on Ph.D. under Cureton: Denise Allard, Lawrence Foster, Nora Yan Shu Liu, Joseph M. Pechinski, Sharon Plowman, Peter Richter, Robert Stallman, and Ali Tooshi.)

PUBLICATIONS*

By THOMAS K. CURETON, JR.

BOOKS

1930

A Water Program for Camps. Philadelphia: P. Blakiston's Son and Co., 1929.

Objective Tests of Swimming. Springfield, Mass., Master's Thesis, Springfield College, 1930.

Recreational Swimming Activities. Privately published, Springfield, Mass., 1930.

The Teaching of Elementary Swimming and Diving. Privately published, Springfield, Mass., 1931.

Physics Applied to Health and Physical Education. Privately published, Springfield, Mass., 1933.

How to Teach Swimming and Diving. New York: Association Press, 1934.

The Teaching and Practice of Intermediate Aquatics. Privately published, Springfield, Mass., 1935.

A Guide to Tests and Measurements in Health and Physical Education. Privately published, Springfield, Mass., 1936.

(Chairman with John Brown, Jr. and John W. Fuhrer). *Official Report, First National Y.M.C.A. Aquatic Conference.* Chicago: George Williams College, May 9-12, 1937.

(Jointly with John Brown, Jr. and John W. Fuhrer). *The New Y.M.C.A. Aquatic Program.* New York: Association Press, 1938.

National Y.M.C.A. Progressive Aquatic Tests (Beginning and Intermediate Level). New York: Association Press, 1938.

(Jointly with John Brown, Jr. and John W. Fuhrer). *National Y.M.C.A. Life Saving and Water Safety Syllabus and Tests.* New York: Association Press, 1939.

Standards for Testing Beginning Swimming, New York: Association Press, 1939.

Scientific Principles Underlying Instruction in Health, Physical Education and Recreation, Syllabus #3930. Berkeley: University of California, 1939.

1940

Physical Fitness Supplement to the Research Quarterly, 12:298-493, 1941. Chairman of Springfield College Committee with J. D. Brock, W. A. Cox, P. V. Karpovich, L. A. Larson, E. W. Pennock, H. S. Seashore and G. B. Affleck.

Physical Fitness Workbook. Champaign, Illinois: (1st edition, planographed), Stipes Publishing Co., 1942.

Warfare Aquatics. Champaign, Illinois: Stipes Publishing Co., 1943.

Physical Fitness Workbook. (2nd edition), Champaign, Illinois: Stipes Publishing Co., 1944.

(With W. J. Huffman, Lyle Welser, R. W. Kireilis, and D. E. Latham). *Endurance of Young Men.* Washington, D.C.: Society for Research in Child Development, National Research Council, Research Monograph, Vol. X, No. 1, 1945.

(With H. T. Friermood, F. S. Lloyd and others). *Y.M.C.A. Learn-to-Swim Campaign,* New York: Association Press, 1946.

*The editor would like to express appreciation to Dr. Maurice Jette' and Mr. Chris Milesis for assistance in compilation of the bibliography.

(With R. H. Pohndorf). *Aquatic Standards for Y.M.C.A. Camps.* New York: Association Press, 1946.

Physical Fitness Workbook. (3rd edition), St. Louis: C. V. Mosby Co., 1947.

Physical Fitness Appraisal and Guidance, St. Louis: C. V. Mosby Co., 1947.

(With H. T. Friermood). *National Y.M.C.A. Aquatic Program,* New York: Association Press, 1948.

Fun in the Water. New York: Association Press, 1949.

(Co-editor and part author). *Research Methods Applied in Health, Physical Education and Recreation.* Washington, D.C.: American Association for Health, Physical Education and Recreation, 1949.

1950

(Co-author). *Measurement and Evaluation Materials in Health, Physical Education and Recreation,* Washington, D.C.: American Association for Health, Physical Education and Recreation, 1950.

(With C. E. Silvia, Lynn R. Russell, and H. T. Friermood). *National Y.M.C.A. Life Saving and Water Safety Student Handbook.* New York: Association Press, 1951.

Physical Fitness of Champion Athletes. Urbana: University of Illinois Press, 1951.

Masters Theses in Health, Physical Education and Recreation, Washington, D.C.: American Association for Health, Physical Education and Recreation, 1952.

(With the Cameron Co.). *The Heartometer in the Field of Physical Education,* Cameron Heartometer Company, 1954. (Summaries written by T. K. Cureton).

(With the Cameron Co. Edited by H. Melterowitz and W. Ruhemann). "Uber Sportmedizinsche Forschung in den U.S.A." *Training, Leistung, Gesundheit.* Frankfurt/Main, Germany: Wilhelm Limpert, 1952. (Summaries written by T. K. Cureton).

"The University of Illinois Sports-Fitness School for Research on Young Boys," *Report of the International Congress on the Essentials of Physical Education for Youth,* Washington, D.C.: American Association for Health, Physical Education and Recreation, 1955.

Effects of Physical Education Upon College Men, privately published (mimeographed, in printed cover), Urbana, Illinois.

University of Illinois Theses Abstracts in Physical Education, 1924-1953, privately published (mimeographed, in printed cover), Urbana, Illinois.

(With Carolyn Bookwalter and Raymond A. Weiss). *Graduate Theses Abstracts, 1938-53.* (New York and Indiana Universities). Urbana, Illinois, 1956.

Graduate Theses Abstracts, 1937-54. (Oregon University, University of Southern California, Springfield College, University of Utah.) Urbana, Illinois. 1956.

(Compiler-editor). *Abstracts of Graduate Theses in Physical Education, Recreation, and Health Education, 1958.* Urbana: School of Physical Education.

Our Wonderful World (Encyclopedia): parts in articles: Vol. 8, "Sports-Fitness School," "Who Can Be An Athlete;" Vol. 2, "Swimming."

(With H. T. Friermood and E. L. Griffin). *Y.M.C.A. National Aquatic Workbook.* New York: Association Press. 1958.

1960

(Compiler-editor with Alan J. Barry). *Abstracts of Graduate Theses in Physical Education, Recreation and Health Education, 1959-60.* Urbana: College of Physical Education.
(With S. C. Staley, Laura J. Huelster and Alan J. Barry). *Exercise and Fitness.* Chicago: The Athletic Institute, 1960.

The World Book Encyclopedia, 1960. Chicago: Field Enterprises Educ. Corp.

(Cureton signed articles)

Physical Education	Vol. 14, Pp. 384-385
Physical Fitness	Vol. 14, Pp. 386-387
Posture	Vol. 14, Pp. 633-636
Pan American	Vol. 14, P. 94
Dumbell or Bar Bell	Vol. 4, P. 307
Weight Lifting	Vol. 19, P. 150
Gymnastics	Vol. 7, P. 430
Gymnasium	Vol. 7, Pp. 430-431
Exercise	Vol. 5, Pp. 336-338
Judo	Vol. 10, Pp. 148-149
Intramural	Vol. 9, P. 278

(Compiler-editor). *Abstracts of Graduate Theses in Physical Education, Recreation and Health Education,* 1960-61, Urbana: College of Physical Education.

(Co-Author with others) *Health and Fitness in the Modern World,* Chicago: The Athletic Institute, 1961.

(Compiler-editor). *Abstracts of Graduate Theses in Physical Education, Recreation and Health Education,* Urbana: College of Physical Education, 1961-62.

Lectures on Health and Fitness in the World of Today, Quezon City: University of the Philippines, 1962.

(Compiler-editor). *Abstracts of Graduate Theses in Physical Education, Recreation and Health Education,* College of Physical Education, University of Illinois, 1963-64.

Physical Fitness and Dynamic Health, New York: The Dial Press, 1965.

Improving the Physical Fitness of Youth, Chicago: University of Chicago Press, (Society for Research in Child Development, Serial No. 95, 1964, Vol. 29, No. 4 Research Monograph). June, 1965.

(Compiler-editor) *Abstracts of Graduate Theses in Physical Education, Recreation and Health Education,* Urbana: College of Physical Education. 1965.

(Ed. by W. Raab) *Prevention of Ischemic Heart Disease,* Springfield, Illinois: C. C. Thomas and Co., 1966. Contributed Chapter XXXIX, "The Relative Value of Various Exercise Programs to Protect Adult Human Subjects from Degenerative Heart Disease."

(Ed. by M. J. Karvonen and Alan J. Barry). *Cardiovascular Effects of Exercise,* Springfield, Illinois: C. C. Thomas and Co., Contributed Chapter 8, with others.

Proceedings of the International Congress of Sport Sciences (Tokyo), "Recent Findings from Dietary Supplement Studies in Relationship to the Possibility for Improving Athletic and Cardiovascular Performances," 1966.

(Compiler-editor). *Abstracts of Graduate Theses in Physical Education and Health Education,* Urbana: College of Physical Education, 1965.

(With Editors of LIFE-TIME Book Division). *The Healthy Life,* New York: Life-Time Pubs., Rockefeller Center, 1966.

Physical Fitness and Dynamic Health. 1967. N.Y.: The Dial Press. *Ibid.* New York: Dell Co.

The Physiological Effects of Exercise Programs on Adults, Springfield, Ill.: C. C. Thomas and Co., 1969.

ARTICLES IN PERIODICAL AND PROFESSIONAL LITERATURE:

1930

"The Stop Watch Method of Testing Speed," *Beach and Pool,* 4: 15-19, (Feb., 1930).

"Relationship of Respiration to Speed Efficiency in Swimming," *Research Quarterly,* 1: 54-70, (Mar., 1930).

"Mechanics of Swimming the Crawl Arm Stroke," *Beach and Pool*, 4: 57-62, (May, 1930).

"Mechanics and Kinesiology of the Crawl Flutter Kick," *Research Quarterly*, 1: 87-121, (Dec., 1930); *Beach and Pool*, 4: 57-62, (May, 1930); *Swimming Pool Data and Reference Annual*, Pp. 41-54, 1935.

"The Psychology of Swimming Instruction," *Beach and Pool*, 5: 162-166, (May, 1931); 5: 244-246, (June, 1931).

"Objective Tests of Swimming," *Beach and Pool*, 5: 306, (July, 1931).

"The Validity of Antero-Posterior Spinal Measurements," *Research Quarterly* 2: 101-113, (Oct., 1931).

"Physics Applied to Physical Education," *Journal of Health and Physical Education*, 3: 22-25, (Jan., 1932).

"The Scope of Coaching Swimming and Diving," *Swimming Pool World*, 1: 13-24, (Mar., 1932).

(Jointly with D. E. Coe). "The Analysis of the Errors in Stop Watch Timing," *Research Quarterly*, 4: 94-109, (May, 1933).

"Problems and Experimental Studies on the Teaching of Swimming and Diving," *Beach and Pool*, 7: 178, (June, 1933).

"A Scientific Pedagogy of Swimming and Diving," *Beach and Pool*, 7: 214, (July, 1933).

"Observations and Tests of Swimming at the 1932 Olympic Games," *Journal of Physical Education*, 7: 214 +, (Aug., 1933); *Swimming Pool Data and Reference Annual*, 1936.

"Coordination Tests in Swimming," *Beach and Pool*, 7: 178, (June, 1933).

"Natural and Artificial Buoyance, Flotation, and Body Balance in the Water," *Beach and Pool*, 7: 272, (Sept., 1933).

"Being Physically Educated Means," Privately published, Springfield, Mass., 1933. (Chart).

"Mechanics of Health and Efficiency," Privately published, Springfield, Mass. 1933. (Chart).

"Diet As Related to Success in Competitive Swimming," *Beach and Pool*. 7: 335, (Nov., 1933); 8: 10, (Jan. 1934).

"How to Teach Swimming and Diving," *Scholastic Coach*, 3: 32-33, (April 1934).

"Course in Beginner's Swimming and Diving Instruction," *Beach and Pool*, 8: 326-9, (Nov., 1934); 8: 356-8, (Dec. 1934).

"Mechanics of the Track Racing Start," *Scholastic Coach*, 4: 14-15, (Jan., 1935).

"Mechanics of Track Running," *Scholastic Coach*, 4: 7-10, (Feb., 1935).

"Mechanics of the Shot Put," *Scholastic Coach*, 4: 7-10, (Mar., 1935).

"Mechanics of the High Jump," *Scholastic Coach*, 4: 9-12, (April, 1935).

"Mechanics of the Broad Jump," *Scholastic Coach*, 4: 8-9, (May, 1935).

"The Validity of Footprints as a Measure of Vertical Height of the Arch and Functional Efficiency of the Foot," *Supplement to the Research Quarterly*, 6: 70-80, (May, 1935).

(With J. S. Wickens and Haskell P. Elder). "Reliability and Objectivity of the Springfield Postural Measurements," *Supplement to the Research Quarterly*, 6: 81-92, (May, 1935).

(With J. S. Wickens). "The Center of Gravity of the Human Body in the Antero-Posterior Plane and Its Relation to Posture, Physical Fitness, and Athletic Ability," *Supplement to the Research Quarterly*, 6: 93-105, (May, 1935).

"Test for Endurance in Speed Swimming," *Supplement to the Research Quarterly*, 6: 106-112, (May, 1935).

"Undergraduate, and Faculty Project Work in Applied Physical Science," *Supplement to the Research Quarterly*, 6: 113-119, (May, 1935).

"Factors Governing Success in Competitive Swimming," *Spalding's Intercollegiate Swimming Guide*, Pp. 48-62, New York: American Sports Publishing Co., 1934; also *Swimming Pool Data and Reference Annual*, 1936.

"Physical Norms for Springfield College Men — Strength and Power Capacity," Privately published, Springfield, Mass., 1936 (Chart).

"Physical Norms for Springfield College Men — Objective Postural Analysis," Privately published, Springfield, Mass., 1936 (Chart).

"Physical Norms for Springfield College Men — Indices for Athletic and Motor Ability (Fundamental Skills)," Privately published, Springfield, Mass., 1936 (Chart).

"Physical Norms for Springfield College Men — Specific Measures of Skeletal Growth," Privately published, Springeld, Mass., 1936 (Chart).

"Physical Norms for Springfield College Men — Objective Flexibility Analysis," Privately published, Springfield, Mass., 1936 (Chart).

"Profile of Health, Athletic Condition and Physical Ability Indices," Privately published, Springfield, Mass., 1936 (Chart).

"Analysis of Vital Capacity As a Test of Condition for High School Boys," *Research Quarterly*, 7: 80-92, (Dec., 1936).

"First National Y.M.C.A. Aquatic Conference," Chicago, Illinois: *Beach and Pool*, 11: 12, (Feb., 1937).

"First National Y.M.C.A. Aquatic Conference," *Beach and Pool*, 11: 15, (June, 1937).

"Outlook for Professional Education in Health, Physical Education and Recreation," *Journal of Physical Education*, 35: 2-3, (Sept.-Oct., 1937).

(With Committee of College Physical Education Association, 1937). "Glossary of Physical Education, Swimming, Diving, Water Sports, Terms."

"Philosophy of the Y.M.C.A. Aquatic Program," *Beach and Pool*, 11: 7, (Oct., 1937).

"Health Appraisal and Guidance in the Y.M.C.A.," (Chapter in *The New Physical Education*, Association Press, 1938).

"Instructor's Work Charts, National Y.M.C.A. Aquatic Program," New York: Association Press, 1938:
Beginning Level (21 Progressive tests).
Intermediate Level (30 Progressive tests).
Life Saving and Water Safety (28 Progressive tests).

"Master Charts, National Y.M.C.A. Aquatic Program," New York: Association Press, 1938.
Beginning Level (21 Progressive tests).
Intermediate Level (30 Progressive tests).
Life Saving and Water Safety (28 Progressive tests).

"New England Aquatic Leadership Conference," *Beach and Pool*, 12: 30, (June, 1938).

"New Y.M.C.A. Aquatic Program," *Recreation*, 32: 262, (July, 1938).

(With John Brown, Jr. and John W. Fuhrer). "Results of the 1937 National Survey of Y.M.C.A. Aquatics," *Beach and Pool*, 12: 28, (June, 1938). Continued: 12: 11, (Sept., 1938); 12: 8, (Oct., 1938); 12: 8, (Nov., 1938); 12: 10, (Dec., 1938); 13: 8, (Jan., 1939).

"Technique of Scaling Silhouettes," Privately published, Springfield, Mass., 1938. (Chart).

"Test Sheets, National Y.M.C.A. Progressive Aquatic Tests." New York: Association Press, 1938.

> Test Sheet No. I, Beginner's Classification Test.
> Test Sheet No. II, Beginner's Middle Length Test.
> Test Sheet No. III, Beginner's Full Length Test.
> Test Sheet No. IV, Low Difficulty Intermediate Swimming and Diving Test.
> Test Sheet No. V, Middle Difficulty Intermediate Swimming and Diving Test.
> Test Sheet No. VI, High Intermediate Swimming, Diving and Pre-Life Saving Test.

"The Y.M.C.A. Aquatic Program," *Physical Education Digest, Health and Recreation,* (Mar., 1938).

"The National Y.M.C.A. Aquatic Program Moves Forward," *Journal of Physical Education,* 36: 23, (Nov.-Dec., 1938).

"Professional Versus Volunteer Leaders in Aquatics," *Beach and Pool,* 13: 12, (Feb., 1939).

"Elementary Principles of Cinematographic Analysis as Aids in Athletic Research," *Research Quarterly,* 10: 3-24, (May, 1939).

"Report of the Commission on the Professional Training of the Y.M.C.A. Physical Education Secretary," *Report and Proceedings of the Physical Director's Society of the Y.M.C.A.'s of North America,* Toronto: Triennial Convention, May 26-29, 1939, Chairman of Commission.

"Institutes, Schools and Field Service with the National Y.M.C.A. Aquatic Program," *Journal of Physical Education,* 36: 83, (May-June, 1939).

"Standards for Testing Beginning Swimming," *Research Quarterly,* 10: 54-59, (Dec., 1939).

"National Y.M.C.A. Aquatic Leadership Training Standards," National Council of the Y.M.C.A., 1939.

"Scientific Principles Underlying Instruction in Health, Physical Education and Recreation," Proceedings (77th Annual Meeting, San Francisco), Washington: National Education Association, 77: 227-228, 1939.

1940

"National Y.M.C.A. Aquatic Program Reviewed and Supported at Detroit," *Journal of Physical Education,* 37: 52, (Jan.-Feb., 1940).

"Index of Springfield College Research, Through December, 1936," Springfield, Mass.: Springfield College (mimeographed). Pp. 48, *Supplementary Sheets for 1937, 1938, 1939, and 1940.*

"Aquatic Program Moves Ahead," *National Council Bulletin* (Y.M.C.A.), 14: No. 2, (April, 1940).

"Progress and Needs of the National Y.M.C.A. Aquatic Program," *Journal of Physical Education,* 37: 62, (May-June, 1940).

"Review of a Decade of Research in Aquatics at Springfield College," *Research Quarterly,* 11: 68-79, (May, 1940).

"The Philosophical or Group Thinking Method of Research," *Research Quarterly,* 11: 63-75, (Oct., 1940).

"Body Build as a Framework of Reference for Interpreting Physical Fitness and Athletic Performance," *Supplement to the Research Quarterly,* 1: 301-330, (May, 1941).

"Weight and Tissue Symmetry Analyses," *Supplement to the Research Quarterly,* 2: 331-347, (May, 1941).

"Bodily Posture as an Indicator of Fitness," *Supplement to the Research Quarterly,* 3: 348-367, (May, 1941).

"Fitness of the Feet and Legs," *Supplement to the Research Quarterly*, 4: 368-380, (May, 1941).

(With Leonard A. Larson). "Strength as an Approach to Physical Fitness," *Supplement to the Research Quarterly*, 6: 391-406, (May, 1941).

"Y.M.C.A. Expands and Improves National Aquatic Program to Carry on Pioneering Work," *Journal of Physical Education*, 38: (March-April, 1941); Continued, 38: 89, (May-June, 1941).

"Leadership Training in Aquatics," Pp. 28-32, *Report on Third Annual Swimming Pool Conference*, Urbana, Illinois: University of Illinois, (Oct. 31 and Nov. 1, 1941).

"Report and Recommendations of the National Committee on Aquatic Leadership," *Research Quarterly*, 13: 520-531, (Dec., 1942).

(With S. C. Staley and G. T. Stafford). "University of Illinois Motor Fitness Test," Champaign: University Print Shop, 1942. Circular 5M7-42-243965.

(With W. D. Price for Intramural Department). "V-Test for Physical Fitness," Champaign, Illinois: University Print Shop, 500-2-42-233135, (Feb., 1942).

"Suggestions for Developing Physical Fitness," *The Physical Educator*, 2: 176-177, (April, 1942).

"Physical Fitness, A National Need," *Journal of Physical Education*, 40: 66-67, (March-April, 1943).

"Improvement in Motor Fitness Associated with Physical Education and Physical Fitness Clinic Work," *Research Quarterly*, 14: 154-157, (May, 1943).

"An Inventory and Screen Test of Motor Fitness for High School and College Men," *The Physical Educator*, 3: 64-74, (Jan., 1943).

(With C. W. Turner and Emma McCloy Layman). "Physical Fitness—A Selected Bibliography," *The Booklist*, 39: No. 10,231,240, Chicago, Illinois: American Library Association.

"A Selected Bibliography on Physical Fitness," *Research Quarterly*, 14: 112-124, (Mar., 1943).

"Warfare Aquatics," *Beach and Pool*, 12: 30, (May, 1943).

"The Swimming Ability of Men," *Illinois Education*, 32: 56, (Oct., 1943).

"Are You Physically Fit?" Champaign, Illinois: McKinley Y.M.C.A. (folder), (Dec., 1943).

"Resuscitation and Water First Aid," *Scholastic Coach*, 12: 9-10, (May, 1943).

"A Prerequisite of Modern Battle-Warfare Aquatics, Part I," *Beach and Pool*, 17: 5, (Oct., 1943).

"Warfare Aquatics, Part II," *Beach and Pool*, 17: 8-9, (Nov., 1943).

"The Unfitness of Young Men in Motor Fitness," *The Journal of the American Medical Association*, 133: 69-74, (Sept. 11, 1943).

"Classification Tests for Physical Fitness," *Scholastic Coach*, 13: 8-11, (Sept., 1943). No. 1.

"A Motor Fitness Screen Test," *Scholastic Coach*, 13: 40-44, (Oct., 1943). No. 2.

"Response of Acceptance," *Journal of Physical Education*, 41: 7, (Sept.-Oct., 1943). 1943 Roberts-Gulick Award to Thomas K. Cureton, Jr.

"The Physiology of Fitness," *Scholastic Coach*, 13: 10-11, (Nov., 1943), No. 3

"The Physiology of Fitness," *Scholastic Coach*, 13: 10-11, (Dec. 1943). No. 4.

"The Physiology of Fitness," *Scholastic Coach*, 14: 40-44, (Jan., 1944). No. 5.

"Physical Fitness, A National Need," *Amateur Athlete*, 15: 3, (Feb., 1944).

"Basic Principles of Physical Fitness for Adults," *Journal of Physical Education*, 41: 51, (Jan.-Feb., 1944).

"Basic Principles of Physical Fitness for Adults," Minneapolis, Minn.: Imperial Printing Co., 1944.

"The Physiology of Fitness," *Scholastic Coach*, 14: 14-18, (March 1944). No. 6.

"Guide for Tracing Research in the Health, Physical Education and Recreation Field," *Research Quarterly*, 15: 150-180, (May, 1944).

"Leadership Training in Physical Fitness and Aquatics," *Journal of Physical Education*, 42: 10-12, (Sept.-Oct., 1944).

"Keep Fit to Live," *Allsports*, 4: 10, (July, 1944).

Review: The U. S. Office of Education Review of the Physical Fitness Workbook as the first such workbook for men in American Colleges. (*Education for Victory*, Vol. 2, No. 24).

"Centennial Conference Report," *Journal of Physical Education*, 42: 5, 6, 10-11. (Sept.-Oct., 1944).

"Leadership Training in Aquatics," *Journal of Physical Education*, 42: 32-43, (Nov.-Dec., 1944).

"Leadership Training in Aquatics," *Progressive Physical Educator*, 27: 5-14, (Dec., 1944).

"What Is Physical Fitness," *Journal of Health and Physical Education*, 16: 111-112, (March, 1945).

(With Lyle Welser and Warren Huffman). "A Short Motor Fitness Test," *Research Quarterly*, 16: 106-119, (May, 1945).

"Meaning of the Y.M.C.A. Leader Examiner Emblem," *Journal of Physical Education*, 42: 94, (May-June, 1945). *Ibid, Beach and Pool*, 19: 9, (July, 1945).

"Aquatic Standards for Y.M.C.A. Camps," *Journal of Physical Education*, 42: 117 +, (July-Aug., 1945).

"Effect of Ultraviolet Radiation on Physical Fitness," *Archives of Physical Medicine*, 26: 641-644, (Oct., 1945).

"Physical Fitness—A No. 1 Health Problem," *Hygeia*, 23: 186-187, 224, (March, 1945).

"Data on Illinois Fitness Experiments," *The Athletic Journal*, 26: 50, (Oct., 1945).

"School of Physical Education, University of Illinois, Publishes Extensive Research Report on Endurance Tests and Exercises," *Illinois Physical Education News*, (Dec., 1945).

(With Mary Evangeline O'Connor). "A Motor Fitness Test for High School Girls," *Research Quarterly*, 16: 302-314, (Dec., 1945).

In *Application of Measurements to Health and Physical Education*, by H. H. Clarke. New York: Prentice-Hall, Inc., 1945. "Tissue Symmetry Analysis," Pp. 104-110; "Posture Measurement," *Ibid;* "Physical Fitness Tests," *Ibid.*

Review: "Endurance of Young Men," *Journal of Health and Physical Education*, 16: 508, (Nov., 1945).

Review: "Endurance Tests and Exercises," *Illinois Physical Education News*, 10: 4, (Dec., 1945).

Review: "Testing in the Field of Physical Education," *School and Society*, 63: 140, (Sat., Feb. 23, 1946).

Review: "What People Are—A Study of Normal Young Men," *The Journal of the American Medical Association*, 130: 378, (Feb., 1946).

Review: "Endurance of Young Men, Analysis of Endurance Exercises and Methods of Evaluating Motor Fitness," *Quarterly Review of Biology*, 21: 97, (Mar., 1946).

Review: "Health in Headlines," *Hygeia*, 24: 80, (March, 1946).

"National Y.M.C.A. Learn to Swim Campaign," *Beach and Pool*, 20: 34, (May, 1946).

"What Makes a Champion," *Beach and Pool,* 20: No. 12,
    I. (Aug., 1946), Pp. 8-9, 19.
    II. (Sept., 1946), Pp. 9, 20.
    III. (Oct., 1946), Pp. 10-11, 22.
    IV. (Nov., 1946, Pp. 9, 20.
    V. (Dec., 1946), Pp. 10, 20-22.

T. K. Cureton, Chairman, Ruth Glassow, Karl W. Bookwalter and Harriet McCormick, "The Measurement of Understanding in Physical Education," Chapter XIII, *Twenty-Fifth Yearbook,* National Society for the Study of Education, Chicago, Illinois: University of Chicago Press, 1946.

(With R. W. Kireilis). "The Relationship of External Fat to Performance in Physical Education Activities," *Research Quarterly,* 18: No. 2, (May, 1947).

(With William Fay). "Science in Sports," *Chicago Sunday Tribune,* (May 18, 1947).

"What's Your Athletic Type," *Science Digest,* 22: No. 3, 1-4, (Sept., 1947).

Review: "Johns Health Practice Inventory," *Mental Measurements Yearbook,* Pp. 423-424. New Brunswick, N. J., Rutgers University, 1947.

"Y.M.C.A. Participation and Representation in the Olympics," *Journal of Physical Education,* 45: 46, (Jan.-Feb., 1948).

"What Makes an Olympic Champion," *Science Illustrated,* 3: 53-55, July, 1948.

"Let Your Body Pick Your Sport," (as told to George Mann), *Esquire,* Pp. 33 +, (Sept., 1948).

(With A. W. Hubbard, J. Sakal and W. Kastrinos). "Variations in a Single Subject of O_2-Intake, Acetylene Minute Volume, O_2 Debt, and R. Q. in 12 Various Exercises Designed as Tests of Maximal Circulatory Capacity," *Proceedings of the American Physiological Society, American Journal of Physiology,* 155: 431-32, (Dec., 1948).

"Doctorate Theses Reported by Graduate Departments of Health, Physical Education and Recreation, 1930-46, Inclusively," *The Research Quarterly,* 20: 21-59, (March, 1949).

"The Second National Y.M.C.A. Aquatic Conference Plans," *Journal of Physical Education,* 46: 52-53, (Mar.-Apr., 1949).

"Motor Performance and Growth," (review), *Science,* 110: 128-29, (July 29, 1949).

"Physical Fitness Test of Top American Athletes (Preliminary Report)," *Amateur Athlete,* 20: No. 7, Pp. 20-21, (July, 1949). *Ibid, Journal of Physical Education,* 47: 8, 24, (1949).

"Second National Y.M.C.A. Aquatic Conference," *Journal of Physical Education,* 46: 37-38 +, (Nov.-Dec., 1949).

(With R. H. Massey), "The Brachial Pulse Wave as a Measure of Cardiovascular Condition," *Federation Proceedings, American Journal of Physiology,* 159: 566, (Dec., 1949).

"A List of Doctorate Theses Reported by Graduate Departments of Health, Physical Education and Recreation," *Quarterly Bulletin of the American Recreation Society,* (Dec., 1949).

Review: "Education of the Body," *The Research Quarterly,* 20: 225-227, (May, 1949).
Review: "Trusler-Arnett Health Knowledge Test," *Mental Measurements Yearbook,* Pp. 424-427, New Brunswick, N.J., Rutgers University, 1949.

1950

"Physical Fitness Tests of Top American Athletes," *Journal of School Health,* 20: No. 2, (Feb., 1950).

(With Alan Stratman). "Physical Fitness Test for Secondary Boys and Girls," *The Research Quarterly,* 21: 47-53, (Mar., 1950).

"Tests Reveal Reasons for Dodds' Ability," *Chicago Tribune*, Sunday, Mar. 5, 1950.

"Six Practical Techniques for Differentiating Strong Versus Weak Hearts and Circulation," *Proceedings 55th Annual Convention, American Association for Health, Physical Education and Recreation*, Dallas, Texas, 1950.

"Prevention of Circulatory Weakness, Have We Overlooked the Obvious?" *Journal of Physical Education*, 47: 126, (July-Aug., 1950).

"Physical Fitness of Swimming Champions—Report on the Physical Fitness of Ralph Wright," *Beach and Pool*, 24: 5, 16 +, (Nov., 1950).

"Heart Minute Volume in All-Out Maximal Endurance Exercises," *Proceedings of the American Physiological Society, American Journal of Physiology*, 163: 706-707, (Dec., 1950).

"Treadmill Tests of Maximal Circulatory-Respiratory Capacity and Metabolic Efficiency," *Proceedings, 55th Annual Convention, American Association for Health, Physical Education and Recreation*, Dallas, Texas, 1950.

"Physical Exercise Dividends," *Journal of Physical Education*, 48: 76, (Mar.-Apr., 1951).

"Exercise to Forestall Heart Disease," *Good Health*, 86: 129, (June, 1951).

"The Hearts of Athletes," *Illinois Medical Journal*, 99: 143, 1951.

"Review of Research to Determine Cardiovascular Condition," (1941-50), *Proceedings of the American Physical Education and Recreation*, 56th Annual Convention, Detroit, 1951.

"Aquatots Tested in Fitness," *The National Y.M.C.A. Aquatic News*, 3: 12-14, (Sept., 1951).

"Report of the National Committee on Aquatic Leadership," (American Association for Health, Physical Education and Recreation), *Proceedings of the American Association for Health, Physical Education and Recreation*, (56th Annual Convention, Detroit, 1951).

"Y.M.C.A. Pioneers Important Steps in Aquatics," *Journal of Physical Education*, 49: Nov.-Dec., 38, 1951.

"Progressive Deterioration is Principal Fitness Problem of Middle-Age—Physical Training Sets the Clock Back," *Journal of Physical Education*, 49: 120-121, (May-June, 1952).

"How to Keep Fit at 50," *Popular Mechanics*, (May, 1952).

"Survival Aquatic Activities for the Emergency," *Journal of Physical Education*, 49: 87-89, March-April, 1952; *The National Y.M.C.A. Aquatic News*, 3: 3-7, (Feb., 1952). (Bibliography).

"Physical Training Produces Important Changes, Psychological and Physiological," *International Symposium of Sports Medicine and Physiology*, XV Olympiad, Helsinki, 1952 (Reprinted in the *Journal of Finnish Medicine*).

"Physical Fitness Improvement of a Middle-Aged Man, with Brief Reviews of Related Studies," *The Research Quarterly*, 23: 149-160, May, 1952.

"Exercise for Executives," *Bulletin of the Industrial Welfare Society, Inc.*, 48 Bryanston Square, London, W 1 (Sports and Social Clubs Conference, Cliftonville, May, 1952).

(With E. D. Michael). "Effects of Physical Training on Cardiac Output at Ground Level and at 15,000 ft. Simulated Altitude." *Research Quarterly*, (A.A.H.P.E.R.), 24: 446-452, 1953.

(With E. D. Michael). "Swimming at the 1952 Olympic Games," *Beach and Pool*, 27: 18, 39, 41, 42.

(With E. D. Michael). "Swimming at the 1952 Olympic Games," *Beach and Pool*, 27: 14, 23, 24.

(With E. D. Michael). "Swimming at the 1952 Olympic Games, *Y.M.C.A. Aquatic News,* 3: 1-6.

(With E. D. Michael). "Diving Aptitude Test," *Y.M.C.A. Aquatic News,* 3: 8, 1952.

(With E. D. Michael). "The Contribution of Swimming to Physical Fitness," *Beach and Pool,* 28: 18 +, June, 1954; Continued July, 1954, P. 16 +; etc.

(With E. D. Michael). "Athletes Have Good Hearts," *Science News Letter,* 66: 10-11, July 3, 1954, as told to Marjorie Van de Water by T. K. Cureton.

(With E. D. Michael). "Regards sur la Recherche Scientifigue Medico—Sportive Aux U.S.A.," (as told by T. K. Cureton to Drs. Jacques Leclerg and Robert Andvivet, Maitres de Recherches a l' I.N.S.) (Initions Nos Sportifs) *INS* 5: 9-11 (May-June, 1952). Joinville, France.

(With E. D. Michael) "Physical Fitness and the Sedentary Worker," *Illinois Certified Accountant* 16: 28-36 +, (July, 1954).

(With E. D. Michael). "Perspective on the National Y.M.C.A. Aquatic Conferences," *Y.M.C.A. Aquatic News,* 5: 2-4, (June, 1954).

"Physical Fitness and the Sedentary Worker," *The Illinois Certified Public Accountant,* 16: 28-36, (June, 1954); (abstract), *The Journal of Accountancy,* 99: 78, (Jan. 1955).

"Comparison of Fifty-Two Middle-Aged Former Athletic Champions with Some 400 Middle-Aged Men and with Normal Young Men," *Proceedings of the American Assn. for Health, Physical Education and Recreation,* Pp. 117-118, 1954.

"Comparison of 55 Middle-Aged Former Athletic Champions with Some 400 Middle-Aged Men and with Normal Young Men," *Am. Journ. of Physical Anthropology,* 12: 294, June, 1954. (Abstract, *Science News Letter,* July 3, 1954).

(With Julian Snyder and Percy Knauth). "The Tip that Led Bannister to Victory," *Sports Illustrated,* 1: 6-9, (Aug. 30, 1954).

"The Contribution of Swimming to Physical Fitness," *Beach and Pool,* 28: 18- 19 +, June, 1954; Part II, 16-17 +, July, 1954; Part III, 17-18, Aug., 1954; Conclusion, Pp. 16-17, Sept., 1954.

"Exercise, Wheat Germ Oil for Middle-Aged Men," *Science News Letter,* 66: 216, (Oct. 2, 1954).

"Preservation of the Middle-Aged Man," *Journal of Physical Education,* 52: 27-29, (Nov.-Dec., 1954).

"Wheat Germ Oil, the Wonder Fuel," *Scholastic Coach,* 24: 36-37 +, (Mar., 1955).

"Results of Moderate Physical Training on Middle-Aged Men," *Bulletin of the Federation Internationale d' Education Physique,* Lund, Sweden, I: 58-59, 1955.

(With W. H. White). "Exercise to Keep Fit," *Sports Illustrated,* 2: 63-65, (Jan. 17, 1955).

"Preservation of the Middle-Aged Man," *Bulletin of the National Council of the Y.M.C.A.,* (Feb., 1955).

(With Bob Allison). "How to Keep Your Family Young," *Redbook,* 104: 30-31, 90-91, (April, 1955).

"Influence of Wheat Germ Oil as a Dietary Supplement in a Program of Conditioning Exercises with Middle-Aged Subjects," *The Research Quarterly,* 26: 391-407, (Dec., 1955).

(With Wayne D. Van Huss) "Relationship of Selected Tests with Energy Metabolism and Swimming Performance," *The Research Quarterly,* 26: 205-221, (May, 1955).

"Shrinkage of Heart Size Associated with Improved Cardiovascular Condition Due to Progressive Physical Training of Three Middle-Aged Men." *Journal of Mental and Physical Rehabilitation,* 10: 75-88 +, (May-June, 1956).

"Physical Fitness, How to Earn It and Keep It," *Journal of Physical Education*, 54: 3-14, (Sept.-Oct., 1956).

"Relationship of Physical Fitness to Athletic Performance and Sports," *Journal of the American Medical Assn.*, 162: 1139-1151, (Nov. 17, 1956).

"The Analysis of Physical Education and Athletic Activities and the Effects Produced by Such Programs," Daytona Beach, Florida: *59th Annual Proceedings*, (College Physical Education Assn.), 1956.

"Physical Fitness Work with Normal Aging Adults," *Jour. of the Assn. for Physical and Mental Rehabilitation*, 11: 145-149, (Sept.-Oct., 1957).

"Post-Exercise Blood Pressures in Maximum Exertion Tests and Relationships to Performance Time, Oxygen Intake and Oxygen Debt, and Peripheral Resistance," *The Journal-Lancet*, (Minneapolis), 77: 81-82, (Mar., 1957).

"Research in Physical Education in the United States," *Physical Education Journal*, 1: No. 9, (Feb.-March, 11-24, 1957).

"You Can Be Physically Fit," *What's New in Home Economics*, 21: 30-31 +, Jan., 1957.

"The Nature of Cardiovascular Condition in Normal Humans," *Journal of the Association for Physical and Mental Rehabilitation*, 11: 186-196, Nov.-Dec., 1957.

"Report Reveals Value of Wheat Germs," *Swimming Age*, 31: 87, 99, 101, April, 1957.

"Technical Analysis of the World's Greatest Swimmers," *Scholastic Coach*, 27: 38-42, (Sept., 1957).

"Science Aids Australian Swimmers," *Athletic Journal*, 38: 40 +, (Mar., 1957).

"What Exercise Can Do for You," *Life and Health*, 72: 14-15, 32 (April, 1957).

"Observations on the 1956 Olympic Games, Swimming and Diving," *National Y.M.C.A. Aquatic News*, No. 4, Pp. 1-7, Apr., 1957; No. 5, Pp. 2-7, (Nov., 1957).

"Improvements in Cardiovascular Condition of Humans Associated with Physical Training, Persistently Performed Sports and Exercises," *Proceedings of the College Physical Education Association*, 60: 82-104, Columbus, Ohio, 1957.

"How to Get the Physical Fitness Ingredient into Sports Education," *Proceedings of the College Physical Education Assn.*, 60: 286-297, Columbus, Ohio, 1957.

"Effects of Physical Education and Athletics Upon the Kraus-Weber and Cureton 18-Item Motor Fitness Tests," *Jour. of Phys. Education*, 55: 37-40, (Nov.-Dec., 1957).

"The Nature of Cardiovascular Condition in Normal Humans" (Part 2). New York: *Journal for Physical and Mental Rehabilitation*. 12: 8-12. (Jan.-Feb., 1958).

"The Nature of Cardiovascular Condition in Normal Humans" (Part 3). New York: *Journal for Physical and Mental Rehabilitation*. 12: 41-49, (Mar.-Apr., 1958).

"Personal Health and Fitness," *Physical Education Journal*, (Melbourne, Australia), (June-July, 1958).

"Effects of Longitudinal Physical Training on the Amplitude of the Highest Precordial T-Wave of the ECG," Rome, Italy: *Medicina Sportiva*. 12: 259-281, 1958.

"The Nature of Cardiovascular Condition in Normal Humans," (Part 4). New York: *Journal for Physical and Mental Rehabilitation*. 12: 113-124 (July-Aug., 1958).

"The Value of Hard Endurance Exercises and Tests to Produce Changes in Weight, Fat, Metabolism and Cardiovascular Condition." Johannesburg, So. Africa: *Vigor*, 2: 12-16, (Sept., 1958).

"The Long Slow Physical Training Fitness Build-Up." *Canadian Aquatic News*, Erindale (Ontario, Canada), 1: 5-10, 17, (Nov., 1958).

"The Effect of Physical Training, Sports and Exercises on Weight, Fat and Tissue

Proportions," Washington, D. C.: *Professional Contributions*, No. 6, American Academy of Physical Education, Nov., 1958.

"L'Exercise Physique Grandue'," *Merite-Nouvelle*, Montreal: Bureaux de L'Executif, (Industrial Acceptance Corporation), 11: 1-4, (Dec., 1958).

"The Case for Physical Fitness," *Think*, New York, Sept., 1958, (Condensed in *Science Digest*, Dec., 1958).

"The Value of Hard Endurance Exercises and Tests to Produce Changes in Weight, Fat, Metabolism and Cardiovascular Condition," Washington, D. C.: *Proceedings of the 61st College Physical Education Assn.*, Pp. 162-171. 1958.

"You Are Middle-Aged at 26," *Pageant*, 14: 58-65, (Feb., 1959).

"Research in Physical Education in the U.S.A.," Pp. 22-32, *Report of the 'World Congress on Physical Education*, Melbourne, 1956, (Australian Physical Education Assn., Victoria, Australia), 1959.

"The Effect of Physical Education and Athletics on Young Boys," Pp. 119-130, *Report of the World Congress of Physical Education*, Victoria, Australia, 1959.

"The Effect of Exercise on Improving Glandular Function," *The Research Quarterly*, 30: 266-284, (Oct., 1959).

"Effect of Physical Training and a Wheat Germ Oil Dietary Supplement upon the T-wave of the ECG and the Bicycle Ergometer Endurance Test," *Medicina Sportiva*, 8: 490-505, (Oct., 1959).

"The Case for Physical Fitness," *English Digest* (London), 60: No. 2, 40-42, (Aug., 1959).

"The Case for Physical Fitness," *Democracy in Action*, 17: 10-15, (Mar.-Apr., 1959).

"The Case for Physical Fitness," *The Los Angeles Police Beat*, 14: 4-8, (Sept., 1959).

(With Charles A. Bucher and others) "Fit for College," Washington, D. C.: *Am. Assn. for Health, Physical Education and Recreation*, 1959, Pp. 24.

"Diet Related to Athletics and Physical Fitness," (Part I), *Journal of Physical Education*, 57: 27-30, (Nov.-Dec., 1959).

"What About Wheat Germ?" *Scholastic Coach*, 29: 24-26 +, (Nov., 1959).

1960

"Suggested Guide Lines for Youth Fitness," Pp. 11-12 in *Suggested Guide Lines for Youth Fitness in Illinois*, Springfield, Illinois (Governor's Office), 1960.

"Scientific Testing of Athletes to Discover Fitness Levels Attained in Various Sports—Differences in Training and Out of Training," *Physical Education Today*, 7: No. 1, 5-6 (March, 1960).

"Scientific Control of Training," *Physical Education Today*, 7: No. 1, 7-9, (March, 1960)..

"What the Heartometer Measures That is of Special Interest and Importance to Physical Educators and Physical Fitness Directors," *Physical Education Today*, 7: No. 1, 10-14, (March, 1960).

"Comparison of Methods for Determining Cardiac Output," *Physical Education Today*, 7: No. 1, 15-20, (March, 1960).

(With Alan Barry). "Warm-up Studies in Athletics," *Physical Education Today*, 7: No. 1, 21-25, (March, 1960).

"Diet in Athletic Conditioning and Training," *Physical Education Today*, 7: No. 1, 27-29, (March, 1960).

"New Techniques of Athletic Training and Conditioning," Tokyo: (privately printed by Japanese Olympic Committee, April 5, 1960); *Ibid, Olympia*, No. 1, Pp. 28-37, (July, 1960).

"The Training and Conditioning of Track and Field Athletes," *Rikujo-Kyogi* (Track and Field Journal), Tokyo: 10: No. 9, 4-13, (July, 1960).

"Nouvelles Technniques d'Entrainment et Mise en Condition Athletiques," *Revue d'Education Physique*, No. 3, 193-218, 1960.

"Diet Related to Athletics and Physical Fitness," *Nabitka Autorska Wychowanic i Sport*, 4: No. 3, 273-386, 1960.

"Diet Related to Athletics and Physical Fitness," Part II, *Journal of Physical Education*, Pp. 59-62, (Jan.-Feb., 1960).

"Diet Related to Athletics and Physical Fitness," Part III, *Journal of Physical Education*, *Pp.* 77-81, (Mar.-Apr., 1960).

"Diet Related to Athletics and Physical Fitness," Part IV, *Journal of Physical Education*, Pp. 104-107, (May-June, 1960).

"Sympathetic Versus Vagus Influence Upon the Contractile Vigor of the Heart," *The Research Quarterly*, 32: 553-557, (Dec., 1961).

"Health and Physical Fitness Tests of Dentists (with Implications)," *Journal of Dental Medicine*, 16: 211-223, (Oct., 1961).

"Putting Physical Fitness Into Physical Education," *Journal of the California Association for Health, Physical Education and Recreation*, 24: 8-10, 11, (Nov.-Dec., 1961).

"Scientific Principles of Human Endurance," *The Australian Journal of Physical Education*, No. 21: 14-24, (Feb.-Mar., 1961).

"Scientific Principles of Human Endurance with Suggestions for Its Development," *The Journal of Physical Education*, 58: 81-86, (Mar.-Apr., 1961).

"New Techniques of Athletic Training and Conditioning," (Part I), *Journal of the Association for Physical and Mental Rehabilitation*, 15: 78-84, 89, (May-June, 1961).

"New Techniques of Athletic Training and Conditioning," (Part II), *Journal of the Association for Physical and Mental Rehabilitation*, 15: 103-107, (July-Aug., 1961).

"Principles of Training and Conditioning," *The Journal of Physical Education*, 59: 37-40, (Nov.-Dec., 1961).

"Ce que le Heartometre revele aux professeurs d'education physique et aux entraineurs," *Revue Education Physique*, 1: 796-802, No. 1, (Sept., 1961).

(With Alan J. Barry) "Factorial Analysis of Physique and Performance in Pre-pubescent Boys," *The Research Quarterly*, *32*: 283-300, (Oct., 1961).

"The Superior Child in Health, Physical Education and Recreation," *Indian Journal of Social Research*, 3: 71-80, (May, 1962).

"New Training Methods and Dietary Supplements Are Responsible for Many of the New Records," *The Athletic Journal*, 42: 12-14 +.

"Entwicklungsprogramme der Korperlichen Ertuchtigung fur Kinder und Erwachesene," *Der Sportarzt* 7: 146-153, 1962.

"Kardio-vaskulare Leistungs fahigkeit und ihre Bewahrung durch korperliche Ubungsprogramme," *Der Sportarzt*, 7: 230-236, 1962.

(With Leroy Sterling). "Factor Analyses of Cardiovascular Variables," *International Journal of Sports Medicine and Physical Fitness*, 2: No. 4, (Nov.-Dec., 1962). (Rome).

(With E. E. Phillips). "Improvements Associated with Alternate Periods of Physical Training and Non-Training," *International Journal of Sports Medicine and Physical Fitness*, 2: No. 4, (Nov.-Dec., 1962.)

"The Training and Seasoning of Muscles, Tendons and Ligaments," *Journal of the Association for Physical and Mental Rehabilitation*, 16: 80-85 (May-June, 1962). Part II: Pp. 103-106 +, (July-Aug., 1962).

"The Principles of Training and Conditioning," *Vyayam* (Saidapet-Madras, India). Y.M.C.A. College of Physical Education, Pp. 13-14, (May, 1962).

"Putting Physical Fitness Into Physical Education," *Journal of the Canadian Assn. for Health, Physical Education and Recreation*, 29: 21-22, 23, (Oct.-Nov., 1962).

"New Training Methods Bring New Records," *Modern Athletics*, 6: 26-28, (July, 1962).

"Improvement of Psychological States by Means of Exercise-Fitness Programs," *The Journal for the Assn. for Physical and Mental Rehabilitation*, 17: 14-25, (Jan.-Feb., 1963).

"Forty-Love—Should Men Over 40 Play Tennis?" *Abbottempo*, 1: 26-29, (Mar. 22, 1963).

"New Techniques of Athletic Training and Conditioning," (in Japanese), 57: 28-37, *Olympia*, No. 1, 1960.

"Principles of Training and Conditioning," (in Japanese), 59: 162-165, No. 2, (June, 1962).

"Results of Moderate Physical Training on Middle-Aged Men," *Louisiana Assn. for Health, Physical Education and Recreation*, 28: No. 2, 16-17, (Mar., 1963).

"Why Research? Professional Perspectives: Hind View, Present View and Future View," *Australian Journal of Physical Education*, No. 28, 14-21, (July, 1963).

"New Training Methods Bring New Records," *Modern Athletics* (London), 6: 26-28, (July, 1962).

"Forty-Love," *The Official USLTA News*, No. 313, 12-13, (Oct., 1963).

"The Nature of Cardiovascular Conditioning and Protection by Exercise-Fitness Programs," *Journal of Physical Education*, 61: 30-34. (Nov.-Dec., 1963).

"Improvements Resulting from a U. S. Navy Underwater Swimming Training Program, "With and Without Dietary Supplements," *The Research Quarterly*, (Dec., 1963).

(With E. V. Doroschuk) "The Relationship of Metabolic, Cardiovascular and Motor Fitness Tests With Endurance Running of Young Boys," *The Journal of Sports Medicine and Physical Fitness*, 3: No. 4, 254, (Dec., 1963) (Abstract).

(With Francis J. Hayden) "A P-Technique Factor Analysis of Cardiovascular Variables," *The Journal of Sports Medicine and Physical Fitness*, 3: No. 4, 253, (Dec., 1963) (Abstract).

"A Physical Fitness Case Study of Joie Ray, Improving Physical Fitness from 60 to 70 Years of Age," *The Journal of the Assn. for Physical and Mental Rehabilitation*, 18: 64-72 + 80, (May-June, 1964).

"Ten Tips on Leading Exercises," Bulletin of *Program Service*, 771 First Ave., New York: Boys' Clubs of America.

(With L. Sterling). "Factor Analyses of Cardiovascular Test Variables," *The Journal of Sports Medicine and Physical Fitness*, 4: No. 1, 1-24, (March, 1964).

"Physical Fitness Changes in Middle-Aged Men Attributable to Equal Eight-Week Periods of Training, Non-Training and Re-Training," *The Journal of Sports Medicine and Physical Fitness*, 4: No. 2, 87-93, June, 1964.

"Results of Dietary Supplementation With Wheat Germ Oil, Wheat Germ and Octacosanol in the Sports-Fitness School With Small Boys," *Proceedings of the International Congress of Sport Sciences*, Tokyo, (Oct., 1964). (Abstract C-52).

(With E. Doroschuk, E. Bernauer, J. Bosco). "Prediction of All-Out Treadmill Running Time in Young Boys in the Sports-Fitness School, University of Illinois," *The Australian Journal of Physical Education*, No. 29: 36-40, (Nov. 1963).

"Cureton's Demonstrations at the First Regional Clinic of the President's Physical Fitness Council," Sacramento, Calif., *Physical Education Newsletter*, No. 18, Vol. 7, 1-2, (May 12, 1963).

(With J. S. Skinner and J. O. Holloszy). "Effects of a Program of Endurance Exercises on Physical Work," *The Amer. Journal of Cardiology*, 14: 747-752, (Dec., 1964).

(With J. O. Holloszy, J. S. Skinner and G. Toro). "Effects of a Six Month Program of Endurance Exercise on the Serum Lipids of Middle-Aged Men," *Amer. Journal of Cardiology*, 14: 753-760, (Dec., 1964).

(With J. O. Holloszy, J. S. Skinner, A. J. Barry). "Effects of Physical Conditioning on Cardiovascular Functioning," *Amer. Journal of Cardiology*, 14: 761-770, (Dec., 1964).

"Making Fitness Experts of Elementary Teachers," *Physical Education Newsletter*, New London: Croft Education Services, 100 Garfield Ave., Vol. 18: Letter 17, (May 1, 1964).

"Summary of Recent Findings from Dietary Supplement Studies in Relationship to the Possibility for Improving Athletic and Cardiovascular Performance," *Report of the International Congress of Sport Sciences*, Tokyo, (Oct. 6, 1964).

The Research Quarterly, 35: 93, (March, 1964). "W. B. Jones and Others, Velocity of Blood Flow and Stroke Volume Obtained from the Pressure Pulse," *Journal of Clin. Invest.* 38: 2087, 1959. (Abstract).

The Journal of the Assn. for Physical and Mental Rehabilitation. "Soviet Studies on Nutrition and Higher Nervous Activity," 18: 171-173, (Nov.-Dec., 1964). (Abstract).

"What Research Reveals about Physical Fitness," in *Nuevas Tendencias*, VIII (Informe de la Conferencia Continental de Educacion Fisica), Piriapolis, S.A., 1965.

"Forty-Love," *The Australian Journal of Sports Medicine*, 1: No. 3, 20-26, (June, 1965).

"New Emphasis for Physical Fitness—How to Get More Fitness into Physical Education," *The Australian Journal of Physical Education*, (4th, 5th and 6th grades) No. 35, Oct.-Nov., 1965).

"Training Youthful Record Breaking Athletes," *The Athletic Journal*, 16:32, Pp. 49-52, (Nov., 1965).

"The Relative Value of Various Exercise-Conditioning Programs to Improve Cardiovascular Status and to Prevent Heart Disease," *First International Conference on Preventive Cardiology*, (Abstracts, 1965).

"A Case Study of Sidney Meadow" (A Dramatic Heart Rehabilitation Case), *Journal of the Association of Physical and Mental Rehabilitation*, 19: 2, 36-43, (March-April, 1965).

"A Case Study Report of Professor E.D.W." (from 58-74 Years of Age, His Fitness Maintenance Program), *Journal of the Association for Physical and Mental Rehabilitation*, 19: 5, (Sept.-Oct., 1965).

"A Fitness Routine—30 Mins. of Non-Stop Exercise," *Physical Education Newsletter*, (Letter 14), Vol. 9, (Mar. 15, 1965).

"Physical Fitness and Testing Activities," *Program Service* (Boys' Clubs of America), (Fall, 1965).

"Physical Fitness Testing and Activities," *Physical Education Newsletter*, (Supplement), 1965.

"The Relative Value of Various Exercise-Conditioning Programs to Improve Cardiovascular Status and to Prevent Heart Disease," (abstract), *The Journal of Sports Medicine and Physical Fitness.* 9: No. 1, 1965.

(With Wilbur Bohm). "Summary of Dietary Supplement Studies Since 1958 which Relate to Bearing Stress or Improving Performance, and a Note on Determining Statistical Reliability in the Same," in *Abstracts of Papers Presented at International Congress of Sport Sciences*, Tokyo, Japan, 1965.

(With Alan Barry). "Measuring Performance and Improvement in Endurance in Circulatory-Respiratory Fitness in Young Boys," *Vigor*, (Pretoria, S.A.), 18: 44-46, (March, 1965).

"Le Role due l'Education Physique dans le Development de la Personality," *Journal of Physical and Mental Rehabilitation*, 19: No. 5, (Sept.-Oct., 1965). (Review).

"Personal Health and Fitness," *Swimming Technique*, (April, 1966).

"The Body of the Whole Man," Pp. 172-181, *Proceedings 1966*, Boston: The Million Dollar Round-Table of the National Association of Life Underwriters, 1966.

"Prevention of Physiological Aging," *Mercury*, 56: 4-5, Los Angeles (Sept., 1966).

"Comparison of Various Factor Analyses of Cardiovascular-Respiratory Test Variables," *The Research Quarterly*, 37: 317-325 (Dec., 1966).

(With Alan J. Barry). "What Does the Research Monograph Reveal? (Improving the Physical Fitness of Youth"), *Australian Journal of Physical Education*, No. 37: 19-24 (June-July, 1966).

(With S. F. du Toit). "Effect of Progressive Physical Training on the Latent Period of Electrical Stimulation of the Left Ventricle of the Human Heart," *Proceedings of the College Physical Education Assn.*, Philadelphia (69th Annual Meeting), 1965.

(With editors). "Cardiovascular Effects of Exercise," *Roche Medical Image*, 8: 32-34 (June, 1966).

(With E. W. Banister, B. C. Abbott and J. W. Pollard). "A Comparative Study of the Brachial Pulse Wave and Its Time Derivatives Among Athletic, Normal and Pathological Subjects," *The Journal of Sports Medicine and Physical Fitness*, 6: 92-99 (June, 1966).

(With W. Raab). "Prevention of Ischemic Heart Disease," In *The relative value of various exercise programs to protect adult human subjects from degenerative heart disease*, Springfield, Ill.: C. C. Thomas.

(With J. L. Berbier, J. C. Muhler). "Improving Dental Practice Through Preventive Measures." In *Physical fitness and dynamic health*. St. Louis: C. V. Mosby.

(With AAHPER). "New Dimensions in Aquatics." *Basic principles of physical fitness work, rules for conducting exercise*. AAHPER, Washington, D.C.

"Physical Fitness and Its Effect on the Mental and Physical Health of the Whole Man." NALU, Washington, D.C.

(With J. W. Blevins). "The Cameron Heartometer in Industrial Medicine." *J. Assn. Phys. and Men. Rehab.* 21: 112-21.

(With S. B. Sward, P. M. Ribisl). "Deterioration Curves and Their Reversal by Physical Fitness Exercise Programs." *70th Proc. Ann. Meet.*, NCPEAM.

"Exercise: Does It Help Ward off Heart Trouble?" *Consumer Rpts.*, 32: 141-45.

"Help Stamp out Middle Age." *Pace*, 3: 28-40.

"What You Should Know About Heart Disease. *Chicago Trib.*, *Supp.*, Aug. 13, 1967.

"You Are Extraordinary," by Roger J. Williams. *Amer. Cor. Ther. J.*, 21: 211-12. (Review).

"The Relative Value of Stress Indicators, Related to Prediction of Strenuous Athletic (Treadmill) Performance," *Biochemistry of Exercise, Medicine and Sport*, 3: 73-80, New York, 1969. (Pub. Karger in Basel, Switzerland).

"Nutritive Aspects of Physical Fitness Work," *Journal of Physical Education*, (Nov.-Dec., 1966).

A Collection of Activities, Routines and Tests for Building Fitness," in *Shaping Up to Quality*, New London, Conn.: Croft Educational Services, 1968.

"Logic (Basic Assumptions) of the Program for Prevention of Ischemic (Including CHD) Heart Disease," 71st Meeting, in *Proceedings of the Annual Meeting, National College Physical Education Association for Men*, (Jan. 10-13, 1968), Houston, Texas.

"What Is Physical Education Research?" *Journal of Health, Physical Education and Recreation*, 30: 95-97 (Oct., 1968).

"Modern Views of Physical Fitness — Physical Fitness for What?" in *Symposium Canadien de la Recreation*, Montreal, P. Q. (June 10-16, 1967) Parks Dept., City of Montreal, 1968.

"The Trends and Hopes of the Physical Fitness Laboratory Work," in *Symposium Canadien de la Recreation*, Montreal, P. Q. (June 10-16, 1967) Parks Dept., City of Montreal, 1968.

"Physical Fitness and Dynamic Health," in *Symposium Canadien de la Recreation*, Montreal, P. Q. (June 10-16, 1967), Parks Dept., City of Montreal, 1968.

"The Training and Seasoning of Muscles, Tendons and Ligaments," in *Symposium Canadien de la Recreation*, Montreal, P. Q. (June 10-16, 1967) Parks Dept., City of Montreal, 1968.

"The Essentials of a Good Physical Fitness Program, The Relative Effectiveness of Various Exercise Programs," *Ibid*.

(With Bradley L. Rothermel and Michael L. Pollock), "AAHPER Physical Fitness Test Score Changes Resulting from an Eight-Week Sports and Physical Fitness Program," *The Research Quarterly*, 39: 1127-1129 (Dec., 1968).

(With B. Don Franks). "Orthogonal Factors of Cardiac Intervals and Their Response to Stress," *The Research Quarterly*, 39: 524-532 (Oct., 1968).

(With B. Don Franks). "Effects of Training on Cardiac Intervals," in *71st Meeting, Proceedings of the Annual Meeting National College Physical Education Association for Men*, (Jan. 10-13, 1968)) Houston, Texas.

(With V. A. Corroll). "Variabilite des mesures d'aptitudes physiques dans differents groupes d'age," in *Biometric Humaine*, Paris, 1967.

(With Mrs. John Boddie). "Cureton of England, Wales and Virginia," in Vol. XII *Historical Southern Families*, Honolulu: P. O. Box 2775, Hawaii 96803.

Relationship of Physical
Activity to Fitness

PHYSICAL ACTIVITY AND RISK FACTORS ASSOCIATED WITH CORONARY HEART DISEASE[1]

HENRY J. MONTOYE

University of Michigan

ABSTRACT

A questionnaire-interview method was used to assess the amount and intensity of habitual physical activity of men age 20-64 in a total community of about 10,000 persons. The men were classified as sedentary, moderately active or active on the basis of their occupational activity, leisure-time activity or a combination of both. Systolic and diastolic blood pressure, serum total cholesterol and glucose tolerance of men in the various activity groups were compared. When activity classification was based upon both occupational and leisure-time activities, the largest differences in the coronary heart disease risk factors appeared. The active men had significantly lower systolic and diastolic blood pressure and significantly lower serum total cholesterol. There were no significant differences in blood glucose.

INTRODUCTION

For many years suggestions have appeared in the literature that regular physical activity somehow plays a role in maintaining the health of the cardiovascular system. For the most part, these suggestions were the result of intuitive impressions of careful observers. Only in comparatively recent times has there been objective scientific work on the problem. Nevertheless, there exists a paucity of evidence that physical activity prevents or delays heart disease in man. The case rests primarily on comparisons among occupational groups in which death certificates and governmental or company records are examined to determine age and cause of death. Reasons why this approach has been employed are obvious. Such data are fairly accessible. Furthermore, it is not difficult to observe differences in physical activity among various occupations. Kraus and Raab (12, pp. 96-97) summarized 17 such studies (the first reported 30 years ago) and there have been at least six additional studies since their book was published. In all but one of the investigations, the more active group experienced fewer deaths due to heart disease when age specific comparisons were made. This sounds impressive and conclusive but these 23 or more studies do not represent different approaches to the problem. Rather, they represent essentially one study repeated 22 times; hence, all of the limitations in the first are present in the others.[2]

[1]This study was supported in part by the Center for Research in Disease of the Heart, the University of Michigan (Dr. Thomas Francis, Jr., Director) under program Project Grant HE-09814 from the National Heart Institute, National Institutes of Health, U.S. Public Health Service and in part by Grant CD-00246 from the National Institutes of Health, U.S. Public Health Service.

[2]For a discussion of limitations of epidemiologic studies of this kind, see Keys (10).

There is little question that one occupational group is more active than another but the men engaged in these occupations may differ in many other respects; namely, diet, "stress," body fatness, smoking habits, etc. There is also the possibility that men who develop impaired health may gravitate to less strenuous occupations. Furthermore, except for one study (18), off-the-job exercise was not seriously studied.

The comment is frequently heard that the problem calls for an intervention study; that is, an experimental investigation in which sedentary subjects initiate an exercise program. In fact, Karvonen (9) quotes an English physician, Heberden, writing in 1802 about heart disease as follows, "I know one who set himself a task of sawing wood half an hour every day, and was nearly cured." The classical approach, if carried out with proper controls, should provide a clear answer to the question of whether a leisure-time exercise program provides protection against coronary heart disease. It was my pleasure to serve for about three years on a committee, organized by Dr. Sam Fox and Dr. Henry L. Taylor under the aegis of the U. S. Public Health Service, to evaluate the feasibility of such an intervention study. An estimate of the number of subjects necessary to undertake an investigation of this kind will have a sobering effect and dampen one's enthusiasm for this approach. Remington and Shork (17) have calculated these estimates. Let us assume the annual incidence of coronary heart disease in sedentary middle-aged men in the United States to be about one percent, not an unreasonable estimate (3). If we assume (a) that a program of exercise would reduce this incidence by about 25 percent, (b) that 10 percent of the men would discontinue the exercise program each year,[3] and (c) the $\propto$ error is set at 5 percent and the power of the test at 95 percent; then we would need to begin with a sample of 12,000 men in the experimental group and 12,000 control subjects, and the experiment would have to continue for five years to detect a significant effect of exercise on coronary heart disease. This is not an impossible task but a formidable one, indeed! The situation is probably not as hopeless as trying to study the effects of smoking on lung cancer utilizing a similar experimental design.

At this point in time, it appears that alternative approaches must be used. Using high risk subjects would help somewhat but would not eliminate the need for very large numbers of subjects. One could exercise people who have already had an infarct (secondary prevention) but this is not quite the same problem. It is also useful to follow a large group of people, periodically collecting physical activity and other data, before the disease manifests itself. This is being attempted in the Tecumseh Study (13). This is also the approach used in the Framingham Study (8) and by Keys and his group (11). But either extremely large numbers of subjects are needed or a long period must elapse before sufficient new coronary heart disease events appear for cause-effects relationships to be studied. It is too early yet for incidence data to be

---

[3]This is likely an optimistic figure. The drop-out rate would probably be considerably higher.

related to exercise habits in a definitive way.

Some species of animals, because of their short life span, can be used for experimental research on cardiovascular disease. Atherosclerosis and infarcts have been produced in many kinds of animals but the applicability of results to human beings is always questionable. Furthermore, with regard to physical exercise, applications require the specification of duration, frequency and intensity, and such quantification cannot be obtained in animal studies.

The Tecumseh Project

For more than 10 years the town of Tecumseh, Michigan, has been the focus of a large scientific research effort, an epidemiologic investigation of an entire American community. By studying the residents of Tecumseh, in particular the younger residents in their community, it is hoped that early signs of predisposition to disease will be revealed among those still healthy and that subtle etiologic factors, both genetic and environmental, which lead to impaired health will be found. This in turn should lead to more effective disease prevention in the future.

A question frequently asked is "why was the community of Tecumseh selected for this investigation?" In the first place, its 10,000 inhabitants represent a population of sufficient size for the results to be significant and yet small enough for the study to be manageable. The population includes 3,000 participants who live in the rural area immediately outside the town limits. Hence, a variety of occupations and socio-economic levels are represented in this setting. The community is 27 miles from the University of Michigan, so it is not difficult for members of the project staff to commute from the University when necessary. Finally, the community was comprised of friendly civic minded people who seemed willing to submit to occasional inconveniences in the interest of science and who had faith that the project would ultimately lead to improved health of the people in Tecumseh, in the nation, and in the world.

The overall procedures include (1) periodic interviews in the home and examinations of the respondents in the clinic, (2) a more frequent surveillance of "minor" medical ailments and personal or family disturbances which might contribute to impaired health, and (3) fringe or side studies involving smaller segments of the population for more intensive study including investigations of more specific scope and studies of the environment outside the family which influence the health of the community members. About 90 percent of all the residents of the community are participating in the study.

An exercise physiology laboratory has been established in the community where treadmill oxygen uptake tests have been administered to over 1,400 respondents. During the last two rounds of examinations, habitual physical activity, both occupational and leisure, has been assessed in males, age 16 and over. Although it is too early to report the relationship of physical activity to overt coronary heart disease, it is possible to study its relationship to risk factors associated with the disease. This is the subject of the present report.

METHODS

Assessment of Habitual Physical Activity

The entire study population was divided into 10, 10 percent random samples by living units and each successive sample interviewed and examined (14). An activity recall questionnaire and interview was employed in 1962-1965 to collect habitual physical activity data on males 16 years of age and over who were not attending school. The professional interviewer, at first contact, delivered a self-administered questionnaire to the respondent. In the questionnaire, inquiries were made about occupation(s), transportation to and from work, major home repairs and maintenance, gardening and sports participation. At next contact the interviewer spent from 30 minutes to an hour with each respondent, completing supplementary questionnaire forms designed to probe for details on each activity. The questionnaire and interview forms were designed to estimate physical activity during the preceding year. In only one general occupation, farming, were the tasks too varied to permit an analysis and quantitative score. For men in this occupation, the interviewer simply determined that the respondent actually worked the farm and these subjects were then grouped in a separate category.

The present report includes data obtained from approximately 80 percent of the males interviewed. Data on the first 20 percent (randomly selected) had been used to develop and refine the questionnaire and interview methods. Data from the following subjects were excluded: males under age 20 and over age 64 because the numbers were too small, respondents who were unemployed at the time of the interview or for whom no information was available on their occupations. The number of subjects, after exclusions, was 1,696.

The energy cost of the 34 leisure activities and of various occupation activities was estimated. This estimate is expressed as a multiple of the basal metabolic rate and is abbreviated as WMR/BMR. A score of 3.0 for bowling indicates that the energy expenditure for bowling is estimated at three times the basal metabolic rate. More strenuous activities were given higher ratios, for example, the ratio for handball is 12. This method of scoring was used to eliminate the necessity of considering the subject's body weight, converting work to calories, etc. It assumes that a task performed by a heavy person raises his metabolism the same amount as for a person weighing less, even though the caloric expenditure may be different. Since the activities recorded generally involved moving one's own body weight, errors in making this assumption are probably not serious. A detailed description of the questionnaire, a complete table of the metabolic costs and the coding system for the various occupation and leisure activities are published elsewhere (16).

Also, the age-specific distribution of leisure-time activities with frequency of participation has been published (2).

Fifteen indices of energy expenditure were calculated for each subject based on the data just described. The age-specific distributions of these indices and their intercorrelations were studied. Several of the indices were quite highly correlated; hence, it was possible to reduce the total to nine. They are described below.

1. The average number of hours per week of occupational work including all occupations of the respondent.
2. The average number of hours per week in which the respondent was engaged in *active* leisure. This does not include hours spent in strictly sedentary activities such as reading, playing cards, etc.
3. A weighted mean WMR/BMR, utilizing the WMR/BMR associated with each of the subject's occupational activities, weighted by the number of hours spent at each. This reflects the total energy expended on the job.
4. A weighted mean WMR/BMR as in #3, but for active leisure. Because of the variation among individuals in time spent, this mean reflects the average rate of energy expenditure for *only* the active leisure and hence does not estimate the total energy expenditure during leisure.
5. A weighted mean WMR/BMR as in #3, but including all leisure activities. This index reflects total energy expenditure during leisure.
6. A weighted mean WMR/BMR as in #3, but including both occupational and leisure activities. This index reflects the total 24-hour daily energy expenditure.
7. Since the highest work-to-basal metabolic ratio reached at regular intervals may be more important to health than average energy expenditure, a peak WMR/BMR was determined for occupation. The highest WMR/BMR attained by an individual was considered his peak if he averaged 1½ hours per week at this level. If not, the next highest ratio was used as the peak provided the time spent at the two levels totaled 1½ hours. The process was continued until a WMR/BMR was reached such that the subject spent 1½ hours a week at levels at least as high. Briefly, the peak WMR/BMR may be defined as the lowest work-to-basal metabolic ratios comprising the most strenuous 1½ hours per week for an individual.
8. Peak WMR/BMR as defined in #7, but for leisure activities only. For those persons who did not report 1½ hours of active leisure a week, a value of 1.8 was assigned as the leisure peak, this being the WMR/BMR designated for quiet leisure.
9. Peak WMR/BMR as defined in #7, but including both occupational and leisure activities.

Next, the respondents were grouped by age as follows: 20-29, 30-39, 40-49, 50-59, and 60-64. Distributions for each of the nine indices and for each of the age groups were examined. Our plan was to classify respondents who were in the lowest 20 percent (for a particular index in a particular age group) as sedentary, the middle 60 percent as moderately active, and the upper 20 percent as active. In most cases, this was possible. However, in the case of hours worked (#1 above), about half of the respondents were placed in the lower group, about 30 percent in the middle group, and about 20 percent in the upper group. In leisure peak (#8 above), about a third were in each of the three groups.

Risk Factors

The present report contains data on only three risk factors associated with coronary heart disease; namely, blood pressure, serum total cholesterol, and glucose tolerance. There is appreciable evidence of an association between hypertension and coronary heart disease (5). Blood pressures of the subjects were taken in the right arm in the sitting position with a mercury sphygmomanometer by a carefully instructed physician. Diastolic pressure was recorded at the disappearance of sound.

The association of high serum total cholesterol with coronary heart disease is also well known and has been observed in the Tecumseh population (3). Blood was drawn in the clinic but the respondents were not necessarily in a post-absorptive state. The sera were frozen for later analysis by the ABELL Method (1).

The relationship between heart disease and hyperglycemia has been reviewed elsewhere (4, 15) and at this stage of knowledge, there is evidence that difficulty in carbohydrate metabolism may be a risk factor in coronary heart disease. The Tecumseh subjects, upon arrival at the clinic, were generally given a 100 gram glucose challenge (6, 7). Venous blood was drawn one hour later into a vacuum tube containing sodium fluoride and refrigerated. The examining physician noted the time of venepuncture and obtained a history of recent meals and snacks. The amount of carbohydrate was estimated from these diet recall records by a dietitian. Blood glucose concentration was determined by the Somogyi-Helson method (19). The relationship between carbohydrate consumed and the glucose tolerance test was used along with age to calculate a glucose score having a mean of 10 for the total population and a standard deviation of one.

In the time and space available, it is not possible to discuss, completely, habitual physical activity as reflected by all nine indices and the CHD risk factors. All of the analyses have been done, but only the most important ones will be discussed at this time. The statistical analysis was the same in each case; namely, a two-way analysis of variance with physical activity classification (sedentary, moderately active, and active) as one variable, and age as the other. Thus, it was possible to calculate F-ratios for two main effects (activity classification and age) and the interaction between the two. In this calculation, separate F-values for physical activity classification and the risk factors being considered, appear for each age group, as well as on F-ratio over all ages.

Of the various physical activity indices the one most closely related to the risk factors is the average WMR/BMR calculated from both occupational and leisure activity (#6 above). Therefore, Figure 1 shows the mean systolic and diastolic blood pressures and serum total cholesterol for the three physical activity classifications using Index 6 over all ages.

FIGURE 1.

Comparison of Mean Systolic and Diastolic Blood Pressure and Serum Total Cholesterol Among Sedentary, Moderately Active and Active Men and Farmers. (Activity classification was by mean WMR/BMR including occupation and leisure, that is, by Index No. 6 in the text.)

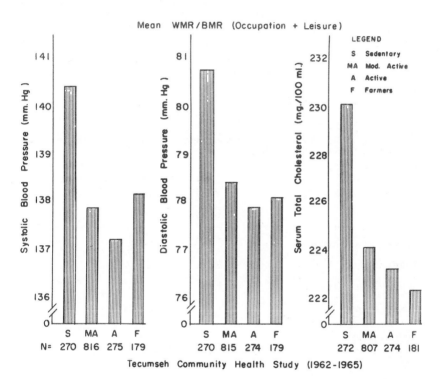

Mean WMR/BMR (Occupation + Leisure)

Tecumseh Community Health Study (1962-1965)

Although all subjects are pooled, any relationship between age and physical activity does not affect the results because the subjects were placed in one of the three categories of physical activities within their own specific age group. The mean values for farmers are included here for comparative purposes, but their data were not included in the analysis of variance. The F-values for these analyses as well as for blood glucose are shown in Table 1. As can be seen in the table, blood pressures and serum total cholesterol are significantly lower in the active men. The mean blood glucose scores for the sedentary, moderately active and active subjects were 10.1, 10.0 and 10.0, respectively, based on approximately the same number of subjects as in the cholesterol and blood pressure analyses. From Table 1 it can be seen that glucose tolerance is not significantly different in the various physical activity groups. Mean systolic and diastolic blood pressure and serum total cholesterol all increased significantly with an increase in age in the subjects (Table 1). Since the blood glucose score was corrected for age, the F-ratio for age was not significant.

When only occupation was used in classifying subjects into various physical activity groups (Indices 3 and 7), some significant differences appeared in diastolic blood pressure and cholesterol but the differences were not as pronounced as when occupation and leisure were combined. When all subjects were classified by leisure only (Indices 2, 4, 5, and 8), no significant differences among activity groups in the risk factors were observed. It is not surprising that combined physical activity (i.e. on the job and during leisure) yield the best correlation with risk factors since there was little correlation between these two sources of physical activity. Hence, one must consider both sources of physical activity to accurately classify men in a total population by habitual physical activity.

TABLE 1.

Comparison of Risk Factors Among Respondents Grouped According to Mean WMR/BMR (occupation and leisure).

CHD Risk Factor	Analysis of Variance (F-Values)		
	Main Effects		Inter-action
	Activity Group	Age	
Systolic Blood Pressure	3.06[a]	13.12[b]	1.98[a]
Diastolic Blood Pressure	4.09[a]	25.26[b]	0.62
Serum Total Cholesterol	4.96[b]	34.84[b]	1.85
Blood Glucose	1.31	0.90	0.74

[a] $0.01 < p < 0.05$

[b] $p < 0.01$

When the respondents were grouped by the average number of hours per week spent at their occupation (Index 1), an interesting pattern developed with regard to systolic blood pressure. The men working about 40 hours or less per week had lower systolic blood pressure than those who worked about 40-50 hours per week, and those who worked over about 50 hours had the highest blood pressure. Although the overall F-value was not quite significant at the five percent level, among men age 25-34, those who worked the longest hours (and in Tecumseh these were primarily in the professional, managerial and business occupations) had significantly higher systolic blood pressure. Hours worked per week was unrelated to diastolic blood pressure, serum total cholesterol or blood glucose.

Next, subjects in the lowest 20 percent as classified by mean occupational WMR/BMR (Index 3) were studied separately. These men, who are all sedentary in their occupation, were subdivided by the leisure indices (Indices 2, 4, 5, and 8). When mean systolic and diastolic blood pressure, serum total cholesterol and blood glucose were compared, the differences among the various sub-groups were not significant.

In summary, therefore, it appears clear that when men in a total population are classified by habitual physical activity, significant differences in certain coronary heart disease risk factors can be observed among the groups. Sedentary men have, on the average, higher resting systolic and diastolic blood pressure and a higher concentration of serum total cholesterol. The differences appear most clearly when participation in both occupational and leisure activity is used to classify the men.

REFERENCES

1. Abell, L. L.; Levy, B. B.; Brodie, B. B.; and Kendall, F. E. A simplified method for the estimation of total cholesterol in serum and demonstration of its specificity. *J. Biol. Chem.* 195:357, 1952.
2. Cunningham, D. A; Montoye, H. J.; Metzner, H. L.; and Keller, J. B. Active leisure time activities as related to age among males in a total population. *J. Gerontology* 23:551-56, 1968.
3. Epstein, F. H. The epidemiology of coronary heart disease: a review. *J. Chron. Dis.* 18:735-74, 1965.
4. Epstein, F. H. Hyperglycemia: a risk factor in coronary heart disease. *Circulation* 36:609-19, 1967.
5. Epstein, F. H. and Hoobler, S. W. Relationship between hypertension and coronary atherosclerosis. *Heart Bulletin* 15:106-10, 1966.
6. Hayner, N. S. The one-hour oral glucose tolerance test. *National Center for Health Statistics*, Series 2, Number 3, U. S. Department of Health, Education and Welfare, July, 1963.
7. Hayner, N. S.; Kjelsberg, M. O.; Epstein, F. H.; and Francis, T. Carbohydrate tolerance and diabetes in a total community, Tecumseh, Michigan. *Diabetes* 14:413-23, 1965.
8. Kannel, W. B.; Kagan, A.; Dawber, T. R.; and Revotskie, N. Epidemiology of coronary heart disease. *Geriatrics* 17:675, 1962.
9. Karvonen, M. J. The relationship of habitual physical activity to disease in the cardiovascular system, pp. 81-89. In Evang, K. and Andersen, K. L. (Ed.), *Physical Activity in Health and Disease.* Baltimore: Williams and Wilkins Co., 1966.
10. Keys, A. Physical activity—promises and problems in regard to cardiovascular disease, Chapter 33, pp. 381-93. In Karvonen, M. J. and Barry, A. J. (Ed.), *Physical Activity and the Heart.* Springfield, Ill.: Charles C. Thomas, 1967.
11. Keys, A., and others. Epidemiological studies related to coronary heart disease: characteristics of men aged 40-59 in seven countries. *Acta. Med. Scand.* Vol. 180, Supplement 460, 1966.
12. Kraus, H. and Raab, W. *Hypokinetic Disease.* Springfield, Ill.: Charles C. Thomas, 1961.
13. Montoye, H. J. and Epstein, F. H. Tecumseh community health study: an investigation of health and disease in an entire community. *J. Sports Med. and Physical Fitness* 5:3-8, 1965.
14. Napier, J. Field methods and response rates in the Tecumseh community health study. *Am. J. Public Health* 52:208-16, 1962.
15. Ostrander, L. D.; Francis, T.; Hayner, N. S.; and Kjelsberg, M. The relationship of cardiovascular disease to hyperglycemia. *Annals of Int. Med.* 62:1188-98, 1965.

16. Reiff, C. G.; Montoye, H. J.; Remington, R. D.; Napier, J. A.; Metzner, H. L.; and Epstein, F. H. Assessment of physical activity by questionnaire and interview. *J. Sports Med. and Physical Fitness* 7:135-42, 1967.
17. Remington, R. D. and Shork, A. Determination of number of subjects needed for experimental epidemiologic studies of the effect of increased physical activity on incidence of coronary heart disease—preliminary consideration. In Karvonen, M. J. and Barry, A. J. (Ed.), *Physical Activity and the Heart.* Springfield, Ill.: Charles C. Thomas, 1967.
18. Shapiro, S.; Weinblatte, E.; Frank, C. W.; and Sager, R. V. The H.I.P. study of incidence and prognosis of coronary heart disease. *J. Chronic Diseases* 18:527-58, 1965.
19. Somogyi, M. Determination of blood sugar. *J. Biol. Chem.* 160:69, 1945.

PHYSIOLOGICAL AND PERCEPTUAL REACTIONS TO EXERTION OF YOUNG MEN DIFFERING IN ACTIVITY AND BODY SIZE[1]

JAMES S. SKINNER
Pennsylvania State University

GUNNAR A. V. BORG
University of Umea (Sweden)

E. R. BUSKIRK
Pennsylvania State University

ABSTRACT

This study investigated two questions: 1) Do people who differ in their level of activity and in body composition also differ in their physical working capacity and physiological response to work? 2) How do these people perceive the work they are doing? The subjects were 26 young men, aged 17-24 years, who were grouped as follows: 6 lean and sedentary (LS); 6 lean and active (LA); 8 heavy and sedentary (HS); and 6 heavy and active (HA).

Each subject was tested on a bicycle ergometer at 75 kgm and 300 kgm. Increments of 300 kgm were then added until a self-imposed maximum was reached. At the end of each 4-minute period, heart rate (HR) was recorded and the subject was asked to rate the level of perceived exertion (RPE).

There was no difference (.05 level) in maximal working capacity between the active subjects (LA and HA) but both did significantly more work than LS subjects. At the same sub-maximal work loads, the active subjects had a lower HR and RPE than the sedentary subjects and the heavier subjects had a lower HR than the lean subjects but no difference in RPE.

When the groups were compared according to 1) their HR and 2) a given percentage of their maximal working capacity, there were no differences in the level of exertion they perceived.

Thus, when work was compared on an absolute basis there were differences which seem to be related to the level of fitness and body composition. When related to working capacity, however, these factors were not of measurable importance.

INTRODUCTION

Exercise physiologists are interested in methods for determining how people react to physical work. Thus, they may use heart rate, blood pressure, oxygen consumption or some other variable to estimate the "strain" on the physiological systems resulting from work. Of these variables, heart

[1]This investigation was supported by PHS Research Grant No. AM 08311 from the Institute of Arthritis and Metabolic Diseases, National Institutes of Health, and by Contract No. 108-67-79, from the National Center for Chronic Disease Control, US PHS.

rate (HR) is one of the easiest to obtain and at a standard work load is considered to be an indicator of the degree of strain an individual is experiencing and an indirect predictor of his physical work capacity (2, 12). Heart rate is an especially good indicator in a given individual as it is linearly related to work load and its energy cost, as estimated by oxygen consumption (1).

Some psychologists are also interested in methods for determining how people react to physical work. A simple rating method has been developed by Borg (3), in which an individual subjectively rates the amount of exertion he perceives that he is doing. Since Borg (3) has shown in a group of healthy people that a high relationship ($r = 0.83$) is present between HR and the subjective rating of perceived exertion (RPE), then the latter also may be a useful indicator of 1) the physiological "strain" and 2) the relative work intensity.

Using this rating scale with various groups of persons, Borg and Linderholm (4, 5) found that the relationship between HR and RPE differs among groups. For example, at low intensities of work, patients with vasoregulatory asthenia and hypertension had a higher HR than healthy control subjects but did not perceive that the amount of exertion was as high. Patients with coronary heart disease, on the other hand, did not react in this way, *i.e.*, at high work intensities they had a lower HR than healthy persons of the same age but they subjectively perceived that they were exerting more. Thus, it appears that additional information can be obtained by observing both the objective-physiological and subjective-psychological responses of various groups to physical work and by relating these findings to other variables present in each group.

Using both of these methods, groups differing in their level of activity and in their body size were compared to determine 1) their physiological response to work and 2) how they perceived the work they were doing.

SUBJECTS

The subjects were 26 young men, aged 17-24 years, who were grouped as follows: lean and sedentary (LS), N = 6; lean and active (LA), N = 6; heavy and sedentary (HS), N = 8; and heavy and active (HA), N = 6. The sedentary subjects were selected among university students who had failed a motor fitness test and were enrolled in a physical conditioning class at the Pennsylvania State University. In each case, the subject was considered by the instructor to be "very unfit," relative to the other poorly conditioned students in the class. These subjects were tested within the first two weeks when the intensity of the activities in the physical conditioning class was low and would not affect the results.

The lean active subjects were distance runners who were in training for competition at the time of testing. The heavy active subjects were football players who had been conditioning themselves for the spring practice sessions which were due to begin within a few weeks of the study.

PROCEDURES

When the subjects reported for testing, their height, weight, grip strength, and leg strength were measured. In addition, three skin-fold measurements (triceps, subscapular, and abdomen) were taken and percent body fat was calculated (7). Electrodes were then put on each subject's chest to record the electrocardiogram and heart rate during and after exercise.

Each subject was exercised on a Monark bicycle ergometer at a work load of 75 kgm/min for four minutes; this was selected so that values could be obtained at a very light, submaximal work load. The work load was then increased to 300 kgm/min for four minutes, after which increments of 300 kgm/min were added each four minutes until the subject reached his self-imposed maximum. Near the end of each four-minute period, heart rate (HR) was recorded and the subject was asked to rate the level of exertion he perceived (RPE), according to a scale graduated from 6 to 20 (7 corresponded to "very, very light" and 19 corresponded to "very, very hard"). The dial indicating the work load was shielded so that the subject was unaware of the actual amount of work he was doing. When the subject attained his self-imposed maximum he stopped pedalling and sat on the bicycle ergometer for three minutes. During this time, HR was recorded immediately, one minute, and three minutes after exercising.

In addition to determining the maximal work load (W_{max}) that each subject could maintain for four minutes, work loads at a HR of 170 (W_{170}), according to Sjöstrand (10) and Wahlund (12), and at an RPE of 17 (W_{R17})* were estimated by interpolation.

An analysis of variance was used to determine whether differences existed among the four groups of subjects. When significant differences were present, Duncan's Multiple Range Test was applied to determine which groups were different.

RESULTS

The physical characteristics of the subjects in this study are shown in Table 1. The HA subjects were taller ($p < 0.05$) than the LS subjects but no other differences in height were found with the other groups. As expected, the lean subjects weighed significantly less ($p < 0.01$) and had a significantly lower percent body fat than the heavy subjects ($p < 0.01$). There was no difference in body weight between the active and sedentary subjects but the active group had less fat ($p < 0.05$).

When performance measures were examined (see Table 2), the HA subjects had significantly more leg strength than the LS or HS subjects ($p < 0.05$). The heavy subjects were stronger than the lean subjects and the active subjects were stronger than the sedentary subjects ($p < 0.05$).

When values for W_{max}, W_{170} or W_{R17} were compared, the same pattern was present, *i.e.,* the LS subjects did less work than the LA or HA

---

*R17 corresponds to a rating of "very hard" on the scale used by the subjects.

subjects and the active group did more work than the sedentary group ($p < 0.01$). There was no significant difference between the lean and heavy subjects.

TABLE I

PHYSICAL CHARACTERISTICS OF SUBJECTS GROUPED ACCORDING TO BODY SIZE AND ACTIVITY STATUS

Group	N	Height (cm.)	Weight (kg.)	Body Fat (%)
Lean-sedentary (LS)	6	173.7 ± 9.5^a	59.4 ± 3.7^b	7.3 ± 1.5^b
Lean-active (LA)	6	178.2 ± 8.4	64.7 ± 6.0^b	4.8 ± 1.2^b
Heavy-sedentary (HS)	8	177.3 ± 6.4	94.1 ± 13.9^b	19.5 ± 5.0^b
Heavy-active (HA)	6	186.0 ± 5.8^a	95.6 ± 14.4^b	15.8 ± 3.3^b
Lean	12	176.0 ± 8.9	62.1 ± 5.5^c	6.1 ± 1.8^c
Heavy	14	181.0 ± 7.4	94.9 ± 13.6^c	17.7 ± 4.6^c
Sedentary	14	175.5 ± 7.8	76.8 ± 20.7	13.4 ± 7.3^d
Active	12	182.1 ± 8.0	80.1 ± 19.3	10.2 ± 6.2^d

[a] LS vs. HA ($p < 0.05$)

[b] LS vs. HS, LS vs. HA, LA vs. HS, LA vs. HA ($p < 0.01$)

[c] Lean vs. Heavy ($p < 0.01$)

[d] Sedentary vs. Active ($p < 0.05$)

TABLE 2

PERFORMANCE MEASURES OF SUBJECTS GROUPED ACCORDING TO BODY SIZE AND ACTIVITY STATUS

Group	N	Leg Strength (kg)	W_{170} (kgm)	W_{R17} (kgm)	W_{max} (kgm)
Lean-sedentary (LS)	6	165 ± 41^a	845 ± 50^b	853 ± 50^b	967 ± 23^b
Lean-active (LA)	6	194 ± 29	1280 ± 212^b	$1202 \pm 111^{b,\,c}$	1365 ± 155^b
Heavy-sedentary (HS)	8	189 ± 50^a	1078 ± 194	986 ± 197^c	1175 ± 199
Heavy-active (HA)	6	250 ± 28^a	1298 ± 268^b	1167 ± 223^b	1356 ± 295^b
Lean	12	178 ± 38^d	1063 ± 273	1028 ± 200	1166 ± 234
Heavy	14	209 ± 52^d	1188 ± 246	1076 ± 221	1265 ± 252
Sedentary	14	179 ± 46^e	961 ± 191^f	919 ± 163^f	1071 ± 181^f
Active	12	219 ± 40^e	1289 ± 231^f	1184 ± 169^f	1360 ± 225^f

[a] LS vs. HA, HS vs. HA ($p < 0.05$)

[b] LS vs. LA, LS vs. HA ($p < 0.01$)

[c] LA vs. HS ($p < 0.05$)

[d] Lean vs. Heavy ($p < 0.05$)

[e] Sedentary vs. Active ($p < 0.05$)

[f] Sedentary vs. Active ($p < 0.01$)

Analysis of the exercise test results was done only on those work loads which all subjects were able to complete (*i.e.,* up to 900 kgm/min). Figure 1 illustrates the effects of increasing work loads on the four groups of sub-

FIGURE 1.

Relationship between heart rate and work load in four groups of young men.

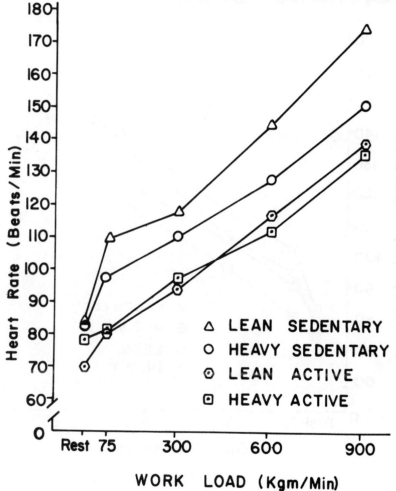

jects. At all four work loads examined, the LS subjects had a significantly higher HR than the LA or HA subjects ($p < 0.01$). At work loads of 75, 600, and 900 kgm/min, the LS subjects had a higher HR than the HS subjects ($p<0.05$). The HS subjects had a higher HR than the LA or HA subjects at 75 kgm/min ($p<0.05$) and a higher HR than the LA subjects at 300 kgm/min.

FIGURE 2.

Relationship between heart rate and work load in young men classified according to activity status and body size.

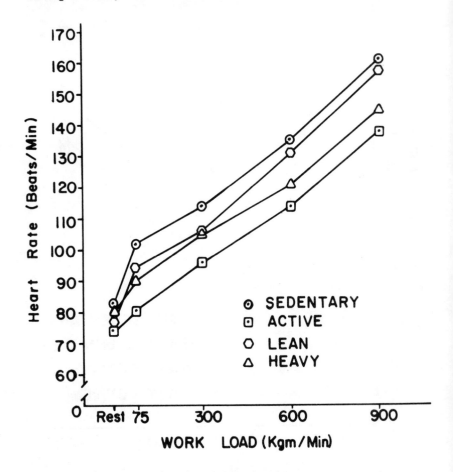

When the subjects were grouped according to body size (Figure 2), no significant differences were present. On the other hand, the active subjects had significantly lower HR's at all work loads ($p<0.01$).

No differences in RPE were observed for any group of subjects at the first two work loads (Figure 3). At the higher work loads, LS subjects had a higher RPE ($p < 0.05$) than the LA or HA subjects, who did not differ

FIGURE 3.

Relationship between ratings of perceived exertion and work load in four groups of young men.

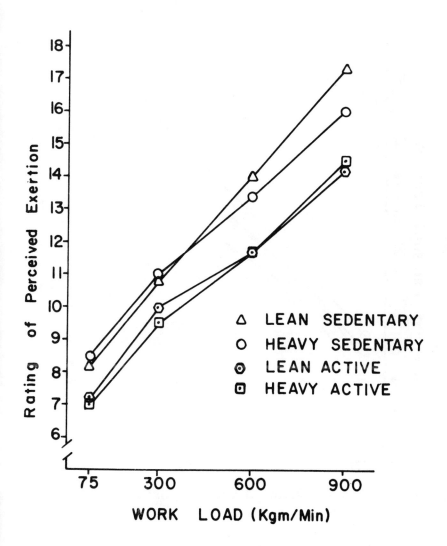

from each other. No differences in RPE were apparent when the subjects were classified by body size but the active subjects perceived less exertion ($p < 0.05$) at the higher two work loads (Figure 4).

FIGURE 4.

Relationship between ratings of perceived exertion and work load in young men classified according to activity status and body size.

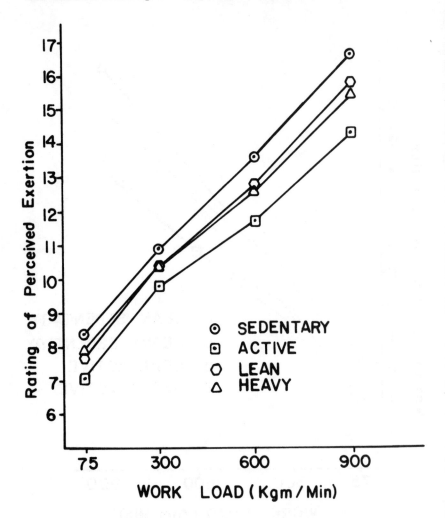

To further examine the relationship between RPE and HR, the values for each group were plotted. As seen in Figure 5, a fairly linear relationship existed for each of the four groups. At the same RPE, LS subjects had a

FIGURE 5.

Relationship between heart rate and ratings of perceived exertion in four groups of young men.

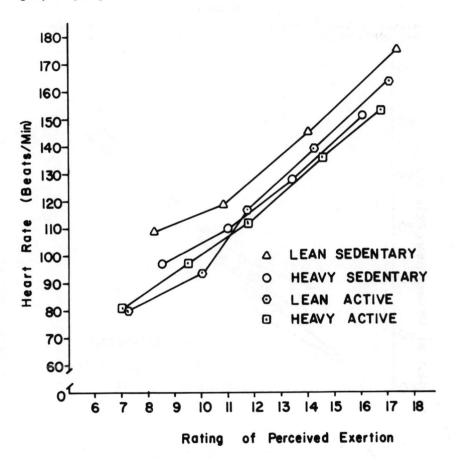

slightly higher HR; no differences were present for the other three groups of subjects. When the groups were reclassified according to activity level or body size, little or no difference was seen.

It was decided to look further into the relationship between RPE and HR to determine whether the same relative amount of physiological stress (HR as a percentage of maximal HR) would be associated with the same amount of perceived stress (RPE). Above 60 percent of maximal HR a linear relationship existed for all groups (Figure 6). When the groups were

FIGURE 6.

Relationship between ratings of perceived exertion and relative strain, as measured by the percentage of maximal heart rate, in four groups of young men.

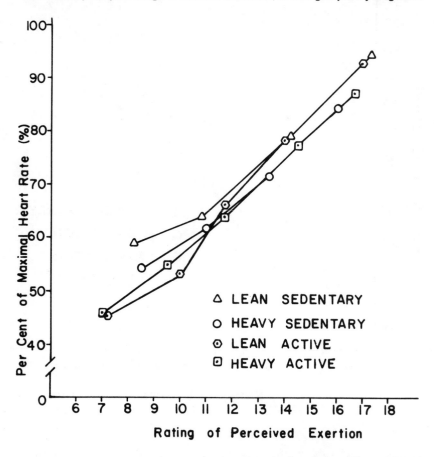

reclassified, values for the active and sedentary subjects fell on the same line and there was little difference between values for the lean and heavy subjects. Looking at the data in another way, no differences were present among any group classifications when their RPE values were related to the percent of the maximal work load (Figures 7 and 8).

FIGURE 7.

Relationship between ratings of perceived exertion and relative strain, as measured by the percentage of maximal work load, in four groups of young men.

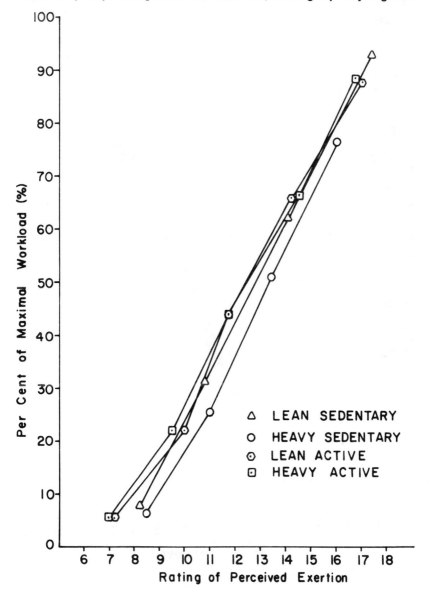

FIGURE 8.

Relationship between ratings of perceived exertion and relative strain, as measured by the percentage of maximal work load, in young men classified according to activity status and body size.

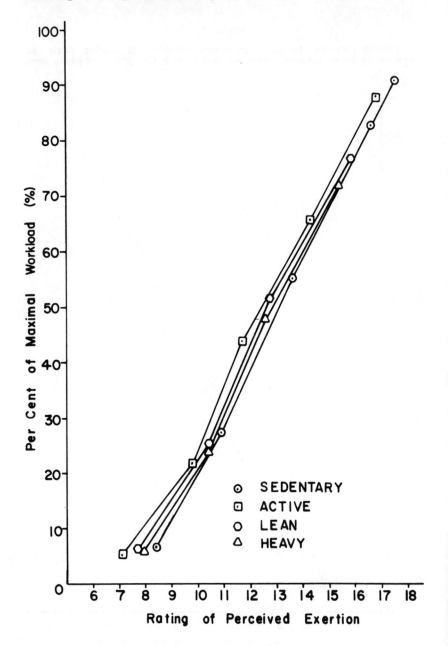

DISCUSSION

The results of this study show the same high relationship between HR and RPE that has been found earlier (3). The subjects appeared to be able to judge how much work they were actually doing, as shown by the linear relationship between RPE and W and by the high correlation ($r = 0.90$) between RPE and HR, a somewhat higher value than the coefficient of 0.83 reported by Borg (3). It should be mentioned, however, that this group was more homogeneous with regard to age and maximal heart rate and more heterogeneous with regard to maximal working capacity than the Swedish group.

It has been suggested that obese people tend to be less active than lean people (8). Also, it has been shown that obese persons are under a substantial handicap in physical performance because of the load they must carry; this excess fat increases the cardiovascular load in submaximal work (9). Thus, it might be hypothesized that obese persons are less active because they experience more "strain" associated with physical work. In this study, there were no differences between lean and heavy subjects in: 1) maximal working capacity, 2) RPE at four submaximal work loads, or 3) RPE at different percentages of maximal HR or work load. However, the heavy subjects in this study had a mean body fat of 16-20 percent and would not be classified as "obese." The greater leg strength in the heavy subjects is one reason why they had slightly higher mean values for maximal work capacity than the lean subjects.

Since most of the subjects' weight was supported by the seat of the bicycle ergometer, the possible effects of body weight on work capacity or on perception of effort may have been obscured. It would have been interesting to determine whether any differences were present between these lean and heavy subjects if they had been tested on a treadmill, where the body mass must be transported and is a factor in energy expenditure. In a recent study on middle-aged men (6), it was found that 27 lean men (72.7 kg body weight and 10 percent body fat) did significantly more work on a treadmill at a HR of 150 and at an RPE of 15 than did 12 heavy men (92.5 kg body weight and 20 percent body fat) of the same age. No differences in HR or in RPE were found for these same men when tested on a bicycle ergometer.

As a result of a physical conditioning program there is usually a decrease in HR at a given submaximal work load and an increase in the maximal working capacity (11). Associated with the differences present between the active and the sedentary subjects in this investigation, the active subjects also had a lower RPE at the same submaximal work loads. As found with the lean and heavy subjects, however, there were no differences in RPE at various percentages of maximal HR or work load.

Since RPE is linearly related to HR, which in turn is related to work done or oxygen consumed, it appears that the subjective perception of effort is related to an individual's maximal capacity. Although the active subjects had a higher maximal working capacity, their perception of the relative amount of physiological strain was the same as that of the sedentary subjects. Since no differences were found between the lean and heavy groups, it does not appear that body size, in the range studied, is of measurable importance to the perception of effort involved in working on a bicycle ergometer.

REFERENCES

1. Åstrand, I. Aerobic work capacity in men and women with special reference to age. *Acta physiologica scandinavica* 49: Supplement 169, 1-92, 1960.
2. Åstrand, P. O. and Rhyming, I. A nomogram for calculation of aerobic capacity (physical fitness) from pulse rate during submaximal work. *Journal of applied physiology* 7:218-21, 1954.
3. Borg, G. A. V. *Physical performance and perceived exertion*. Lund: Gleerup, 1962.
4. Borg, G. A. V. and Linderholm, H. Exercise performance and perceived exertion in patients with coronary insufficiency, arterial hypertension and vascoregulatory asthenia. *Acta medica scandinavica,* in press.
5. Borg, G. A. V. and Linderholm, H. Perceived exertion and pulse rate during graded exercise in various age groups. *Acta medica scandinavica* 472:194-206, 1967.
6. Borg, G. A. V.; Skinner, J. S. and Buskirk, E. R. Physiological and perceptive indicators of physical stress in a group of middle-aged men who possess characteristics associated with the development of coronary heart disease. To be published.
7. Buskirk, E. R. Unpublished data.
8. Chirico, A. M. and Stunkard, A. J. Physical activity and human obesity. *New England journal of medicine* 263:935-940, 1960.
9. Miller, A. T. and Blyth, C. S. Influence of body type and body fat content on the metabolic cost of work. *Journal of applied physiology* 8:139-141, 1955.
10. Sjöstrand, T. Changes in the respiratory organs of workmen at an ore smelting works. *Acta medica scandinavica,* Supplement 196:687-699, 1947.
11. Skinner, J. S.; Holloszy, J. O. and Cureton, T. K. Effects of a program of endurance exercises on physical work capacity and anthropometric measurements of fifteen middle-aged men. *The American journal of cardiology* 14:747-752, 1964.
12. Wåhlund, H. Determination of physical working capacity. *Acta medica scandinavica,* Supplement 215, 1948.

BLOOD BIOCHEMICAL CHANGES IN MAN ASSOCIATED WITH PHYSICAL TRAINING

GUY MÉTIVIER

GUY BRISSON

JEAN-PIERRE DES GROSSEILLIERS
University of Ottawa

ABSTRACT

The purpose of the study was to determine the possible effects of a relatively strenuous work bout on certain hematological and blood biochemical indices in trained and untrained male subjects. Two groups of subjects were separated on the basis of their maximal oxygen intake capacity during an all-out treadmill run, but later redistributed according to their maximal pulse rate curve during a strenuous ergometer exercise.

Venous blood samples were collected from all subjects in a basal state, immediately before the experiment, every 10 minutes during, 60, 90, and 150 minutes following the work (pedalling a Monark ergometer for 30 minutes set at 750 kpm, 60 rpm).

The analysis of variance technique when applied to some 15 blood parameters yielded significant differences "within groups" in the following: glucose, total protein, albumin, bilirubin, electrolytes, alkaline phosphatase, hematocrit and serum glutamic-oxalacetic transaminase. When the "between groups" variance was considered, significant differences were recorded in the glucose, calcium, alkaline phosphatase and hemoglobin. It was concluded that in all subjects, the changes reflected hemoconcentration and a more efficient endocrinological control in the trained subjects.

INTRODUCTION

It is often difficult to interpret long, sustained endurance feats by morphological, physiological or psychological explanations. The basic characteristics which differentiate the trained from the untrained athlete may rest most probably at the cellular level, and long endurance exercise capacity may be based upon the proper channeling of certain intrinsic cellular forces toward efficient physio-psychological pathways.

In order to understand the basic physiological mechanism which could differentiate between trained and untrained athletes, applied physiologists have investigated various physiological aspects of man in motion with a multitude of methods and techniques.

The literature up to five years ago offered much information concerning the relationship between exercise and hemo-dynamic, cardio-pulmonary, biomechanical and psycho-physiological parameters. The direct study of cells during work has proved to be most difficult; however, examination of blood before, during, and after exercise can yield precious information as to cellular changes during the work bout.

PROBLEM

The present experiment proposed to investigate hematological and bio-chemical changes in blood of untrained and trained subjects submitted to a standardized work load.

SUBJECTS

Seventy-five subjects were examined for oxygen uptake capacity and five were chosen and classified as trained and untrained respectively according to their maximum value. By definition, trained subjects were chosen from those who obtained a value equal or superior to 3.52 1/m of O_2 during an all-out treadmill run. The non-trained subjects group was made up of those persons who could not attain this previously chosen value.

In order to evaluate the results more thoroughly, a second distribution was made based upon the pulse rate value obtained above 180 beats per minute at any time during the standardized test on a bicycle ergometer. This new distribution yielded a group of seven trained and a group of three non-trained individuals.

METHOD

All subjects selected for the experiment reported to the laboratory in a post-absorptive state three mornings of the same week at which time 30 cc. of blood were taken from the brachial vein. Subsequently, hematological and biochemical analyses were made on the samples within 24 hours by means of a technicon sequential automatic analyzer and other well stand-ardized techniques.

Upon termination of these preliminary testing sessions, each subject ap-peared in the lab (in a post-absorptive state) for the experiment during a morning of each of the two weeks which followed.

Testing Protocol

Upon the subject's arrival in the laboratory the day of the experiment, he rested on a bed for 10 minutes following which a catheter was introduced in the right brachial vein. After a 20 minute rest, the subject was taken to the main laboratory and seated comfortably on a Monark bicycle ergometer fitted with overhead respiratory gases collection equipment. The heart fre-quencies were recorded by means of an electrocardiograph. The work bout consisted of pedalling the ergometer set at 2.5 KPM 60 times per minute for 30 minutes. Blood samples were taken every 10 minutes during the exer-cise, immediately following, 60, 90 and 150 minutes after the test.

Statistical Treatments

The analysis of variance for groups with equal N as outlined by Winer (13) was applied to the data pertaining to the first grouping, and a modifi-cation of the same design for groups with unequal N was applied to the data of the second distribution. The data were presented graphically in terms of differences between pre-exercise values and consecutive ones.

RESULTS

There were significant changes (.05 level) in all parameters, except urea nitrogen in the "within groups" in both distributions of subjects. Upon analysis of the "between groups" for the redistributed subjects, there were significant differences in cortisol, glucose, calcium, alkaline phosphatase and hemoglobin. The first classification of the subjects yielded significant differences in cortisol and hemoglobin only.

The data may be interpreted as meaning that the exercise bout did produce marked changes in all parameters, except in urea nitrogen, no matter how the groups were distributed; however, some parameters (glucose, calcium, alkaline phosphatase) were more subject to changes depending upon the relative degree of effort by each subject.

TABLE I
TESTS OF SIGNIFICANCE

Parameters	5 TRAINED VS. 5 UNTRAINED			7 TRAINED VS. 3 UNTRAINED		
	F_1***	F_2	F_3	F_1	F_2	F_3
Cortisol	10.51*	6.96***	6.06	23.58**	5.93***	4.61***
Glucose	2.33	2.53*	1.31	26.81***	9.26***	8.35***
Total Proteins	0	73.76***	6.12***	0.26	95.33***	3.00*
Albumin	0.30	82.99***	2.06	2.10	106.23***	4.91***
Bilirubin	0.21	10.42***	0.96	0.36	12.07***	4.02**
BUN	2.17	3.98**	0.96	0	0.22	0.09
Calcium	1.79	25.02***	0.94	13.82**	26.96***	1.71
Chlorides	1.32	7.19***	1.93	0.71	5.99***	0.47
Potassium	0.63	25.96***	1.90	1.18	25.68***	2.51
Alkaline P'ase	3.72	10.55***	2.93*	14.30**	20.67***	2.16
SGOT	0.16	5.39***	1.79	0.08	8.42***	3.38
Sodium	0.01	13.34***	0.84	0.06	14.33***	1.35
Hemoglobin	5.73*	66.11***	1.74	7.43*	66.13***	2.51*
Hematocrit	1.21	67.08***	0.62	2.50	37.37***	3.25

        * significant at 5%   ****Legend:

      ** significant at 1% F_1 = Between Trw

    *** significant at .1% F_2 = Within Effects of Exercise

                                 F_3 = Interaction

Ionic and Enzymatic Changes

The significant changes recorded in the electrolytes were probably caused by the state of dehydration developed in the subjects during the 30 minute work bout. This increase in electrolytes could be a result also of decreased

renal tubular reabsorption (10) caused by a sudden vasoconstriction of renal
arterioles. This latter phenomenon was more evident during the post-
exercise period where there was a decrease in the serum ions; at this time the
kidney resumes its normal activities (Figures 1-4).

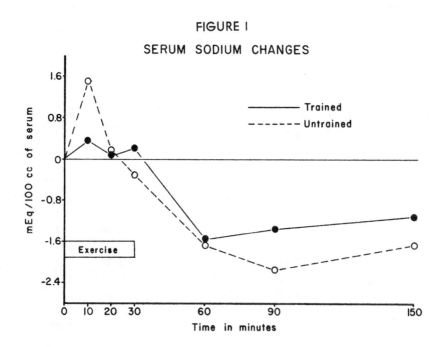

FIGURE I

SERUM SODIUM CHANGES

It is to be noted also that during work the enzyme and electrolyte levels
of trained subjects were considerably lower than those of untrained individuals. Based upon results of preliminary work (7, 8, 9) it is postulated
that trained subjects may possess an intrinsic cellular mechanism for retain-

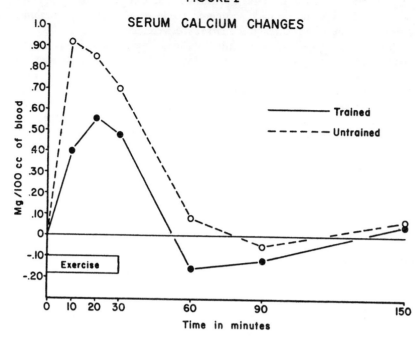

FIGURE 2

SERUM CALCIUM CHANGES

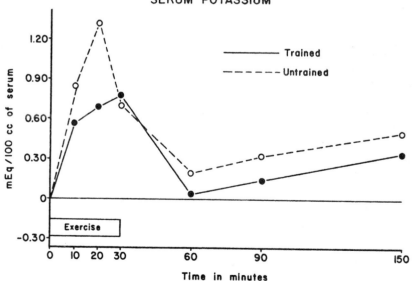

FIGURE 3

SERUM POTASSIUM

ing inorganic materials in intra- and extracellular compartments of muscles. This hypothesis would be made possible by the increased cellular permeability presumably caused by adrenomedullary hypersecretions.

The state of hypercalcemia in the untrained group could signify a maladaptation to the physical stress whereby possibly a demineralization of bones indicated by the increased level of alkaline phosphatase which itself suggests increased osteoblastic activity (7).

The increase in S.G.O.T. during work might be the result of an hypoxic condition and could have increased the cellular membrane's permeability, thus releasing the enzyme in the serum. This increased permeability is a result

FIGURE 4

SERUM CHLORIDE CHANGES

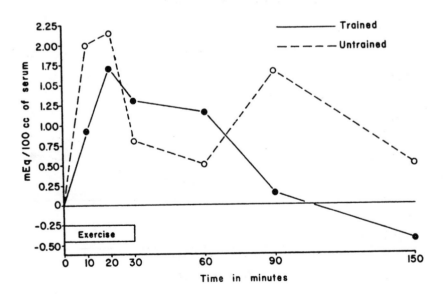

of cathecholamine secretion initiated by the hypoxic condition (5). Cohen (1) suggested that S.O.T. in the serum may play a role in muscle contraction and would enter the Krebs cycle. Since trained subjects usually have a high VO_2 capacity, and are also capable of encountering a greater O_2 debt than untrained athletes, it follows that this last hypothesis may hold true. Inference to this effect may be made in respect to the work of Fowler and others (3) where it was found that the increase in serum activity was related to the previous training of the person and the severity of the exercise over a 15 minute period.

FIGURE 5

SERUM ALKALINE PHOSPHATASE CHANGES

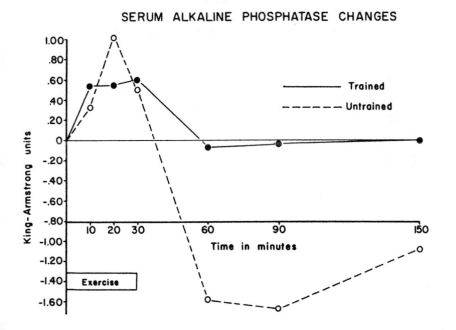

Hematological and Biochemical Changes

The increase of hematocrit, glucose and proteins during the exercise period may be related to the state of dehydration produced. Following the work bout, it is probable that these proteins were reabsorbed by the tissues or distributed within the interstitial fluids. The hypothesis that trained athletes possess a special cellular retention mechanism could explain partly the progressive decrease in albumin concentration. The latter protein controls the somewhat osmotic balance between fluid compartments.

According to the protein profile, it seemed that in trained subjects, the blood plasma volume was restored sooner after work than in untrained individuals (Figures 7-11).

FIGURE 6

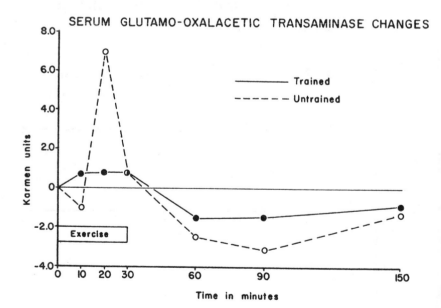

SERUM GLUTAMO-OXALACETIC TRANSAMINASE CHANGES

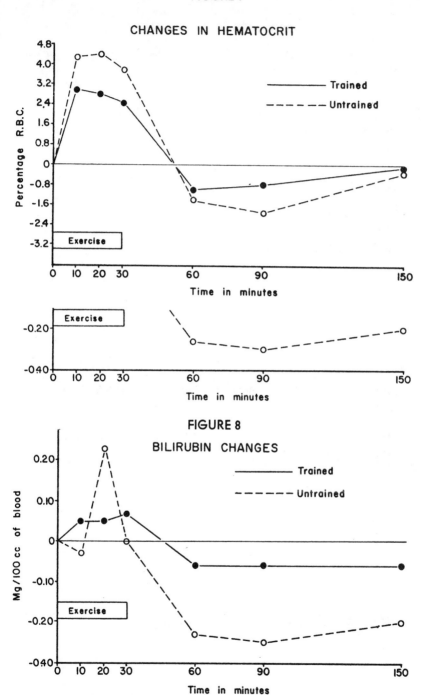

FIGURE 7

CHANGES IN HEMATOCRIT

FIGURE 8

BILIRUBIN CHANGES

FIGURE 9

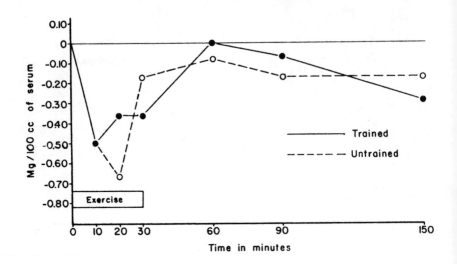

FIGURE 10

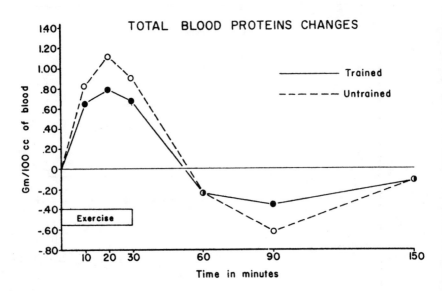

FIGURE 11

HEMOGLOBIN CHANGES

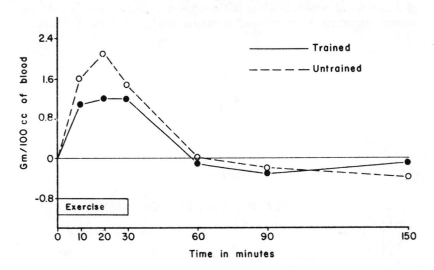

FIGURE 12

SERUM ALBUMIN CHANGES

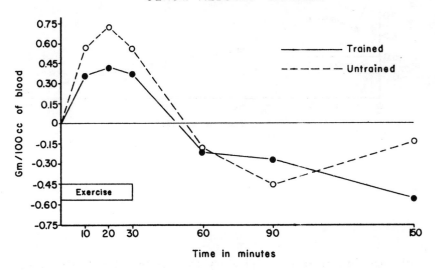

Cortisol and Glucose Changes

There were significant differences within and between groups in plasma cortisol, and the curve for trained subjects was much different than that of the untrained persons involved in the experiment (Figure 13). For the untrained individuals, plasma cortisol increased steadily until the 30th minute

FIGURE 13

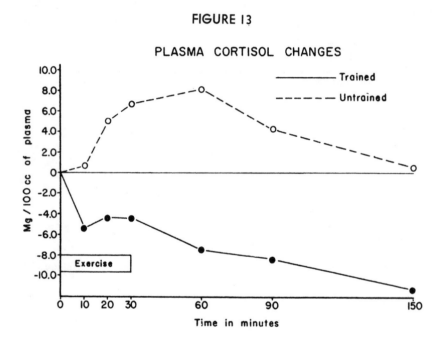

following the exercise and progressively decreased thereafter. In the trained subjects, there was a marked decrease in this substance during the first 10 minutes followed by a slight increase to the end of the work period. At the termination of the work period, a gradual decline was observed. The blood serum glucose remained relatively stable in the trained subjects, but showed a sudden rise during work for the untrained subjects, possibly indicating increased gluconeogenesis (Figure 14).

FIGURE 14

BLOOD GLUCOSE CHANGES

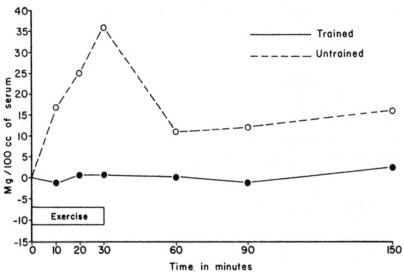

It was reported by Karlson and Lardy (6) that cortisol was a necessary activator of enzymes in the process of gluconeogenesis, thus explaining its presence in plasma during the working period for the untrained persons.

In the trained individuals, however, the adequate carbohydrate reserves "in situ," proper oxygen transport mechanism and well controlled pyruvic and lactic acid levels did not necessitate increased gluconeogenesis. For this reason, an increase in secretion of the aforementioned hormone was not necessary. On the other hand, we know from the work of Williams (13), Vermeulen (12), and Gray and Bacharach (4) that the stroma of the erythrocytes absorbed a certain quantity of cortisol. During the period of work and recovery, this substance could have been absorbed by these cells as their number was considerably increased.

CONCLUSION

The Effects of Muscular Exercise

The work bout caused a state of hemoconcentration as indicated by an increase in total blood protein, albumin, and hemoglobin and confirmed by the high hematocrit value. Electrolytes played an important role during exercise in stabilizing osmotic pressures. The parallelism between serum, calcium and alkaline phosphatase curves during and after the exercise suggested an increased osteoblastic activity and bone calcium mobilization.

The non-trained subjects may have been stressed more and may have developed an hypoxic condition as it was suggested by the increase in S.G.O.T.

The untrained person seemed to possess different carbohydrate metabolism controls than the trained person as revealed by the cortisol and glucose data collected.

Trained vs. Untrained

The trained subjects appeared to be able to stabilize bodily functions during stressful situations. The untrained participant showed an increased production of blood glucose and an inability to utilize it. This rise in glucose associated with the non-trained individuals reflected an accentuated gluconeogenetic process as indicated by an elevated cortisol level.

REFERENCES

1. Cohen, P. Transamination with purified enzyme preparations (transaminase) *J. Biol. Chem*. 136: 565-601, 1940.
2. Critz, J. and Merrick, A. Serum glutamic - oxalacetic transaminase levels after exercise in men. *Proc. Soc. Exp. Biol. Med*. 109: 608-10, 1962.
3. Fowler, W. M., and others. Changes in serum enzyme levels after exercise in trained and untrained subjects. *J. Appl. Physiol*. 17: 943, 1962.
4. Gray, C. H. and Bacharach, A. O. *Hormones in Blood, Vol. 2*. London and New York: Academic Press, 1967.
5. Highman, B.; Maling, Hano; and Thompsons, E. Serum transaminase and alkaline phosphatase levels after large doses of norephonephrine and epinephrine in dogs. *Am. Journ. Physiol*. 196: 436-40, 1959.
6. Karlson, P. New concepts on the mode of action of hormones. *Persp. Biol. Med*. 6: 203-14, 1963.
7. Lardy, H. A., and others. Metabolic and hormonal regulation of phosphoenol-pyruvate synthesis. *Advances in Enzyme regulation* 2:39-47, 1964.
8. Métivier, Guy. Changements Hematologiques et Biochimiques chez des Athlètes Durant un Effort Prolongé. Scientific Paper presented at the 35 Congrés Annuel de l' ACFAS, University of Sherbrooke, 1967.

9. Métivier, Guy. Enzymatic and ionic changes in man associated with physical work. Research Paper presented at the 1 er Congrés International de la Biochimie de l' Effort, Bruxelles, 1968.

10. Métivier, Guy. Blood changes in man during sustained exercise. Research Paper presented to CAHPER Convention, Montreal, 1966.

11. Sheer, Robert. Studies on the Renal Concentrating Mechanism. *Journ. of Clin. Invest.* 38:8, 1959.

12. Turner, C. D. *General Endocrinology.* Philadelphia: W. B. Saunders Co., 1961.

13. Vermeulen, A. Role of the erythrocytes in transport and metabolism of 4 - C cortisol. *Acta Endocr.* 37: 348-52, 1961.

14. Williams, R. H. *Textbooks of endocrinology.* Toronto: W. B. Saunders Co., 1968.

15. Winer, B. S. *Statistical principles in experimental design.* New York: McGraw-Hill Books Company, 1962.

RELATIONSHIPS BETWEEN HYPERURICEMIA AND GOUT, HEREDITARY AND BEHAVIOR FACTORS, AND CARDIOVASCULAR DISEASE — WITH SPECIAL EMPHASIS ON THE ROLE OF ACUTE AND CHRONIC PHYSICAL EXERCISE

JAMES S. BOSCO
San Jose State College

JOHN E. GREENLEAF
NASA-Ames Research Center

ABSTRACT

Numerous factors can influence serum uric acid concentration in healthy individuals: genetic factors, age and sex, body type, drugs, diet, occupation and social class status, achievement-oriented behavior and drive, acute physical exercise and chronic physical exercise. Statistical studies on monozygotic and dizygotic twin pairs have suggested that in males the mechanisms controlling the normal serum uric acid levels are influenced more by environmental factors whereas in females, hereditary factors predominate. Significantly higher mean serum uric acid values have been reported in both high school and college athletes when contrasted with comparably aged samples from "normal" populations. Three factors have been suggested which, singly or in combination, may contribute to high serum uric acid values in athletes: (a) acute and/or chronic physical exercise, (b) genetic predisposition, and (c) achievement-oriented behavior. Some epidemiological studies report significant but low positive correlations between high serum uric acid levels and psycho-social characteristics such as intelligence, *achieved* social status, and "drive," but it is still not clear whether they reflect *inherent* personal characteristics, environmental factors, e.g., participation in athletics or both. The increase in serum uric acid with acute physical exercise is well documented. The causal relationship between muscular exercise and elevated serum uric acid is still not clear, but inhibition of uric acid excretion with a corresponding rise in its concentration in the blood is the most probable explanation. The effects of chronic physical exercise (training) on serum uric acid have not been studied systematically. Strenuous conditioning (a season of competitive water polo) has been shown to *decrease* significantly the mean serum uric acid value of a sample of college athletes. Probable explanations for this result are (a) a relatively constant turnover of urate accompanied by a progressively increasing plasma volume and/or (b) an absolute increase in uric acid excretion.

INTRODUCTION

Many factors influence serum uric acid concentration in healthy people: age and sex (44), body type (18), drugs (19), diet (38), occupation and social class status (13), achievement-oriented behavior and drive (7), acute physical exercise (39, 54) chronic physical exercise (4, 42) and genetic factors (44, 59).

The relationship between serum uric acid concentration, gout, and gouty arthritis has been under investigation for almost 200 years (59) but only recently has hyperuricemia been reported to be associated with coronary heart disease (18, 22, 45), hypercholesterolemia (24), hypertriglyceridemia (2) and hypertension (6, 10) with much greater frequency than in the general population.

Older studies have shown that acute physical exercise of various intensity and duration produced a rise in serum uric acid concentration in both men (39) and women (54). More recently, a positive relationship in male high school students was found between serum uric acid concentration and the degree of participation in combined scholastic and athletic activities (13). In another study, healthy high school athletes not in peak training had elevated serum uric acid values (46). The same results were obtained in a sample of 29 healthy college athletes not in peak condition (20).

Given (a) the association between serum uric acid concentration, gout, and cardiovascular disease, (b) the uncertain role of chronic exercise on serum uric acid values and (c) the growing inclination of physicians to prescribe graded physical exercise as both a preventive measure (65) and a rehabilitation procedure (26), the purpose of this paper is to explore in greater depth the relationship between hyperuricemia and gout and cardiovascular disease including a consideration of hereditary and behavioral factors — with special emphasis on the role of physical exercise.

REVIEW OF HYPERURICEMIA

Hyperuricemia and Gout

In 1876 Garrod (59) observed the blood of gouty patients contained more uric acid than that of normal persons. Since then there has developed a greater understanding of the relationship between hyperuricemia and gout. Seegmiller, *et al.* (59) proposed a working hypothesis to account for several but not all of the steps in the pathogenesis of an acute attack of gouty arthritis: (a) crystals of monosodium urate deposited from hyperuricemic body fluids must be present in the joint tissue, (b) an inflammatory reaction to the crystals must develop and (c) the inflammatory reaction must be propagated by the addition of more urate crystals to the area of inflammation.

The cause of hyperuricemia in gouty patients has not been determined absolutely but there seems to be general agreement that the cause is due to

(a) excessive production of uric acid, (b) normal production but diminished ability of the kidneys to excrete uric acid or (c) a combination of both (37, 48, 57, 58).

It seems important that uric acid levels be maintained as low as possible because Hall, *et al.* (22) found that among those subjects who had serum uric acid levels of 8.0 mg/100 ml or higher, 36% had gouty arthritis and among those who had uric acid levels above 9.0 mg/100 ml, 40% had renal calculi. Among those subjects who had uric acid levels above 12 mg/100 ml, 50% had renal calculi (66).

Regardless of its cause, the level of hyperuricemia is correlated directly with the presence of tophi (59). These tophi can be reduced by administration of uricosuric agents (drugs) that lower the concentration of uric acid in body fluids by promoting its excretion from the kidneys (35). Therefore, two questions are raised regarding exercise: (a) are bouts of acute vigorous exercise contraindicated for individuals with a tendency toward hyperuricemia and (b) what, if any, is the value of carefully controlled chronic exercise in the prevention of hyperuricemia?

Hyperuricemia in Selected Populations

Epidemiological studies have shown that populations vary in mean serum uric acid levels (Table 1) and that frequency distributions are normal in some instances and skewed positively in others (20, 21, 36, 44). Hyperuricemia is more common than gout and both are more common in males than in females (20, 21, 22). For males, the lower limit of "hyperuricemia" is placed generally at about 7.0 mg/100 ml. when measured by the enzymatic spectrophotometric method (40) and urate crystal precipitation is uncommon below this level (59). Uric acid values measured by the colorimetric method are usually 0.2-0.6 mg/100 ml. higher than the enzymatic method (27). Serum uric acid values above 7.0 mg/100 ml. are not uncommon in adult males but are relatively rare in premenopausal women. This observation parallels the known incidence of clinical gout (44). In the same study, 9.2 percent of the male population over 20 years of age were hyperuricemic (above 7.0 mg/100 ml.). This is particularly important in view of the fact that the Framingham Heart Disease study (22) has reported that the risk of gout developing within a 10-year period is approximately one in five for middle-aged men with serum uric acid levels above 7.0 mg/100 ml.

Montoye (46) in a recent study of high school athletes not at peak training, reported elevated serum uric acid values. Greenleaf, *et al.* (20) measured serum sodium urate concentrations in 29 healthy Caucasian male college athletes and found an unexpected number (52 percent) had levels of 6.0 mg/100 ml. or greater and 14 percent had levels of 7.0 mg/100 ml. or greater. Similar data from a group of healthy, physically active women showed no abnormal increase in serum uric acid, (Table 1) whereas the mean of a population of male athletes (20) was significantly higher than that of

Emmerson and Sandilands' (16) "normal" population. The study (20) demonstrated yet another asymptomatic group, college athletes, in whom elevated urates may exist and not necessarily reflect a disease state. Three factors might be identified which, singly or in combination, may have contributed to the high uric acid values in high school and college athletes — acute and/or chronic physical exercise, genetic predisposition and achievement-oriented behavior.

Table I

Comparison of Some Representative Serum Uric Acid Values in Males and Females**

Reference	No. Cases	Occupation Age	Serum Uric Acid Conc. (mg/100 ml)			
			(Mean ±S.D.)	(Range)	(> 5.9)	(> 6.9)
MALES						
Mikkelsen, et al. (44) (Americans)	2,987	Various 4-80+	4.9±1.4*	1.0-13.6	20.8	7.4
Mikkelsen, et al. (44) (Americans)	153	Various 20-24	5.6±1.3*	2.6-13.6	28.8	11.1
Emmerson, et al. (16) (Australians)	100	Students 20-30	5.6±1.0†‡	3.5-8.4	32.0	7.0
Dreyfuss, et al. (12) (Israelis)	21 (18 + 3)	Students 20-30	5.4±1.1§	4.1-7.4	33.3	9.5
Dunn, et al. (13) (Americans)	331	Executives 40-60	5.7±1.2*	——	43.3	16.5
Dunn, et al. (13) (Americans)	76	Ph.D. Scientists	5.3±1.2*	——	26.3	9.2
Dunn, et al. (13) (Americans)	532	Craftsmen 40-60	4.8±1.1*	——	12.6	3.5
Greenleaf, et al. (20) (Americans)	29	Athletes 21-31	6.1±1.0‡	3.6-11.4	51.7	13.8
FEMALES					(> 4.9)	(> 5.9)
Mikkelsen, et al. (44) (Americans)	3,013	Various 4-80+	4.2±1.2*	1.0-11.9	21.9	7.2
Mikkelsen, et al. (44) (Americans)	277	Various 25-29	4.0±1.2*	1.0-11.6	16.2	5.4
Emmerson, et al. (16) (Australians)	100	Nurses 20-25	4.5±0.7†‡	2.5-6.4	30.0	1.0
Greenleaf, et al. (20) (Americans)	11	Physical Education Teachers 24-33	4.6±0.7‡	3.0-6.4	27.3	9.1

*Liddle, et al. J. Lab. Clin. Med. 54: 903, 1959. (Enzymatic method)
†Feichtmeir, et al. Am. J. Clin. Path 25: 833, 1955. (Enzymatic method)
‡Henry, et al. Am. J. Clin. Path. 28: 152, 1957. (Colorimetric method)
§Hepler, et al. Am J. Clin. Path. 22: 72, 1952. (Colorimetric method)
**From Greenleaf, et al. Am. Corr. Ther. J. 23: 66, 1969.

Hyperuricemia and Heredity

Little is known about the relative role of genetic factors in the control of serum uric acid levels in humans although several studies have suggested inborn differences between various ethnic groups and communities apparently unexplainable by diet, drugs, or other diseases (25, 60, 61). The kind of experimental design used in these studies is typified by that of Hauge and Harvald (25) in which 261 relatives of gouty subjects were compared with 266 relatives on non-gouty matched controls. Their results indicated a clear "familiality" for hyperuricemia, gout, and urinary calculi. Another epidemiological study on Indians in Arizona and Montana concluded, however, that the trait of hyperuricemia is, for the most part, not a genetic one but is largely determined by environmental factors (49). Epidemiological and familial studies have been criticized by Blumberg (3), since they do not differentiate between heredity and environmental factors.

A most comprehensive genetic study was done by Boyle, *et al.* (5) on 112 pairs of male and female twins. They compared the mean intrapair variance of serum uric acid levels in monozygotic (genetically identical) twin pairs and contrasted it with the mean intrapair variance of dizygotic (genetically non-identical) twin pairs. A genetic influence would predominate if the variance between the monozygotic twin pairs were smaller than the variance in the dizygotic pairs. This did indeed occur in the females ($p < .001$). However, just the opposite occurred in the males, i.e., there was a larger but not statistically significant variance in the monozygotes. Their results suggest that in males the mechanisms controlling the normal serum uric acid levels are influenced more by environmental factors whereas in females, hereditary factors predominate. This may account for the greater variation in means and variances reported in male populations (Table 1).

Apparently, no studies have attempted to demonstrate a genetic influence on the elevated serum uric acid levels reported in athletes. Future research should attempt to elucidate exact mechanisms and differentiate between hereditary and environmental factors.

Hyperuricemia and Psycho-social Factors

A number of epidemiological studies have shown significant but low positive correlations between high serum uric acid levels and psycho-social characteristics such as intelligence, *achieved* social status and "drive" (7, 13, 30, 45, 62). A small but statistically significant correlation ($r = 0.07$) between serum uric acid levels and intelligence was found in army inductees (62). A positive association between serum uric acid levels and "achieved" social status was observed in students, craftsmen, executives and scientists (13). A positive relationship ($r = 0.66$) was shown in university professors, between serum uric acid levels and "drive," achievement and leadership (7). This was the highest correlation coefficient reported between a behavioral variable and serum uric acid. Kasl, *et al.* (30) found higher serum uric acid levels in children who were highly motivated academically. Montoye, *et al.* (45) reported a significantly higher serum uric acid concentration (by 0.5 mg/100 ml) in a subgroup of Michigan business executives compared to comparably aged men from a larger population.

Recently, several researchers have attempted to measure serum uric acid before, during and after psychological and/or physical stress (31, 36, 52, 53). These studies are in general agreement that serum acid concentration rises approximately 0.5 - 1.0 mg/100 ml during periods of *anticipation* of demanding situations but that it falls approximately 0.5 - 2.0 mg/100 ml *during* periods of intense physical and psychological overload. A crucial area of differentiation between persons with high serum uric acid levels and those with elevated serum cholesterol was in how the individual perceived his current life situation. Persons with high serum uric acid concentrations seemed to view current life stresses as enjoyable challenges, while individuals with high cholesterol viewed those stresses as overburdening (31, 36, 52).

The results of these studies appear to support an association between the hyperuricemic state and certain behavior patterns. However, they also suggest that it is still far from clear whether they reflect inherent personal characteristics, environmental factors reflected in a different "style of life," or both. In view of the elevated serum uric acid concentrations reported in athletes out of training, the challenge is to determine if the cause is due to achievement-oriented personality, physical activity, etc.

Hyperuricemia and Cardiovascular Disease

Epidemiological studies of coronary heart disease have identified characteristics which, to some extent, are associated with an increased liability to cardiovascular disease. The Framingham study (22) demonstrates that the predominant factors are high serum lipid patterns, hypertension, obesity, smoking and inactivity. Two metabolic disorders, gout and diabetes, are also postulated as predisposing to coronary heart disease. Therefore, it would seem important to ascertain whether elevated serum uric acid contributes to the development of coronary heart disease, since effective treatment for hyperuricemia by use of drugs is available. For the same reason, it would also be important to know if chronic physical exercise had any preventive or controlling effect on hyperuricemia. By the same token, the hyperuricemic effect of acute exercise (see following section) may contraindicate participation in acute strenuous exercise for hyperuricemic individuals.

Despite the apparent association between obesity and atherosclerosis, studies of relationships between hyperuricemia in individuals with or without gout and atherosclerosis have been undertaken only in recent years. Probably the earliest systematic study of this kind was that of Gertler, *et al.* (18) who found hyperuricemia to be four times as prevalent in a group of 92 men who had suffered a myocardial infarction before the age of 40 than in control subjects. Since then various investigations have demonstrated positive but low correlations between gout and arteriosclerosis (15), myocardial infarction (34), cerebral thrombosis (23), essential hypertension (32), diabetes mellitus (64) and familial xanthomatosis (29), all of which (gout excepted) are caused by or associated with atherosclerosis (1).

However, there are many unresolved questions concerning the relationships between the above diseases, hyperuricemia, gout and the various lipids that might influence them. For example, some studies (6, 11, 28, 32, 33), but not all (65) have reported hyperuricemia in hypertensive patients without typical gouty arthritis.

Some investigators have reported a positive correlation between cholesterol and uric acid (35, 56) while others (1, 14) failed to find significant correlations between serum concentrations of either cholesterol or triglyceride and uric acid. It is quite likely these serum fractions vary independently of one another (55).

Finally, a great deal of interest has centered around the positive relationship of obesity and/or weight and hyperuricemia, with several researchers (1, 7, 18, 32) reporting positive but low correlations and others (4, 63) reporting little or no correlation. Probable reasons for confusion in this area may be found in the failure to differentiate clearly between obesity (relative quantity of fat) and absolute body weight. If the association between weight and serum uric acid concentration is a real one, it may contribute to the higher levels found in athletes. Athletes are generally taller and heavier than their non-athletic counterparts (46).

Hyperuricemia and Acute Exercise

Acute exercise is defined as a *single* bout of exercise and its immediate physiological effects.

The experimental studies (39, 41, 47, 51, 54, 67) are practically unanimous in reporting increases in serum uric acid with acute exercise. Researchers reported an increase of 0.9-1.5 mg/100 ml with single bouts of short, strenuous exercise (54); a rise of 0.4-2.6 mg/100 ml following a marathon race (39); a rise of 1.0 mg/100 ml following one half hour of muscular endurance exercises (41); a very small rise (0.2 mg/100 ml) after one hour of exercise (51); a rise of 0.5 mg/100 ml after 30 minutes of running (47) and a slight increase (0.2 mg/100 ml) in serum uric acid in 20 healthy young male subjects who did light muscular exercise for 30 minutes (67).

Neither the causal relationship between muscular exercise and elevated serum uric acid nor the underlying physiological mechanisms have been clarified exactly, but it is accepted generally that the hyperlactacidemia associated with exercise causes a decrease in urinary urate clearance by inducing an increase in tubular reabsorption of urate in the kidneys, resulting in a corresponding rise in its concentration in the blood (47). Further substantiating this argument is the work of Michael (43) who reported a close correlation between *artificially induced* hyperlactacidemia and inhibition of uric acid excretion. However, many other substances have been shown to inhibit uric acid excretion. For example, uric acid excretion by the kidneys has been inhibited by hyperlipidemia and/or induced ketosis (50).

Hyperuricemia and Chronic Exercise

Chronic exercise (training) is defined as an intermittent series of *single* bouts of exercise (usually progressively strenuous in nature) and their *cumulative* physiological effects. The question of concern is whether the effects of chronic exercise are identical, basically, to those of acute exercise.

The attempts to elucidate the effects of chronic exercise on serum uric acid concentration have resulted in (a) epidemiological studies on athletes (13, 20, 46) wherein the effects of chronic exercise are *implied* and (b) experimental studies (4, 8, 9, 42, 52, 53) wherein the longitudinal effects of training are *observed*.

In the former type of study, Dunn, *et al.* (13) observed a positive relationship in male high school students between serum uric acid and the degree of participation in combined scholastic and athletic activities but no relationship between serum uric acid and athletic participation only. Significantly elevated serum uric acid values (by 0.6 mg/100 ml) were reported in high school athletes (46) and in college athletes (20) not at peak training, suggesting that decreased activity was associated with higher uric acid. In another study, Montoye, *et al.* (45) observed in a group of business executives, a direct relationship between physical activity and serum uric acid. In the most active group, uric acid averaged 6.5 mg and that of the least active was 5.8 mg/100 ml. This seemingly paradoxical relationship between activity levels and serum uric acid levels can be explained if it is assumed that activity levels of relatively sedentary people, i.e., executives, are more closely dependent upon a "drive"-achievement factor, therefore having higher serum uric acid. This would also explain why athletes have higher serum uric acid when out of training — a "drive"-hereditary factor "sets" the resting level but chronic exercise (training) decreases it.

Few studies have attempted to measure uric acid during longitudinal physical training. The results of these studies have been conflicting and confusing. Serum uric acid in Marine recruits did not change at the end of a training period (8) while in a second study, (9) uric acid decreased. Rahe and Arthur (53) noted a decrease of 1.6 mg/100 ml in serum uric acid during underwater demolition training. In a second study Rahe, *et al.* (52) observed statistically significant elevations in serum uric acid when trainees were eagerly performing new and challenging (early in training) strenuous activities, and significant decreases of 0.9 - 1.3 mg/100 ml when the men undertook prolonged, unpleasant activities.

The two most recent studies have reported conflicting results. Mann, *et al.* (42) studied the effects on unfit adult men of six months of physical training consisting of a series of calisthenics with alternate periods of walking, jogging and running. The mean serum uric acid concentration increased slightly (about 0.5 mg/100 ml). They proposed that the increase was due possibly to an increase in muscle mass of their subjects or to repetitive hyper-lactacidemia.

Bosco, *et al.* (4) investigated the effect of eight weeks of chronic exercise on serum uric acid concentration. The sample was composed of 30 normal, healthy, college-aged students: 10 athletes in training (athletic group), 10 moderately active physical education class participants (training group) and 10 relatively sedentary individuals (control group). Serum uric acid concentration was measured at the beginning, periodically during an eight-week training period and after a four-week "deconditioning" period. It was found that chronic physical exercise lowered serum uric acid 0.3 to 3.2 mg/100 ml in 80% of the subjects in the athletic and training groups, particularly in those subjects with initially elevated values of 7.0 - 8.5 mg/100 ml (Fig. 1). Their most important finding was a significant ($p < 0.05$) decrease

FIGURE 1.

Shift in Serum Uric Acid Concentration after Eight Weeks of Exercise at Three Intensity levels.

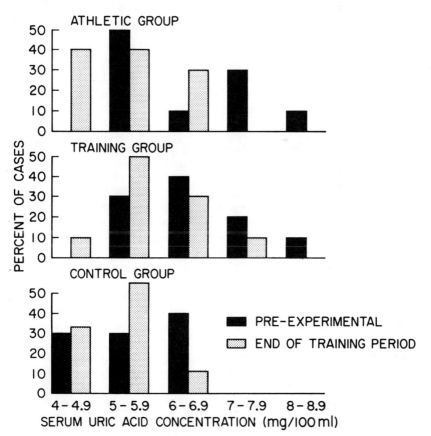

in serum uric acid in the athletic group which underwent an extremely strenuous exercise program in comparison to the other groups (Fig. 2).

FIGURE 2.*

Within-group changes in serum uric acid concentration. The uric acid values at the end of the experiment (training) period are compared with the pre-experimental values.

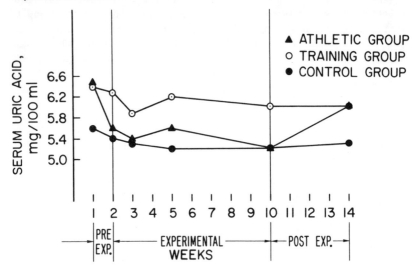

*From Bosco, et al. Amer. J. Cardiol. 25: 47, 1970.

Factors which could have contributed to the lowering of serum uric acid concentration with chronic exercise (training) were classified (4) as follows: (A) *primary* effects on uric acid metabolism *per se* due to exercise stimuli, and (B) *secondary* reactions of uric acid due to the effects of exercise on some other variable, e.g., lipid or amino acid metabolism. The *primary* effects were: (a) a decrease in uric acid production with constant excretion, (b) an increased excretion with constant production, (c) no change in uric acid turnover rate, but a progressively increasing plasma volume and (d) some influence of diurnal and/or seasonal variations on uric acid metabolism. The two most likely *primary* effects explaining lowering of serum uric acid during chronic exercise (training) were: (a) a relatively constant turnover of urate accompanied by a progressively increasing plasma volume and (b) an absolute increase in urinary uric acid excretion. The failure of Calvy, *et al.* (8, 9) and Mann, *et al.* (42) to obtain a decrease in serum uric acid concentration with chronic exercise (training) may have been due to the high fat diet used by Calvy's subjects and the increase in fat intake by Mann's subjects which would tend to decrease uric acid excretion (50) thereby maintaining higher blood levels. More complete answers await the research that will, in one study (a) control dietary intake, (b) control the amount of exercise and (c) measure serum uric acid concentration, plasma volume, and urinary excretion of uric acid.

REFERENCES

1. Benedek, T. G. Correlations of serum uric acid and lipid concentrations in normal, gouty, and atherosclerotic men. *Ann. int. med.* 66: 851, 1967.
2. Berkowitz, D. Blood lipid and uric acid interrelationships. *J.A.M.A.* 190: 856, 1964.
3. Blumberg, B. S. Heredity of gout and hyperuricemia. *Arth. rheum.* 8: 627, 1965.
4. Bosco, J. S., Greenleaf, J. E., Kaye, R. L. and Averkin, E. G. Reduction of serum uric acid in young men during physical training. *Amer. j. cardiol.* 25: 47, 1970.
5. Boyle, J. A., Grieg, W. R., Jasani, M. K., Duncan, A., Diver, M. and Buchanan, W. W. Relative roles of genetic and environmental factors in the control of serum uric acid levels in normouricaemic subjects. *Ann. rheum. dis.* 26: 234, 1967.
6. Breckenridge, A. Hypertension and hyperuricaemia. *Lancet* 1: 15, 1966.
7. Brooks, G. W. and Mueller, E. Serum urate concentration among university professors. Relation to drive, achievement, and leadership. *J.A.M.A.* 195: 415, 1966.
8. Calvy, G. L., Cady, L.D., Mufson, M.A., Nierman, J. and Gertler, M. M. Serum lipids and enzymes. Their levels after high-caloric, high-fat intake and vigorous exercise regimen in Marine Corps recruit personnel. *J.A.M.A.* 183: 1, 1963.
9. Calvy, G. L., Coffin, L. H., Jr., Gertler, M. M. and Cady, L. D. The effect of strenuous exercise on serum lipids and enzymes. *Military med.* 129: 1012, 1964.
10. Cannon, P. J., Stason, W. B., Demartini, F. E., Sommers, S. C. and Laragh, J. H. Hyperuricemia in primary and renal hypertension. *New eng. j. med.* 275: 457, 1966.
11. Dollery, C. T., Duncan, H. and Schumer, G. Hyperuricemia related to treatment of hypertension. *Brit. med. j.* 2: 832, 1960.
12. Dreyfuss, F. and Czaczkes, J. W. Blood cholesterol and uric acid of healthy medical students under stress of an examination. *A.M.A. arch. int. med.* 103: 708, 1959.
13. Dunn, J. P., Brooks, G. W., Mausner, J., Rodnan, G. P. and Cobb S. Social class gradient of serum uric acid levels in males. *J.A.M.A.* 185: 431, 1963.
14. Dunn, J. P. and Moses, C. Correlation of serum lipids with uric acid and blood sugar in normal males. *Metabolism.* 14: 788, 1965.
15. Eidlitz, M. Uric acid and arteriosclerosis. *Lancet.* 2: 1046, 1961.
16. Emmerson, B. T. and Sandilands, P. The normal range of plasma urate levels. *Australian ann. med.* 12: 46, 1963.
17. Garrod, A. B. *A treatise on gout and rheumatic gout: rheumatoid arthritis.* Third edition. London: Longmans, Green and Co., 1876, p. 88, cited by Seegmiller, *et al., New eng. j. med.* 268: 712, 1963.
18. Gertler, M. M., Garn, S. M. and Levine, S. A. Serum uric acid in relation to age and physique in health and in coronary heart disease. *Ann. int. med.* 34: 1421, 1951.
19. Grayzel, A. I., Liddle, L. and Seegmiller, J. E. Diagnostic significance of hyperuricemia in arthritis. *New eng. j. med.* 265: 763, 1961.
20. Greenleaf, J. E., Kaye, R. L. and Bosco, J. S. Elevated serum uric acid concentration in college athletes: a preliminary study. *Am. corr. ther. j.* 23: 66, 1969.
21. Gresham, G. E. Hyperuricemia. An epidemiologic review. *Arch. environ. health.* 11: 863, 1965.
22. Hall, A. P., Barry, P. E., Dawber, T. R. and McNamara, P. M. Epidemiology of gout and hyperuricemia. A long-term population study. *Am. j. med.* 42: 27, 1967.
23. Hansen, O. E. Acute gouty arthritis provoked by cerebrovascular disease. *Acta med. scand.* 178: 423, 1965.
24. Harris-Jones, J. N. Hyperuricaemia and essential hypercholesterolaemia. *Lancet* 1: 857, 1957.
25. Hauge, M. and Harvald, B. Heredity in gout and hyperuricemia. *Acta med. scand.* 152: 247, 1955.

26. Hellerstein, H. K. and Ford, A. B. Rehabilitation of the cardiac patient. *J.A.M.A.* 164: 225, 1957.

27. Henry, R. J., Sobel, C. and Kim, J. A modified carbonate-phosphotungstate method for the determination of uric acid and comparison with the spectrophotometric uricase method. *Am. j. clin. path.* 28: 152, 1957.

28. Itskovitz, H. D. and Sellers, A. M. Gout and hyperuricemia after adrenolectomy for hypertension. *New eng. j. med.* 268: 1105, 1963.

29. Jensen, J., Blankenhorn, D. H. and Kornerup, V. Blood-uric-acid levels in familial hypercholesterolaemia. *Lancet* 1: 298, 1966.

30. Kasl, S. V., Brooks, G. W. and Cobb, S. Serum urate concentrations in male high-school students. A predictor of college attendance. *J.A.M.A.* 198: 713, 1966.

31. Kasl, S. V., Cobb, S. and Brooks, G. W. Changes in serum uric acid and cholesterol levels in men undergoing job loss. *J.A.M.A.* 206: 1500, 1968.

32. Kinsey, D., Walther, R., Sise, H. S., Whitelaw, G. and Smithwick, R. Incidence of hyperuricemia in 400 hypertensive patients (abstract). *Circulation.* 24: 972, 1961.

33. Köelbel, F., Gregonova, I. and Sonka, J. Hyperuricemia in hypertension. *Lancet* 1: 519, 1965.

34. Kohn, P. M. and Prozan, G. B. Hyperuricemia — relationship to hypercholesterolemia and acute myocardial infarction. *J.A.M.A.* 170: 1909, 1959.

35. Kuzell, W. G., Glover, R. P., Gibbs, J. O. and Blau, R. A. Effect of sulphinpyrazone on total serum cholesterol in gout: a long term study. *Am. j. med. sci.* 248: 164, 1964.

36. Lanese, R. R., Gresham, G. E. and Keller, M. D. Behavioral and physiological characteristics in hyperuricemia. *J.A.M.A.* 207: 1878, 1969.

37. Lathem, W. and Rodnan, G. P. Impairment of uric acid excretion in gout. *J. clin. invest.* 41: 1955, 1962.

38. Lennox, W. G. A study of the retention of uric acid during fasting. *J. biol. chem.* 66: 521, 1925.

39. Levine, S. A., Gordon B. and Derick, C. L. Some changes in the chemical constituents of the blood following a marathon race. With special reference to the development of hypoglycemia. *J.A.M.A.* 82: 1778, 1924.

40. Liddle, L., Seegmiller, J. E. and Laster, L. The enzymatic spectrophotometric method for determination of uric acid. *J. lab. clin. med.* 54: 903, 1959.

41. Lucke, H. Über Schwankungen des endogenen Harnsaurestoffwechsels des Normalen und deren Regulation. *Ztschr. f. exper. med.* 56: 251, 1927 (English translation).

42. Mann, G. V., Garrett, H. L., Fahri, A., Murray, H. and Billings, F. T. Exercise to prevent coronary heart disease. *Am. j. med.* 46: 12, 1969.

43. Michael, S. T. The relation of uric acid excretion to blood lactic acid in man. *Am. j. physiol.* 141: 71, 1944.

44. Mikkelsen, W. M., Dodge, H. J. and Valkenburg, H. The distribution of serum uric acid values in a population unselected as to gout or hyperuricemia. Tecumseh, Michigan 1959-1960. *Am. j. med.* 39: 242, 1965.

45. Montoye, H. J., Faulkener, J. A., Dodge, H. J. Mikkelsen, W. M., Willis, P. W., III and Block, W. D. Serum uric acid concentration among business executives. With observations on other coronary heart disease risk factors. *Ann. int. med.* 66: 838, 1967.

46. Montoye, H. J., Howard, G. E. and Wood, J. H. Observations of some hemochemical and anthropometric measurements in athletes. *J. sports med. physical fitness* 7: 35, 1967.

47. Nichols, J., Miller, A. T., Jr. and Hiatt, E. P. Influence of muscular exercise on uric acid excretion in man. *J. appl. physiol.* 3: 501, 1951.

48. Nugent, C. A. and Tyler, F. H. The renal excretion of uric acid in patients with gout and in non-gouty subjects. *J. clin. invest.* 38: 1890, 1959.

49. O'Brien, W. M., Burch, T. A. and Bunim, J. J. Genetics of hyperuricaemia in Blackfeet and Pima Indians. *Ann. rheum. dis.* 25: 117, 1966.

50. Ogryzlo, M. A. Hyperuricemia induced by high fat diets and starvation. *Arth. rheum.* 8: 799, 1965.

51. Quick, A. J. The effect of exercise on the excretion of uric acid. *J. biol. chem.* 110: 107, 1935.
52. Rahe, R. H., Rubin, R. T., Arthur, R. J. and Clark, B. R. Serum uric acid and cholesterol variability. *J.A.M.A.* 206: 2875, 1968.
53. Rahe, R. H. and Arthur, R. J. Stressful underwater demolition training. Serum urate and cholesterol variability. *J.A.M.A.* 202: 1052, 1967.
54. Rakestraw, N. W. Chemical factors in fatigue. I. The effect of muscular exercise upon certain common blood constituents. *J. biol. chem.* 47: 565, 1921.
55. Schaefer, L. E. Serum cholesterol—triglyceride distribution in a "normal" New York City population *Am. j. med.* 36: 262, 1964.
56. Schoenfeld, M. R. and Goldberger, E. Serum cholesterol—uric acid correlations. *Metabolism* 12: 74, 1963.
57. Seegmiller, J. E., Grazel, A. I., Howell, R. R. and Plato, C. The renal excretion of uric acid in gout. *J. clin. invest.* 41: 1094, 1962.
58. Seegmiller, J. E., Grazel, A. I., Laster, L. and Liddle, L. Uric acid production in gout. *J. clin. invest.* 40: 1304, 1961.
59. Seegmiller, J. E., Laster, L. and Howell, R. R. Biochemistry of uric acid and its relation to gout. *New eng. j. med.* 268: 712-716 (Mar 28), 764-773 (Apr 4), 821-827 (Apr 11) 1963.
60. Smyth, C. J., Cotterman, C. W. and Freyberg, R. H., Jr. The genetics of gout and hyperuricemia—an analysis of 19 families. *J. clin. invest.* 27: 749, 1948.
61. Stecher, R. M., Hersh, A. H. and Solomon, W. M. The heredity of gout and its relationship to familial hyperuricemia. *Ann. int. med.* 31: 595, 1949.
62. Stetten, D., Jr. and Hearon, J. Z. Intellectual level measured by army classification battery and serum uric acid concentration. *Science.* 129: 1737, 1959.
63. Tibblin, G. High blood pressure in men aged 50: a population study of men born in 1913. *Acta med. scand.* Supp. 470, 1-84, 1967.
64. Whitehouse, F. W. and Cleary, W. J., Jr. Diabetes mellitus in patients with gout. *J.A.M.A.,* 197: 73, 1966.
65. Wolffe, J. B. Continued vigorous physical activity as a possible factor in the prevention of atherosclerosis. *Circulation* 16: 517, 1957.
66. Yü, T. F. and Gutman, A. B. Uric acid nephrolithiasis in gout. Predisposing factors. *Ann. int. med.* 67: 1133, 1967.
67. Zachau-Christiansen, B. The rise in the serum uric acid during muscular exercise. *Scand. j. clin. lab. invest.* 11: 57, 1959.

SELECTED PHYSICAL FITNESS CHARACTERISTICS OF PROFESSIONAL BASEBALL PLAYERS

BRADLEY LeGEORGE ROTHERMEL
University of Illinois
Chicago Circle Campus

ABSTRACT

The purpose of this investigation was to observe and evaluate selected physical fitness characteristics manifested by samples of professional baseball players and to compare by a non-parametric statistical method the mean differences between the professional baseball players and samples of comparably aged, normal college males on these characteristics. Thirty-five professional baseball players ranging in age from 18 to 28 years were subjected to a battery of 93 physique, cardiovascular-respiratory, and motor fitness test items administered at eight testing stations during the final three weeks of spring training and the initial two weeks of the 1964 baseball season. Of the 32 physique characteristics selected for measurement the professional baseball players were discovered to differ significantly from the normal college males on 27, 26 of which were perceived to represent better fitness for the baseball group. Of the 42 cardiovascular-respiratory characteristics selected for measurement the professional baseball players were discovered to possess significantly better scores in seven characteristics, significantly lower than normal scores in 13 characteristics, and average scores in the remaining 20 variables. Of the 19 motor performance characteristics selected for measurement the professional baseball players averaged significantly better scores in 12. In the remaining seven characteristics their scores were average.

PURPOSE

The purpose of this investigation was to observe and evaluate selected physical fitness characteristics manifested by a sample of professional baseball players and to compare by statistical treatment the differences between the professional baseball players and samples of normal men of a comparable age on the characteristics selected for measurement.

NEED FOR THE INVESTIGATION

Experiments designed to measure changes in physical fitness due to participation in various activities are important, and the difficulties inherent in controlling such investigation are recognized. Another approach to the problem of determining the effects of participation in a particular sports activity is to test the present status of champions or professionals engaged in that activity because the best performers in a given sport should manifest the physical characteristics of that sport. Identification of these characteristics, then, would have great practical value to the physical education profession both from the performance and fitness points of view.

Need for the present experiment in the field of baseball became even more evident when a review of physical education literature revealed that no investigation of this type had ever been conducted in this area at the time (spring, 1964) when this experiment was initiated. However, before the results were finalized, results of a similar investigation conducted by Golding (5) were presented. A review of that article as well as all additional articles related to this investigation was offered by Rothermel (7).

METHODOLOGY

A sample of 35 professional baseball players who volunteered as subjects and who ranged in age from 18 to 28 years were subjected to a battery of 93 physique, cardiovascular-respiratory, and motor fitness test items.

Eight areas were selected as stations for administration of the tests: 1) The Physical Fitness Laboratory at the University of Illinois, 2) The Kinesiotherapy Laboratory at the University of Illinois; 3) Maricopa Inn, Mesa, Ariz. (spring training headquarters of the Chicago National League Ball Club); 4) Rendezvous Park, Mesa, Ariz. (winter home of the professional baseball club just mentioned); 5) Jackrabbit Field, Mesa, Ariz. (winter home of Salt Lake City, Utah, Class AAA-Pacific Coast League; Ft. Worth, Texas, of the Class AA-Texas League; Wenatchee, Wash., of the Class A-Northwest League; St. Cloud, Minn., of the Class A-Northern League; and Caldwell, Idaho, of the Rookie Class-Pioneer League); 6) Wrigley Field, Chicago, Ill. (summer headquarters of the Chicago National League Ball Club); 7) Busch Stadium, St. Louis, Mo. (summer headquarters of the St. Louis National League Ball Club) and 8) White Sox Park, Chicago, Ill. (summer headquarters of the Chicago American League Ball Club).

Nearly all tests were administered during the final three weeks of spring training and the initial two weeks of the 1964 baseball season when, according to a review of literature and personal interviews with individuals who were perceived to be experts in the area of baseball training and conditioning, players had attained maximum fitness levels for baseball players.

Since interest was focused on present status, only one determination was completed on each test. A retest was administered only when error by the tester, lack of cooperation by the subject, or improper functioning of equipment or instruments was suspected. All testing was conducted and/or supervised by the writer. One highly qualified member of the University of Illinois teaching staff who formerly played major league baseball provided assistance in administration of some tests.

Order of testing for subjects who were able to complete the entire battery was:

Round I (in the post-absorptive state)

A. Electrocardiogram
B. Schneider Test
C. Heartometer Test

Round II
   A. Bone, Muscle, and Fat Determinations
   B. Flexibility Measurements
   C. Reaction Time Tests
   D. Strength Measurements
   E. Vital Capacity Test
   F. Expiratory Force Test
   G. Breath-Holding Test
   H. Five-Minute Step Test

Round III
   A. Agility Tests
   B. Balance Tests
   C. Power Tests

A complete listing of individual test items is presented in Table 1. A minimum of two days was necessary for satisfactory completion of all test items because a reasonable amount of rest commensurable with the severity of the activity was allowed between tests of the maximum (all-out) variety. Not all the subjects submitted to the entire battery of tests since some objected to performing various tests of the more strenuous nature. However, each score obtained was expected to represent maximum effort on a particular test item.

In addition to ascertaining the means and standard deviations for each of the test items (variables) investigated within the sample of professional baseball players, the primary objective of the present investigation was to compare the sample of professional baseball players with the samples of comparably aged (18 to 28 years of age), normal college men. For the purpose of this investigation normal college men were defined as individuals who were not ill or under medical treatment, who were not members of college athletic teams and who appeared to be representative of typical college males.

The hypothesis of interest was that the professional baseball players would differ significantly from the normal population in the physical fitness characteristics investigated. It was further hypothesized that in selected characteristics investigated, professional baseball players would differ in the direction of better fitness.

To test the hypothesis a one-sample, nonparametric test was selected. Employment of this test enabled each raw score in the sample of professional baseball players to be compared with the mean of the corresponding normal sample by converting the measurements of the ball players from data which were essentially continuous into a discrete dichotomy, i.e., representing the raw scores as falling above or below the mean of the normal sample.

By using Siegel's (8) computational formula

$$z = \frac{(x\text{-}NP) \pm .5}{\sqrt{NPQ}}$$

and two tables, the researcher was able to determine whether or not the observed difference between the scores obtaind by the group of baseball players and the mean of normal sample were significant.

PRESENTATION OF DATA

The data procured from this investigation are presented in Table 1.

DISCUSSION

Physique Characteristics

Of the 32 physique characteristics selected for measurement the professional baseball players were discovered to differ significantly from normal college males on 27. Of these 27 signicant differences, 26 were in the direction which was considered to represent better fitness for the sample of professional baseball players.

The professional baseball players averaged significantly taller and heavier than the normals. In surface area, a measure representing a relationship between height and weight, the professional baseball players averaged significantly greater than normals as in weight residual. Although a standing height of 67.50 inches and a weight of 150 pounds was recorded among the professional baseball players, the data indicated that on the average taller and heavier individuals are most likely to succeed in professional baseball.

The professional baseball players averaged significantly greater than the normal college males in chest breadth, chest depth, normal chest girth, maximum chest girth, minimum chest girth, chest expansion, abdominal girth, maximum chest girth minus abdominal girth, shoulder width, hip width, and arm span. The professional baseball players then, were characterized generally by higher than average over-all skeletal components.

Professional baseball players averaged significantly greater than the normal group in biceps girth, abdominal girth, thigh girth, calf girth, and ankle girth. Higher than average muscle girth appeared to be characteristic of professional players.

The professional baseball players were discovered to possess significantly less superficial fat than normals in the cheeks, abdomen, hips, front thighs, and rear thighs. The average of the baseball group also possessed significantly less total fat than the average college male. The data indicated that less than average superficial fat appeared to be characteristic of individuals who succeeded in baseball.

On the basis of the data obtained from 32 physique characteristics investigated it was concluded that the professional baseball players were characterized by being structurally larger than normal and possessing superior physique characteristics.

Cardiovascular Characteristics

Of the 38 cardiovascular characteristics selected for measurement the professional baseball players were discovered to possess significantly better scores than normals in seven characteristics and significantly lower scores than normals in nine characteristics.

TABLE I

PRESENTATION OF DATA

No. Variable	M_1	Source of M_1	$S.D._1$	N_1	M_2	$S.D._2$	N_2	+	-	0	z
Physique Items:											
1 Height (in.)	68.840	3:128	2.680	335	71.890	2.335	35	33	2	0	5.071*
2 Weight (lbs.)	151.000	3:128	22.350	334	182.570	14.957	35	34	1	0	5.409*
3 Surface Area (sq. m.)	1.894	2:293	0.145	54	2.025	0.106	35	31	4	0	4.395*
4 Reciprocal Ponderal Index	12.680	4:331	0.450	793	12.682	0.298	35	19	14	2	0.696
5 Chest Breadth (in.)	11.020	3:128	0.797	332	12.685	0.521	34	34	0	0	5.659*
6 Chest Depth (in.)	7.420	3:128	0.763	334	8.185	0.682	34	29	5	0	3.944*
7 Normal Chest Girth (in.)	35.000	2:22	2.100	644	37.500	0.839	26	26	0	0	4.903*
8 Maximum Chest Girth (in.)	35.500	3:129	2.320	332	39.785	1.328	26	26	0	0	4.903*
9 Minimum Chest Girth (in.)	33.490	3:129	2.250	332	36.146	1.156	26	26	0	0	4.903*
10 Chest Expansion (in.)	3.240	3:129	0.826	380	3.638	0.453	26	20	6	0	2.550*
11 Abdominal Girth (in.)	30.790	2:22	2.140	239	32.754	1.787	26	23	3	0	3.726*
12 Maximum Chest Minus Abdominal Girth (in.)	4.480	3:129	2.350	301	7.031	1.626	26	26	0	0	4.903*
13 Shoulder Width (in.)	13.490	2:30	1.600	197	15.000	0.314	26	26	0	0	4.903*
14 Hip Width (in.)	11.590	3:128	0.800	335	13.190	1.096	34	31	3	0	4.630*
15 Ankle Girth (in.)	8.740	3:128	0.673	333	9.788	0.691	34	32	2	0	4.973*
16 Calf Girth (in.)	13.860	3:131	1.020	331	14.932	1.108	34	32	2	0	4.973*
17 Gluteal Girth (in.)	35.650	3:131	2.360	332	35.400	1.974	33	17	16	0	0.000
18 Thigh Girth (in.)	20.130	3:131	1.980	331	23.742	1.342	33	33	0	0	5.570*
19 Biceps Girth (in.)	11.450	3:131	1.100	332	12.500	0.534	13	13	0	0	3.344*
20 Cheek Fat (mm.)	21.102	3:132	3.462	332	15.600	3.498	34	2	32	0	-5.316*
21 Abdominal Fat (mm.)	24.020	3:132	8.085	332	21.210	9.543	34	9	25	0	-2.915*
22 Hip Fat (mm.)	27.290	3:132	8.210	332	22.530	8.863	34	7	27	0	-3.601*
23 Gluteal Fat (mm.)	33.825	3:132	8.145	332	33.980	13.879	34	23	11	0	1.886
24 Front Thigh Fat (mm.)	27.560	3:132	6.910	332	17.760	6.867	34	5	29	0	-4.287*
25 Rear Thigh Fat (mm.)	26.260	3:132	8.420	332	22.620	9.374	34	11	23	0	-2.229*
26 Total Fat (mm.)	160.00	3:132	43.000	332	139.740	44.395	34	11	23	0	-2.229*
27 Arm Span (in.)	70.730	2:22	3.000	273	74.200	3.728	16	16	0	0	3.750*
28 Weighted Skeletal Index	150.590	1:140	16.000	110	179.067	16.375	33	32	1	0	5.222*
29 Muscle Girth Index	146.010	11:38	15.400	80	148.288	14.068	33	19	14	0	0.696
30 Weighted Adipose Index	193.840	11:38	37.120	80	250.897	60.121	33	28	5	0	3.829*
31 Predicted Weight					171.797	18.222	33				
32 Weight Residual	4.854	1:140	7.680	110	10.352	12.895	33	25	8	0	2.785*

Table 1 (Continued)

No. Variable	M_1	Source of M_1	$S.D._1$	N_1	M_2	$S.D._2$	N_2	+	-	0	z
Cardiovascular Items:											
A. Basal Electrocardiogram-Lead V											
33 P-Wave Amplitude (mm.)	1.520	12:58	0.390	81	1.500	0.270	31	11	20	0	-1.796
34. R-Wave Amplitude (mm.)	24.510	12:58	5.276	49	24.420	4.578	31	15	16	0	- .359
35 T-Wave Amplitude (mm.)	10.260	12:58	3.256	81	10.390	3.029	31	12	19	0	-1.437
36 PQR Interval (sec.)	0.175	12:58	0.018	81	0.172	0.130	31	11	20	0	-1.796
37 QRS Interval (sec.)	0.028	6:63	0.070	61	0.050	0.010	31	11	11	0	- .213
38 Work Time (sec.)	0.312	12:59	0.027	81	0.296	0.027	31	11	20	0	-1.796
39 Rest Time (sec.)	0.748	12:59	0.126	81	0.713	0.098	31	11	20	0	-1.796
40 Rest to Work Ratio	2.526	12:59	0.345	81	2.395	0.370	31	11	20	0	-1.796
B. Heart Rates, Blood Pressures, and Pulse Pressures (Sphygmomanometer)											
41 Lying Pulse Rate (beats/min.)	72.530	3:135	10.840	821	59.000	7.191	29	0	29	0	-5.199*
42 Standing Pulse Rate (beats/min.)	84.570	3:135	12.920	835	83.620	11.602	29	19	10	0	1.857
43 Pulse Rate Change Lying to Standing	12.140	3:135	11:880	821	24.690	9.749	29	25	4	0	3.713*
44 Lying Systolic Blood Pressure (mm. Hg)	121.660	3:136	11.450	834	109.590	9.083	29	4	25	0	-3.713*
45 Lying Diastolic Blood Pressure (mm. Hg)	76.270	3:135	9.050	945	73.830	7.637	29	10	19	0	-1.857
46 Lying Pulse Pressure (mm. Hg)	48.144	3:227	12.960	110	35.760	8.862	29	3	26	0	-4.085*
47 Standing Systolic Blood Pressure (mm. Hg)	123.660	3:136	12.648	824	113.900	7.862	29	3	26	0	-4.085*
48 Standing Diastolic Blood Pressure (mm. Hg)	85.490	3:135	9.570	826	87.240	10.249	29	17	12	0	0.743
49 Standing Pulse Pressure (mm. Hg)	40.482	1:227	9.865	109	26.660	8.198	29	1	28	0	-4.827*
50 Pulse Pressure Change Lying to Standing	-8.234	1:227	9.130	109	5.970	13.062	29	25	4	0	3.713*
60 Systolic Time (cm.)	0.277	1:278	0.037	110	0.260	0.031	31	9	22	0	-2.514⁻
61 Diastolic Time (cm.)	0.513	1:278	0.137	110	0.575	0.126	31	20	11	0	1.437
62 Cycle Time (cm.)	0.780	1:278	0.150	110	0.835	0.121	31	20	8	3	2.079*
63 Rest to Work Ratio	1.897	1:271	0.551	110	2.268	0.639	31	23	8	0	2.514*
64 Fatigue Ratio	0.392	1:271	0.128	110	0.408	0.106	31	16	15	0	0.000
65 Pulse Rate (beats/min.)	79.160	1:271	12.680	110	73.560	8.850	32	6	26	0	-3.712*
66 Systolic Blood Pressure (mm. Hg)	118.455	1:225	13.450	110	112.530	9.770	32	7	25	0	-3.359*
67 Diastolic Blood Pressure (mm. Hg)	72.775	1:226	11.550	110	84.970	6.766	32	32	0	0	5.480*
68 Pulse Pressure (mm. Hg)	47.360	1:227	12.050	110	27.560	9.443	32	1	31	0	-5.480*
69 Total of Three 30-Second Pulse Rate Counts, After 5-Minute Step Test	168.540	3:135	31.200	127	169.090	9.102	35	20	15	0	0.676

Table 1 (Continued)

No. Variable	M_1	Source of M_1	$S.D._1$	N_1	M_2	$S.D._2$	N_2	+	-	0	z
Respiratory Items:											
70 Vital Capacity (in.^{3}, 37° C.)	385.330	3:129	42.400	316	325.370	34.327	35	0	35	0	-6.085*
71 Vital Capacity Norm					352.030	34.280	35				
72 Vital Capacity Residual (in.^{3})	16.360	1:345	42.400	110	-26.940	32.494	35	3	32	0	-5.071*
73 Maximum Expiratory Blow (mm. Hg)	162.910	1:353	48.500	110	139.000	34.496	34	10	24	0	-2.572*
74 Breath-Holding (Sec.) After 1 - Min. Step-Up (17 in., 30/min.)	21.310	3:134	9.660	63	15.410	8.634	34	4	30	0	-4.630*
Motor Performance Items:											
A. Reaction Time											
75 Visual Reaction Time (sec.)	0.350	2:97	0.075	150	0.295	0.029	34	1	33	0	-5.659*
76 Auditory Reaction Time (sec.)	0.340	2:97	0.075	150	0.266	0.030	34	0	34	0	-6.002*
77 Visual-Auditory Reaction Time (sec.)	0.310	2:97	0.075	150	0.280	0.031	34	7	27	0	-3.601*
B. Strength											
78 Right Grip (lbs.)	128.400	3:131	17.100	422	147.300	21.322	35	27	8	0	3.043*
79 Left Grip (lbs.)	121.500	3:131	16.430	420	135.400	28.949	35	22	13	0	1.352
80 Back (lbs.)	361.900	3:131	88.800	436	396.900	70.199	32	22	10	0	1.944
81 Legs (lbs.)	521.500	3:131	146.600	455	542.300	100.273	32	16	16	0	- .177
82 Total Strength (lbs.)	905.080	3:110	159.200	106	1214.060	160.847	32	32	0	0	5.480*
83 Strength ÷ Body Weight	5.870	3:110	0.970	106	6.628	0.839	32	27	5	0	3.712*
C. Power											
84 Vertical Jump (in.)	20.560	3:137	3.786	3116	21.750	1.478	28	23	5	0	2.457*
D. Flexibility											
85 Right Ankle (degrees)	56.410	3:133	10.950	707	67.000	7.047	12	12	0	0	3.180*
86 Left Ankle (degrees)	56.410	3:133	10.950	707	64.000	7.262	12	11	1	0	2.630*
87 Trunk Flexion Forward (in.)	12.080	3:133	3.700	647	9.654	3.286	35	7	28	0	-3.719*
88 Trunk Extension Backward (in.)	11.450	3:133	3.220	551	16.654	3.916	35	33	2	0	5.071*
89 Shoulder Flexibility (in.)	12.900	3:133	3.180	576	12.820	4.707	35	14	21	0	-1.352
E. Agility											
90 Illinois Agility Run (sec.)	20.720	10:21	1.704	100	16.500	1.136	20	0	20	0	-4.696*
F. Balance											
91 Balance Beam Test	15.320	9:50	1.184	22	15.480	1.810	21	9	12	0	- .873
G. Muscular Endurance											
92 Chins (no.)	9.810	3:138	3.320	381	9.852	3.101	27	14	13	0	0.000
93 Dips (no.)	10.670	3:138	4.770	3117	10.276	3.827	29	14	15	0	- .371

M_1 = The mean of the normal sample.

Source of M_1 = The source from which the writer obtained the mean of the normal sample. The first number refers to the number of the reference in the list of references and the second number refers to the page number. For example, 3:128 referred to Cureton, *Physical Fitness Workbook*, p. 128.

S. D.$_1$= The standard deviation of the normal sample.

N_1 = The number of cases in the normal sample.

M_2 = The mean of the sample of professional baseball players.

S.D.$_2$ = The standard deviation of the sample of professional baseball players.

N_2 = The number of cases in the sample of professional baseball players.

+   = The number of professional baseball players who scored above M_1.

-    = The number of professional baseball players who scored below M_1.

0   = The number of professional baseball players who scores equaled M_1.

z   = A score representing an area under the unit normal curve. (A z score prefixed by a minus denoted a variable for which the mean score of the professional baseball sample was below the mean score of the sample of normal college males. A minus z score should not necessarily be construed as an indication that the professional baseball players were less fit than the normal group on a particular variable since in certain instances a lower mean score represented superior performance, e.g., auditory reaction time. A z score prefixed by a plus denoted a variable for which the mean score of the sample of professional baseball players was above the mean score of the normals. In like manner, a plus z score should not necessarily be construed as an indication that the professional baseball players were fitter than the normal group on a particular variable since in some instances a higher mean score represented inferior performance, e. g., Weighted Adipose Index.)

* = A score which was significant at the 5% level.

None of the differences between the professional baseball players and the normals on the nine electrocardiograph measures were discovered to be significant. In general, the professional baseball players possessed average wave amplitudes representing magnitude of electrical potentials across the heart muscle and average time measures representing cardiac efficiency.

Participation in baseball, apparently, did not maintain or develop the higher pulse wave amplitudes typically possessed by trained, endurance athletes.

Professional baseball players averaged significantly better scores than normals in lying pulse rate, change in pulse pressure lying to standing terminal pulse rate after bench step and significantly lower scores than normals in change in pulse rate lying to standing, lying systolic blood pressure, lying pulse pressure, standing systolic blood pressure, and standing pulse pressure. Results of these comparisons indicated that participation in baseball over a period of years maintained the heart at an average level of efficiency, at least, in quiet, static postures.

Of the 16 heartometer characteristics selected for measurement, the professional baseball players averaged better scores than normals in four, namely obliquity angle, rest-to-work ratio, pulse rate, and diastolic blood pressure; and lower scores than normals in four, notably diastolic amplitude, diastolic surge amplitude, systolic blood pressure, and pulse pressure. In general, the professional baseball players possessed average brachial pulse waves indicating that participation in baseball produced average cardiovascular fitness as interpreted from the heartometer.

On the basis of the data obtained in this investigation it was concluded that professional baseball players were characterized by average cardiovascular fitness.

Respiratory Characteristics

Since the professional baseball players were discovered to possess significantly lower scores in the four respiratory tests, i.e., vital capacity, vital capacity residual, maximum expiratory force, and breath-holding after a one-minute bench step, it was concluded that they were characterized by lower than average respiratory fitness.

Motor Performance Characteristics

Nineteen motor performance variables were selected for comparison between the professional baseball players and the normal college males. In 12 characteristics professional baseball players were discovered to possess significantly better than average scores while in the remaining seven characteristics their scores were average.

Faster than average reaction time was highly characteristic of the professional baseball players since they averaged significantly faster than normals in visual (.295 vs. .350 seconds), auditory (.266 vs. .340 seconds), and visual-auditory (.280 vs. .310 seconds) total body reaction times and since almost every professional baseball player scored better than the average normal male.

The professional baseball players averaged significantly greater than normals in three of the six strength measures, namely, right grip, total strength, and strength divided by body weight. Therefore, professional baseball players were characterized by average to high levels of strength when compared to normal college men.

Professional baseball players were significantly more flexible in the right ankle, left ankle, trunk flexion forward-inches from the floor, and trunk extension backward. When compared with normals, professional baseball players were characterized by an average to a high degree of flexibility.

Professional baseball players possessed significantly more power as measured by the vertical jump and significantly more agility as measured by the agility run.

No differences between the two groups were noted in balance and muscular endurance.

On the basis of that data procured in this investigation it was concluded that average to superior motor fitness characteristics were possessed by individuals who participated in baseball professionally.

REFERENCES

1. Cureton, Thomas K. *Physical fitness appraisal and guidance.* St. Louis: The C. V. Mosby Company, 1947.
2. _____. *Physical fitness of champion athletes.* Urbana, Illinois: University of Illinois Press, 1951.
3. _____. *Physical fitness workbook.* St. Louis: The C. V. Mosby Company, 1947.
4. _____. Weight and tissue symmetry analysis. *Res. quart.* 2: 331-347, May, 1941.
5. Golding, L. A. Physical fitness of major league baseball players. *J. Ariz. Assoc. hlth. phys. educ. rec.* 10: 1, Fall, 1966.
6. Massey, B. H. *Prediction of all-out treadmill running from electrocardiogram measurements.* Unpublished master's thesis, University of Illinois, 1947.
7. Rothermel, Bradley L., and Breen, J. L. *Conditioning in baseball and team sports.* A paper presented at the American Association for the Advancement of Science, Dallas, Texas, December 27, 1968.
8. Siegel, S. *Nonparametric statistics for the behavioral sciences.* New York: McGraw-Hill Book Company, 1956.
9. Sterling, L. F. *Effect of badminton on physical fitness.* Unpublished master's thesis, University of Illinois, 1955.
10. Sternloff, R. E. *Prediction of civilian flying grades from physical fitness tests.* Unpublished master's thesis, University of Illinois, 1947.
11. Wells, H. P. *Relationships between physical fitness and psychological variables.* Unpublished doctoral dissertation, University of Illinois, 1958.
12. Wolf, J. G. *Electrocardiogram standards for normal young men.* Unpublished master's thesis, University of Illinois, 1947.

SOME OBSERVATIONS ON SELECTED ELECTROPHYSICAL COMPONENTS OF THE RESTING CARDIAC CYCLES OF WORLD CHAMPIONSHIP WRESTLERS[1]

DAVID E. CUNDIFF
University of Toledo

CHARLES B. CORBIN
Texas A & M University

ABSTRACT

Selected electrophysical components of the resting cardiac cycles of 51 world championship wrestlers and eight coaches (former champions) were studied during the 1966 World Championships. Athletes from various countries (USA, USSR, South Africa, Turkey, Iran and Japan) were found to differ with respect to the following measures: heart rate (60/R to R' interval), total systole (Q to second heart sound), the pre-ejection period of the carotid pulse wave (Q to carotid upstroke), and diastole (second heart sound to Q). The South African wrestlers exhibited the highest heart rates and the shortest time intervals for systole and diastole; wrestlers from the United States exhibited the longest time interval for diastole and lowest heart rate. When former athletes were compared to current champions, they were found to have shorter diastolic time intervals.

INTRODUCTION

Recent advances in multi-channel equipment have rendered possible the simultaneous measurement of the mechanical and electrical events of the cardiac cycle. Using such equipment, Franks and Cureton (6) determined the existence of four non-overlapping intervals (ejection period, diastole, isovolumetric contraction period (ICP) and electromechanical lag) which they believe should be measured and interpreted separately. Raab (19, 20) has long maintained that sedentary habits increase the sympathetic dominance of the autonomic nervous system (ANS) and that trained subjects exhibit parasympathetic dominance (slow heart rate and longer ICP). Habner and Rochelle (9) compared the ANS activity between physically trained (track and field) and untrained individuals. They found runners displayed a parasympathetic tendency on five of six tests of ANS balance at rest (heart rate was one test used), although the procedure for testing the subjects on ANS balance was questionable since the trained athletes had a 6-10 mile workout four hours before the testing session. Glick and Braunwald (8) did not subscribe to the view that an increase in one part of ANS decreases the tone of the other. They presented evidence which indicated both parts of ANS could be increased in tone simultaneously. Rushmer (21) indicated the myocardium received its blood supply while the heart was in diastole. Allowing for some blood flow during systole, it seems probable that the length of rest would be important to the long-range health of the heart.

---

[1] Drs. Charles B. Corbin and John Burt were responsible for data collection for this study.

FIGURE 1

Simultaneous physiograph recording and measurement of cardiac cycle intervals.

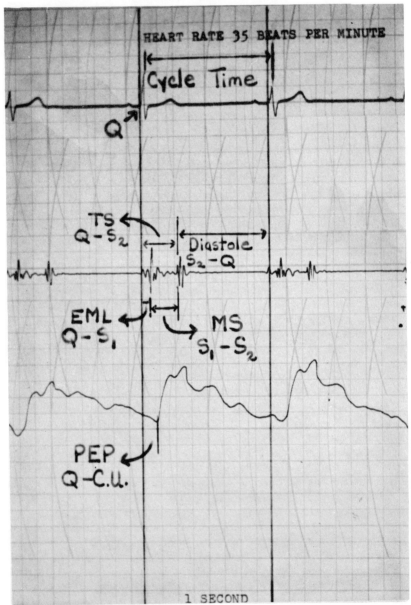

HEART RATE 35 BEATS PER MINUTE

Cycle Time

Q

TS
Q-S₂

Diastole
S₂-Q

EML
Q-S₁

MS
S₁-S₂

PEP
Q-C.U.

1 SECOND

In the present study the following cardiac cycle intervals were investigated (see Figure 1): a) *Cycle time* (CT) measured from R-R' (next R) on

ECG; heart rate = 60/R-R'. b) *Electromechanical lag* (EML) or Q of ECG to first heart sound (S_1), the time between onset of excitation and onset of contraction (A-V valve closure) measured by the downward deflection of Q to first major vibration of S_1 (11). c) *Pre-ejection period* (PEP) or Q to carotid upstroke, measured from the onset of excitation to beginning of carotid upstroke (10). d) *Total systole* (TS), the interval between Q and the end of ejection (closure of semi-lunar valves) as measured by the first major component of S_2 (24). e) *Mechanical systole* (MS) or the interval between S_1 and S_2 (25). f) *Diastole,* the interval between S_2 and Q (26).

REVIEW OF LITERATURE

Although a great deal of study has been directed toward the measurement of cardiac cycle intervals and their interpretation, few investigations have been carried out with championship athletes. The following is a brief review of studies in which cardiac cycle intervals were investigated in subjects, ranging from 4 to 97 years of age with varying physical conditions (sedentary normals, heart disease and distance runners).

McKusick (16) described factors which affect the amplitude and length or quickness of the heart sound. The youthful heart was described as displaying "snappy" heart sounds. The administration of adrenalin, which caused little or no change in intravascular pressures, accentuated S_1. Other factors affecting EML length were the quickness of valve closure and the physical quality of the valve. According to Luisada (15), the normal EML was close to 0.05 seconds. He found that this interval was usually prolonged in heart diseases other than mitral stenosis and was shortest in children. According to Craige (3), the normal EML should not exceed 0.074 seconds. Leatham, and others (14) measured EML in 80 children from 4 to 16 years of age. The intervals ranged between 0.04 to 0.06 seconds with a mean of 0.04 seconds for younger and 0.05 seconds for older children. In a study involving a large number of subjects (1,085; age range from 16 to 85 years with differences in health and physical condition), Hyman (11) stated that the EML was shortest when normal physiologic conditions were present and longest when any one or more of the sequential reaction factors became temporarily or permanently altered. He found that athletes exhibited the shortest mean EML (0.058 seconds) followed by normal subjects (good fitness = 0.072 seconds) and normal subjects (poor fitness = 0.080 seconds). Subjects with various degrees of cardiovascular disease had the longest intervals.

Harrison, and others (10) determined the effects of normal aging on the duration of selected intervals of the cardiac cycle. They appraised 65 healthy subjects aged 9 to 97 years and found that the PEP became slightly longer with advancing age. The linear shortening of the pulse-transmission time with age and a slight increase in the isovolumetric contraction time also cited in the study helped explain the paradox of variation in reported pre-ejection intervals. Wolferth and Mangolies (26) found a PEP of 0.111 seconds, whereas three other authors reported a time of 0.120 seconds (1, 2, 13).

McKusick (16) listed the following factors as affecting the length of TS and MS: sex (female), bradycardia, increased diastolic volume, increased resistance to systolic ejection and alkalosis resulting in prolongation; and sex (male), tackycardia, reduced diastolic volume (i.e., inspiration), epinephrine, acidosis, fever and digitalis resulting in shortening. Nixon and Wagner (18) used a needle inserted into the brachial artery to compare normal subjects with ones that exhibited mitral incompetence. TS was shorter for the disabled (0.26-0.37 seconds compared to 0.37 seconds mean for normals). Harrison, and others (10) found the duration of ejection to increase markedly with longer cycle length and slightly with age.

PROCEDURES

Wrestlers and former champions (coaches) were tested in Toledo, Ohio, during the 1966 Amateur Wrestling World Championships. Athletes and coaches from USA, USSR, South Africa, Turkey, Iran and Japan were tested before the start of competition. The E & M Physiograph was utilized to re-

TABLE I

SUBJECT GROUPING

	Age Group	Mean Age	No.
Wrestlers	18-33	24.8	51
Coaches	36-53	43.1	8

WRESTLERS WT. CLASSIFICATION AND COACHES

Group No.	Classification	No. of Subjects
1	114.5	6
2	125.5	5
3	138.5	7
4	154.5	9
5	171.5	8
6	191.5	8
7	213.5	3
8	Hwt.	5
9	Coaches	8

GROUPS BY COUNTRIES (wrestlers only)

1	USA	9
2	USSR	5
3	South Africa	7
4	Turkey	7
5	Iran	15
6	Japan	8

cord simultaneous ECG's, carotid pulse waves (Sanborn transducer type) and heart sounds (E & M Instrument Company), while the subjects were resting in their dormitory rooms. Most recordings were taken between 4:00 and 9:00 p.m. at one testing session. From these recordings selected cardiac cycle intervals were measured (Figure 1). The average of five consecutive intervals was recorded for each subject. Additional data recorded and compared were age, height, weight and heart rate. The data were analyzed by means of one-way ANOVA's for unequal N's. Comparisons were made among nine groups (eight standard weight classes of wrestlers and one group of coaches) and among wrestlers from various countries (see Table 1 for division and number of groups). F values were tested for significance at the .05 level. Where necessary, Duncan's multiple range test (22, 7) was used to determine significant differences among groups.

RESULTS AND DISCUSSION

Table 2 gives the means and standard deviations for variables with significant F ratios for the comparison of athletes (according to weight class) and coaches. Diastole was the only cycle interval with a significant F value. The summary results of the Duncan Multiple Range test are presented in Table 3. Group 9 (coaches) yielded the shortest diastole while Group 3 (138.5 pound) had the longest diastole.

When the wrestlers and coaches were compared, no significant differences were obtained in heart rate. Franks and Cureton (5) have found diastole and heart rate to be highly related. Although the coaches had been out of world-class competition for a number of years, diastole was the only

TABLE 2

SUMMARY OF RESULTS FOR ANOVA'S

Group	N	Mean Age	sd	Mean Wt.	sd	Mean Ht.	sd	Mean HR	sd	Diastole	sd
1	6	21.8	1.6	116.3	1.6	63.9	0.9	55.8	12.2	.655	.15
2	5	21.4	3.2	124.0	5.6	64.4	1.7	59.7	29.8	.723	.30
3	7	26.1	4.0	139.1	3.7	65.2	1.9	51.2	12.8	.807	.25
4	9	25.4	3.8	152.7	2.6	68.0	2.2	58.5	13.6	.652	.23
5	8	25.8	4.6	171.5	3.0	68.4	1.9	60.0	11.2	.574	.18
6	8	27.0	4.3	193.6	2.8	71.0	2.3	57.9	7.6	.610	.12
7	3	21.3	4.9	210.0	6.2	71.9	0.2	54.8	5.8	.678	.10
8	5	25.4	2.9	225.8	8.3	73.4	3.9	55.8	13.8	.712	.30
9	8	43.1	7.2	177.6	29.3	67.8	2.4	74.0	11.9	.353	.18
		F=16.19[a]		F=12.74[a]		F=56.59[a]		F=NS[c]		F=2.49[b]	

[a] $p < .01$
[b] $p < .05$
[c] Not significant

interval measured which was adversely affected by this absence of training and competition. However, the importance of this finding should not be overlooked, especially when diastole is translated into percent of resting time of the cardiac cycle. The hearts of the coaches rested only 43% of the cycle while the hearts of wrestlers (Group 3) rested 69% of the cycle.

Factors such as height and weight seemed to have no detectable effect on the cardiac cycle intervals. As indicated in Table 2, height and weight produced significant F ratios (.01 level) but no differences in cardiac cycle inter-

TABLE 3
SUMMARY RESULTS OF DUNCAN MULTIPLE RANGE[a]

Variable	Groups[b]								
Age	9	6	3	5	4	8	1	2	7
	43.1	27.0	26.1	25.8	25.4	25.4	21.8	21.4	21.3
Height	8	7	6	5	4	9	3	2	1
	73.4	71.9	71.0	68.4	68.0	67.8	65.2	64.6	63.9
Weight	8	7	6	9	5	4	3	2	1
	225.8	210.0	193.6	177.6	171.5	152.7	139.1	124.0	116.3
Diastole	3	2	8	7	1	4	6	5	9
	0.807	0.723	0.712	0.678	0.654	0.652	0.610	0.574	0.353

[a]All means underlined by same line are not significantly different (.05 level). Means not underlined by the same line are significantly different.
[b]Refer to Table 1 for identity of groups.

vals were observed when wrestlers were compared by weight classes. Also, age (the coaches were significantly older) apparently had no adverse effect on cycle intervals except diastole.

The comparison of wrestlers (coaches eliminated) by countries, is presented in Table 4. Total systole, PEP, diastole and cycle time (heart rate) yielded significant F ratios. Table 5 gives the summary results of Duncan's Multiple Range test. There were no significant F ratios in age, weight and height. The South African team yielded scores which were on the less desirable end of the continuum in three variables (TS, diastole, cycle time), while the USA appeared on the more desirable end of the continuum in three variables (PEP, diastole, cycle time).

When the comparison of teams by countries are expressed in terms of percentages of diastole to cycle time, the mean team diastoles of South Africa were 52%, USA 66% and the USSR 59%. When the resting time was converted into minutes/hour, the South African hearts rested 31 minutes/hour compared to a resting time of 40 minutes/hour for the hearts of the USA wrestlers.

In reviewing the results of the competition, the South African team members failed to win a match while the USSR and USA teams finished second and third respectively. Morgan (17) studied the personality characteristics of English speaking wrestlers at the same championships. The Mann-Whitney U test showed the South African team to be significantly more neurotic than the USA wrestlers. He also computed Rank-Order correlations between performance (number of rounds the wrestler remained in tournament) and the dimension of extraversion and neuroticism. A significant correlation $(+.50)$ was observed between extraversion and performance in the tournament.

TABLE 4

					SUMMARY OF RESULTS FOR ANOVA'S WRESTLERS BY COUNTRIES						
Country	No	Age	Height	Weight	HR	sd	TS	sd	PEP	sd	Diastole	sd
USA	9	24.4	68.8	157.7	46.4	5.8	.445	.01	.184	.01	.867	.17
USSR	5	25.8	66.8	169.6	52.2	9.1	.451	.03	.270	.07	.734	.24
So. Africa	7	23.1	68.2	158.2	75.2	19.9	.403	.05	.200	.03	.437	.15
Turkey	7	28.4	67.8	167.0	50.6	5.8	.451	.02	.196	.02	.755	.29
Iran	15	24.9	68.6	161.8	59.8	10.5	.424	.03	.231	.08	.609	.16
Japan	8	22.5	67.4	171.6	56.0	10.0	.431	.03	.175	.02	.670	.19
		$F=NS^c$	$F=NS^c$	$F=NS^c$	$F=6.43^a$		$F=3.05^b$		$F=2.89^b$		$F=5.16^a$	

[a] $p < .01$

[b] $p < .05$

[c] Not Significant

One South African wrestler had a heart rate of 112. It was found that this particular wrestler had lost 10 pounds in two days. Four of the nine wrestlers from the USA had weight losses from five to fifteen pounds in two days. Two of the seven South African wrestlers indicated a weight loss of 10 to 13 pounds. No other country reported weight losses, but it can be fairly assumed that a similar number of wrestlers from the other countries also lost weight but did not report it for various reasons. One wrestler from the USA recorded a heart rate of 35.4/minute and the Russian, Medvid, who won the heavyweight class competition recorded a heart rate of 36.8/minute.

TABLE 5
SUMMARY RESULTS OF DUNCAN MULTIPLE RANGE[a]

Variable	Group[b]					
TS (sec.)	4	2	1	6	5	3
	0.451	0.451	0.445	0.431	0.424	0.403
PEP (sec.)	2	5	3	4	1	6
	0.270	0.231	0.200	0.196	0.186	0.175
Diastole (sec.)	1	4	2	6	5	3
	0.867	0.755	0.734	0.670	0.609	0.437
Heart Rate (b/min)	1	4	2	6	5	3
	45.8	49.9	50.6	54.5	58.1	71.3
Cycle Time	1.311	1.202	1.186	1.101	1.032	0.841

[a]All means underlined by same line are not significantly different (.05 level). Means not underlined by the same line are significantly different.
[b]Refer to Table 1 for identity of groups.

Table 6 gives a comparison of cardiac cycle intervals for three different studies. The most striking difference in interval length occurred in the EML. The EML of 0.084 seconds in the present study would be considered out of normal range (too long) according to Craige (3). For the 51 wrestlers in the present study, the heart rate is lower than most studies have reported and may partially explain the lengthened EML. In addition, the considerable loss of weight (body water loss resulting in a diminished blood volume; i.e., greater blood viscosity) may be another factor. Karnegis and Wang (12) suggested that a diminished effective force in the closing of the mitral valve could cause a delay in closure and thus result in prolonged EML interval.

Although the other intervals appear to relate closely, care should be taken when comparing intervals obtained on different testing equipment and under varying conditions.

TABLE 6
COMPARISON OF CARDIAC INTERVALS IN PRESENT STUDY WITH THOSE REPORTED IN LITERATURE

Variable	Present Study	Franks and Cureton (5)	Cundiff (4)
Number	51	61	27
Age	24.8	34	43.4
EML	0.084	0.051	0.057
MS	0.348	0.340	0.347
TS	0.432	0.392	0.411
Diastole	0.672	0.546	0.533
R-R'	1.104	0.937	0.909
HR	54.3	64	66

SUMMARY

The findings of this study, considered in relation to the population, conditions and design used, warrant the following observations:

1. Highly trained wrestlers did not exhibit differences in cardiac cycle intervals when compared on the basis of wrestling weight.
2. Diastole was a more sensitive measure of cardiovascular condition than heart rate even though both measures are highly related.
3. The EML's of world championship wrestlers were longer than those reported in the literature and may have been the result of increased blood viscosity caused by dehydration.
4. The performance of the South African team in the championships was to some extent reflected in the electrophysical measures investigated in this study.

REFERENCES

1. Battro, A., and others. Asincromismo de la contraccion ventricular en el bloqueo de rama. *Rev. argentina de cardiol.* 3: 325-59, 1936-37.
2. Castex, M. R., and others. Diagnosis of the site of origin of ventricular extrasystoles in human beings. *Arch. int. med.* 67:76-90, 1941.
3. Craige, E. Phonocardiographic studies in mitral stenosis. *New eng. j. med.* 257: 650, 1957.
4. Cundiff, D. E. Training changes in the sympatho-adrenal system determined by cardiac cycle hemodynamics, oxygen intake and eosinopenia. Unpublished doctor dissertation, University of Illinois, 1966.
5. Franks, B. D. and Cureton, T. K., Jr. Orthogonal factors of cardiac intervals and their response to stress. *Res. quart.* 39: 524-32, 1968.
6. _____. Orthogonal factors and norms for time components of the left ventricle. *Abstracts of research papers/1969 convention.* Washington, D.C. AAHPER, 1969.
7. Freund, J. E., and others. *Manual of experimental statistics.* Englewood Cliffs, N.J.: Prentice Hall, Inc., 1960.
8. Glick, Gerald and Braunwald, E. Relative roles of the sympathetic and parasympathetic nervous systems in the reflex control of heart rate. *Cir. res.* 16: 363-75, 1965.
9. Hahner, R. H. and Rochelle, R. H. A comparison of autonomic nervous system activity between physically trained and untrained individuals. *Res. quart.* 39: 975-82, 1968.
10. Harrison, T. R., and others. The relation of age to the duration of contraction, ejection, and relaxation of the normal human heart. *Am. heart j.* 67: 189-99, 1964.
11. Hyman, A. S. The Q-first heart sound interval in athletes at rest and after exercise. *J. of sports med. and phy. fit.* 4: 199-200, 1964.
12. Karnegis, J. N. and Wang, Y. Q-first interval of the phonocardiograph studies in hypertensives. *Brit. heart j.* 28: 240-43, 1966.
13. Kossmann, C. E. and Goldberg, H. H. Sequence of ventricular stimulation and contraction in a case of anomalous AV excitation. *Am. heart j.* 33: 308-18, 1947.
14. Leatham, A., and others. Ausculatory and phonocardiographic findings in healthy children with systolic murmurs. *Brit. heart j.* 25: 451-59, 1963.
15. Luisada, A. A. *From ausculatation to phonocardiography.* St. Louis: C. V. Mosby Co., 1965.
16. McKusick, V. *Cardiovascular sound in health and disease.* Baltimore: William and Wilkins Co., 1958.
17. Morgan, William P. Personality characteristics of wrestlers participating in the world championships. *J. of sports med. and phy. fit.* 8: 212-16, 1968.
18. Nixon, P. G. F. and Wagner, G. R. The duration of left ventricular systole in mitral incompetence. *Brit. heart j.* 24: 464-68, 1962.
19. Raab, W. Training, physical inactivity and the cardiac dynamic cycle. *J. of sports med. and phy. fit.* 6:38-47, 1966.
20. _____. The nonvascular metabolic myocardial vulnerability factor in "coronary heart disease." Fundamentals of pathogenesis, treatment, and prevention. *Am. heart j.* 66: 685-705, 1963.
21. Rushmer, Robert F. *Cardiovascular dynamics* (2nd ed.). Philadelphia: W. B. Saunders Co., 1961.
22. Steel, R. G. D. and Torrie, J. H. *Principles and procedures of statistics (with special reference to the biological sciences).* New York: McGraw-Hill Inc., 1960.
23. Weissler, A. M., and others. Observations on the delayed first heart sound in mitral stenosis and hypertension. *Cir.* 18: 165, 1958.
24. Weissler, A. M., and others. The effects of deslanoside on the duration of the phases of ventricular systole in man. *Am. j. cardiol.* 15: 153-61, 1958.
25. Wiggers, C. J. Studies on the consecutive phases of the cardiac cycle. *Am. j. of physiol.* 56: 439-59, 1921.
26. Wolferth, C. C. and Mangolies, A. Asynchronism in contraction of the ventricles in the so-called common type of bundle branch block. *Am. heart j.* 10: 425-58, 1935.

THE ROLE OF EXERCISE IN THE PERFORMANCE
OF A SIMPLE MENTAL TASK

DAVID GIESE

ROBERT McADAM
University of Minnesota

GEORGE MILTON
Kansas State Teachers College

PETER WANG
Tulane University

ABSTRACT

One hundred fifty-seven male college students in the physical education service classes were divided at random into four treatment groups. It was found that groups which rested or exercised and then performed a simple 15-minute mental task surpassed in performance those groups which received classroom instruction or took a pencil and paper test and then undertook the mental exercise. However, the difference in performance was not statistically significant. Since similar trends were noted in each of three separate studies in this series, further analysis of combined studies showed the rest groups to be significantly superior to the classroom instruction and the test-taking groups (.05 level of significance), but not superior to the exercise group. Patterns of performance in terms of the onset of mistakes and the variability of performance were different for the exercise groups than for the other groups.

INTRODUCTION

The temporary and the enduring physiological changes brought about by exercise have been — and continue to be — the main thrust of exercise research. Although the integrated nature of man has long been recognized, it is only quite recently that systematic experimentation has taken place which asks questions concerning the potential of exercise for modifying the psychological and the sociological aspects of man's behavior.

One line of studies (5, 7, 8) has sought to show the parallel between achievement in physical performance and achievement in mental performance. These have been pursued with mixed, high, medium and low mental ability groups. In general, significant relationships do not appear to be present. The exception to this seems to appear when one examines only extremely high or extremely low mental ability groups.

Another line of studies (2, 4) has sought to relate perceptual skill or changes in perceptual skill to varying levels of motor development. The rationale for this is based partly on the theory that patterned movements give specific direction to neurological development which results in heightened function of the cortex. Another theory held within this group is that the kinesthetically keen have greater awareness of themselves in space and

117

are therefore better oriented to the acquisition and interpretation of information which comes to them through the senses. There are not, at this time, clear generalizations which can be made concerning the findings in this line of investigation.

Still others have attempted to study changes in mental performance with exposure to exercise either of a long term or a short term duration. The brain, comprising only 2% of the body's weight, consumes 25% of the blood's oxygen supply in a full cycle of circulation (10). It may be conjectured that that which will increase the circulation of the blood to the brain may, in the process, increase the capacity of it to function.

Wetmore (9) found that high school freshmen who participated in physical activity classes two mornings each week showed improvement in general academic average, numbers of honor grades, and reduced failing grades, while the control group (not taking activity classes) showed no change in the same period of time. Oliver (7), using matched groups of educationally subnormal boys, found that the exercise group improved significantly over a period of time on mental test scores and also did better than the control group. Gutin (3) found no significant difference between an exercise and a control group which performed a complex mental task after a 12 week physical conditioning program. There were, however, significant changes in the performance on the mental task by those within the groups who had made significant changes in physical fitness.

In more recent work, McAdam and Wang (6) have tested the value of a single exposure to exercise as it related to performance of a simple mental task. A moderate exercise which was circulatory promoting but not fatiguing did not appear to have any different effect upon mental performance than did a rest period. However, subjects doing either of these did perform better than subjects who performed other experimental treatments. Because these trends emerged in the early work, a series of studies (none of which have yet been reported in the literature and of which this is the third) with new design and modified hypothesis has been undertaken.

THE PROBLEM

It was the purpose of this study to determine to what extent a single exposure to exercise would modify the performance of male college students in a paper and pencil symbol-substitution type task. It was hypothesized that there was no difference in performance on the mental task between groups which exercised and those which did not.

In pursuit of this question, 157 male college students were selected at random from within each physical education service class and placed in one of four groups. All treatment groups were given a preliminary paper and pencil type test (Figures 1 & 2) of 15 minute duration in the same setting. Varied treatments were then administered. After exposure to the treatment, they returned to the original setting for a post-treatment test which was an alternate form of the first paper and pencil test.

In the 15 minute treatment period, group 1 executed a run-jog-walk — which was designed to promote a mild sweat, but to avoid fatigue. Group 2 lay upon soft mats in a room adjacent to the gymnasium and listened to sleep promoting music. Group 3, in another room adjacent to the gymnasium, viewed a film on the volleyball serve. The film was chosen because it was informative but not particularly exciting or stimulating. Group 4 remained in the setting of the pre-treatment test and as soon as alternate test forms were distributed, everyone took the second paper and pencil test. Upon completion of the treatments, groups 1, 2 and 3 returned (without vigorous movement) to the original setting for a 15 minute post-treatment test.

FIGURE I
SAMPLE–SIMPLE MENTAL TASK
FORM A

A –(15)

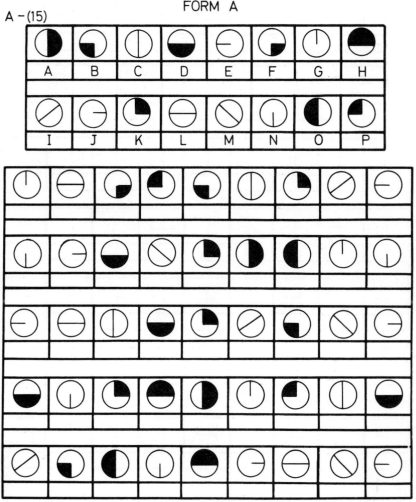

THE TASK

The mental task consisted of learning to associate a letter of the alphabet with a symbol as given in a key at the top of each page of the test. (1) The key consisted of 16 symbols with the associated letter shown below each symbol and was exactly the same for all pages of the test.

The subjects were carefully instructed to assign to each symbol the correct letter without skipping symbols and to work as accurately and as

FIGURE 2
SAMPLE–SIMPLE MENTAL TASK
FORM B

B–(3)

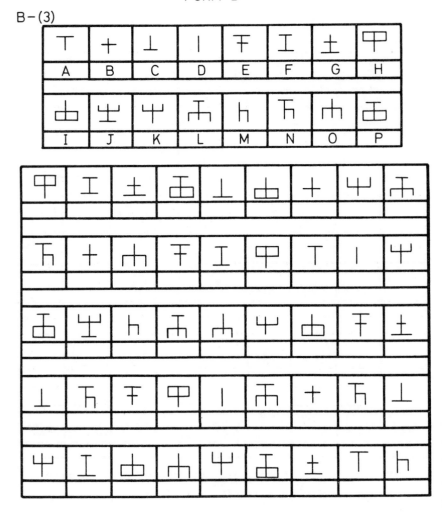

quickly as possible. Each 30 seconds the word "mark" was called by the test administrator at which time the student placed a large X over the symbol which was being identified at that time. In this way, minute-by-minute progress of the subject's work could be recorded.

In prior tests it was determined that there was evidence of stability and consistency in performance in both forms of this test. Because the explicit instructions in administering the test emphasized accuracy, errors were held to a minimum to the point that the relationship of total answers to correct answers yielded an r of .98 in Form A and .97 in Form B. Fluctuation in total responses minute-by-minute were also small although there was evidence of a slight upward trend in performance, indicating that learning of the task was taking place. Lastly, test-retest correlations of the performance of

FIGURE 3

POST TREATMENT PERFORMANCE
SCORES IN SIMPLE MENTAL TASK
EXPERIMENT #3

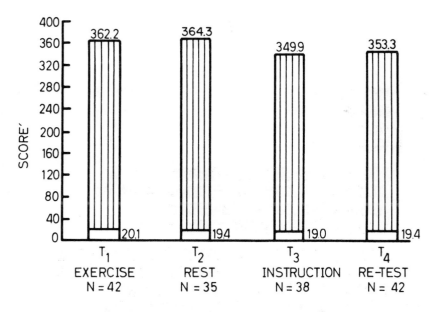

group 4 (immediate retest group) supports the hypothesis that these are essentially similar tasks and evoke consistent performance from the subjects.

RESULTS

An attempt to determine several characteristics of performance on this task was made. In the first question — namely what is the effect of the various treatments upon the performance of a simple mental task — the null hypothesis was tested (Figure 3). Since a significant F was not attained following an analysis of variance (F = .46), the hypothesis was not rejected. This finding verified results of earlier studies in this series. An analysis of co-variance using 15 minute pre-treatment performance scores as a base raised the F value (F = 1.49), but not to a level that could be considered significant. This finding also verified results of the two preceding studies in this series. In all experiments one trend was striking. The post-treatment 15 minute rest and exercise groups' performances exceeded the performances of the other two treatment groups (Figure 4). These definite traces of similar performance, though too weak to yield significant F ratios, were repeated in each of the experiments in this series.

FIGURE 4

15 MINUTES, POST TREATMENT PERFORMANCE SCORES IN REPLICATED EXPERIMENTS

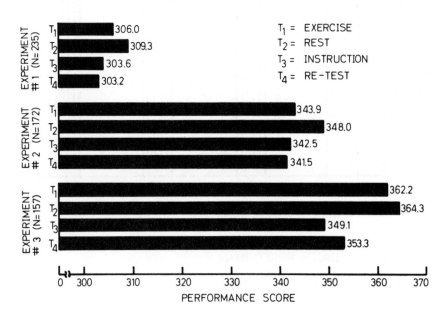

A second means of limiting the effect of the individual subject variability on the performance of this simple mental task was to block into high, medium, and low groups based on pre-treatment test totals. The post-post-treatment means for 1, 5, 10, 15 minute intervals are shown in Table 1. The effectiveness of the blocking variable is demonstrated by the F ratio of 87.4, significant well beyond the .01 level. The F ratio corresponding to the dif-

TABLE 1

BLOCKING INTO HIGH, MEDIUM, AND LOW GROUPS BASED ON POST TREATMENT PERFORMANCE ON ON SIMPLE MENTAL TASK (EXPERIMENT #3)

Minutes ⟶		1M	5M	10M	15M
T_1 (Exercise)	H	22.5	121	226	424
	M	19.1	95	217	348
	L	18.2	88	190	301
T_2 (Rest)	H	22.5	119	261	417
	M	18.8	96	214	341
	L	14.6	80	187	301
T_3 (Instruction)	H	21.1	113	259	420
	M	19.7	99	220	349
	L	16.7	80	185	301
T_4 (Re-test)	H	23.1	116	255	408
	M	17.9	95	210	333
	L	15.6	83	181	294

ferences among treatments was .64, while the interaction F ratio was .04. These findings, except for the interaction F ratio, replicate the findings of the two previous studies in this series.

Two other characteristics of performance in this task deserve attention. In all previous studies in this series it was noted that variability of 15 minute post-treatment performance in the exercise group tended to be higher than for the other groups. In this study, when viewed in terms of range and in terms of subjects performing very well and very poorly (though not in terms of standard deviations), the exercise group once again showed great variability in performance compared to the other groups (Figure 5). This would tend to support the subjective testimony of those who "swear by" and those who "swear at" exercise as a stimulus to productivity. (No attempt to identify subjective judgment with performance scores was made in this study.)

FIGURE 5

VARIABILITY OF PERFORMANCE IN POST TREATMENT SIMPLE MENTAL TASK EXPERIMENT # 3

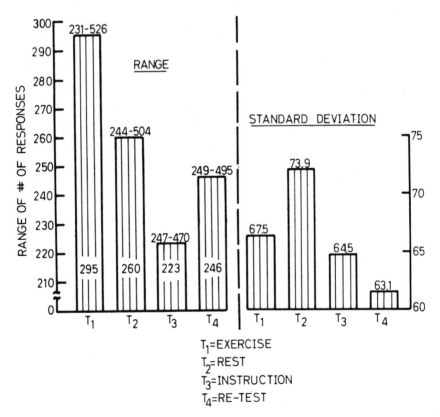

T₁=EXERCISE
T₂=REST
T₃=INSTRUCTION
T₄=RE-TEST

One other variable was studied though not tested for significance. It seemed to the investigators that if a treatment were actually effective, the subjects participating in that treatment would *not* tend to error early in the performance of the task. Figure 6 illustrates the relative percentage in each treatment group making errors in the first minute of performance.

FIGURE 6

PERCENT OF CASES MAKING ERROR IN POST TREATMENT SIMPLE MENTAL TASK

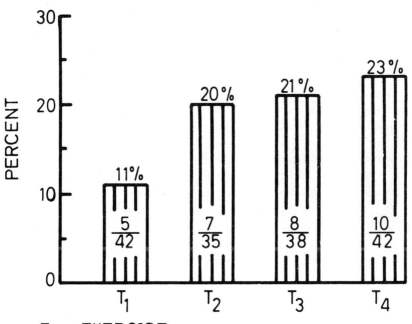

T_1 = EXERCISE

T_2 = REST

T_3 = INSTRUCTION

T_4 = RE-TEST

While the tendency for relatively few mistakes in the exercise group (compared to the other groups) in the early stage of performance is replicated in all studies of this series, unlike the previous studies, in this one the advantage "washes out" by the end of the testing period.

An Analysis of Composite Studies

The presence of persistent patterns in each study in the series raised new questions. While it was not possible to demonstrate statistically significant differences in each study, the consistency and relative position of mean performance over the studies deserved further analysis. An effort to do this was made by comparing the difference among the treatments with the degree of consistency of the mean scores over the several studies. This was done through a two-way analysis of variance with one observation per cell, namely the mean score of each treatment, replication (Table 2). There is noted a consistency among the treatment means across the three replications as the mean square for interactions was very small.

The variability of total scores among the three replications when treatment scores are combined to find a total score for that replication was then examined and was found to be significant at the .01 level when compared with the interaction variability.

There are at least two possible explanations for this occurrence. In the one case, subjects in experiment 1 were from a state teachers college while subjects from experiments 2 and 3 were from a liberal arts university. These actually might have represented essentially different segments of the adult male college population. Secondly, while the post-treatment simple mental task requirement was the same for all groups, the pre-treatment simple mental task was actually of shorter duration for schools in experiment 1 and 2.

The variability among the treatment means (when one combines the three replications) is again large compared to the variability of treatments within replications. This is significant at the .05 level. This would indicate that in spite of some slight within-population difference, consistent and significant trends in group performance emerged.

A modified Newman Keuls paired means method was used to further examine the reasons for the significant F ratio (Table 3). It appeared that of all combinations only two were significant at the .05 level. This procedure showed the T_2 group (rest) to be significantly better in 15 minute post-treatment performance than the T_3 group (instruction) and the T_4 group (immediate retest). It was not, however, significantly different from the T_1 group (exercise). Also, as would be expected from the previously mentioned pattern of similarity of performance between the rest and the exercise groups, the exercise group approached but did not quite reach the .05 level of significance when compared with the T_3 and T_4 groups.

The heightening effect which rest tends to have upon human performance in both physical and mental tasks has long been observed and often demonstrated. In this series of experiments the 15 minute performance of groups of subjects who rested is clearly differentiated from the performance of groups of subjects who took typical classroom instruction, or who took a paper and pencil test for the same period of time. The rest groups' 15 minute performance was not, however, differentiated from the exercise groups' performance. Objective evidence that exercise of this kind and of this intensity

TABLE 2

MEAN 15 MINUTE PERFORMANCE SCORES FOR 3 SEPARATE EXPERIMENTS

Experiments→	1	2	3
T_1 (Exercise)	306.0	343.9	362.2
T_2 (Rest)	309.3	348.0	364.3
T_3 (Instruction)	303.6	342.5	349.1
T_4 (Re-test)	303.2	341.5	353.3

TWO WAY ANALYSIS OF VARIANCE COMBINING 3 EXPERIMENTS INVOLVING SAME TREATMENT

Source of Variability	df	ss	ms	F
Treatments	3	153.04	51.013	5.97
Experiments	2	5,769.14	2,884.570	337.46
Interaction	6	51.29	8.548	

yields performance which approximates in some ways and even exceeds in other ways the effects of rest has not been previously demonstrated.

TABLE 3

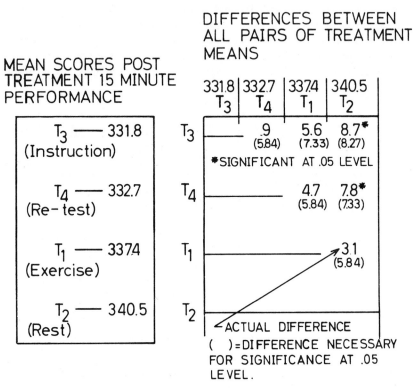

MEAN SCORES POST TREATMENT 15 MINUTE PERFORMANCE

DIFFERENCES BETWEEN ALL PAIRS OF TREATMENT MEANS

	331.8 T_3	332.7 T_4	337.4 T_1	340.5 T_2
T_3 — 331.8 (Instruction)	T_3	.9 (5.84)	5.6 (7.33)	8.7* (8.27)
				*SIGNIFICANT AT .05 LEVEL
T_4 — 332.7 (Re-test)	T_4		4.7 (5.84)	7.8* (7.33)
T_1 — 337.4 (Exercise)	T_1			3.1 (5.84)
T_2 — 340.5 (Rest)	T_2			

ACTUAL DIFFERENCE
( ) = DIFFERENCE NECESSARY FOR SIGNIFICANCE AT .05 LEVEL.

CONCLUSION

The hypothesis that there is no significant difference in simple mental task performance following the four different treatments used was not rejected in this experiment. The finding replicated results of two previous experiments in this series. The exercise group showed two tendencies not shown by the other treatment groups: 1) in general, greater variability of performance on the mental task following the treatment period and, 2) relatively fewer making errors early and fewer making any errors through the 15 minute simple mental performance task. These findings were essentially replications of the results of the previous studies in this series.

Since non-significant but obviously similar patterns of performance developed in each of the studies in this series, an analysis of combined data brought new information to the surface. In the total 15 minute simple mental task performance, the groups of subjects who rested proved to be significantly superior (.05 level) to the groups taking classroom instruction and groups taking paper and pencil tests as treatments. However, the rest groups were not significantly better in performance than the exercise groups.

REFERENCES

1. Ammons, Carol H. A task for the study of perceptual learning and performance variables. *Perceptual Motor Skills* 5: 11-14, 1955.
2. Godfrey, Barbara B. Motor therapy and school achievement. *Journal of Health, Physical Education and Recreation* 35: 65-66, 1964.
3. Gutin, Bernard. Effects of increase in physical fitness and mental ability following physical and mental stress. *Research Quarterly* 37: 211-20, 1966.
4. Halgren, Marvin R. Opus in see sharp. *Education* 81: 369-71, 1961.
5. Hart, Marcia E. and Shay, Clayton. Relationships between physical fitness and academic success. *Research Quarterly* 35: 443-45, 1964.
6. McAdam, Robert and Wang, Yuan Kai. Performance of a simple mental task following various treatments. *Research Quarterly* 38: 208-11, 1967.
7. Oliver, James N. The effect of physical conditioning exercises on the mental characteristics of educationally sub-normal boys. *British Journal of Education Psychology* 28: 155-65, 1958.
8. Rarick, G. Lawrence and McKee, Robert. A study of twenty third grade children exhibiting extreme levels of achievement on tests of motor efficiency. *Research Quarterly* 20: 142-52, 1949.
9. Wetmore, Reagh. Testing the effectiveness of individual incentives. *Journal of Health, Physical Education and Recreation* 32: 31-2, 1961.
10. Wilson, John Rowan, and others. *The Mind*. New York: Time, Inc., 1964.

Effects of Training
on Fitness

EFFECTS OF TRAINING ON MIDDLE-AGED MEN

HASKELL P. ELDER
Long Beach Y.M.C.A., Calif.

ABSTRACT

This study was conducted to determine the effects upon cardiovascular fitness, flexibility, adipose tissue, and vital capacity residual that result from participation in a program of continuous, rhythmical exercises and jogging, 30-45 minutes per day, three days per week (Mondays, Wednesdays, Fridays) for three months. The Cameron Heartometer and Cureton Progressive Pulse Ratio Test were used to determine the level of cardiovascular fitness. The Cureton Tests were used to determine the level of shoulder and trunk flexibility. Lange calipers were used to measure adipose tissue at the six points suggested by Cureton. A Collins wet spirometer was used to measure vital capacity and the residual was computed from Cureton's equation. All subjects were volunteers between the ages of 24 and 72 years; the mean age was 45 years, eight months. N varied from 38 to 100 subjects; 83 subjects completed pre- and post-training trials on most tests. The t-ratio technique was used to determine the significance of the difference between pre-training and post-training data.

The training group made the following significant changes ($p < .05$): (1) improved cardiovascular efficiency (9 out of 13 tests used); (2) flexibility (all three tests); and, (3) reduced the amount of body fat as indicated by skinfold measurements (5 out of 6 measurements used). The change in vital capacity residual was not significant.

PURPOSE

That middle-aged men in general need exercise to improve cardiovascular fitness, restore flexibility, reduce accumulation of excess fat, and maintain breathing capacity is hardly debatable. There is a divergence of opinion, however, regarding what form the exercise should take, how often it should be engaged in, and for how long it must be continued to achieve significant changes in these fitness parameters.

In establishing a fitness program for men at the Downtown Branch of the Long Beach (California) Y.M.C.A., decisions regarding type of exercise program to be used, frequency and length of workout periods, and overall duration of the program were initially made arbitrarily. In part, the decisions were dictated by costs, administrative expediency, and availability of physical facilities. However, it was recognized that to capture interest and encourage participation it was only prudent to offer a program which would be initially attractive in regard to these factors. A pilot program was offered involving 12 middle-aged men who worked out 30 to 45 minutes per day, three days per week for three months in a program of continuous, rhythmical exercise and jogging closely patterned after a program outlined by

Cureton (1). This approach showed reasonable promise of producing significant changes in physical fitness and it therefore was decided that this would
be the basic format of the program. This study was subsequently designed
to investigate the effectiveness of the program after the first full year of
operation.

METHOD

Subjects

The subjects used in this study were volunteers who paid a fee to participate. They ranged in age from 24 years, six months to 73 years, two months
with a mean of 45 years, eight months. They ranged in height from 60 to
76.5 inches with a mean of 70.2 inches. They ranged in weight from 130
to 290 pounds with a mean of 183 pounds.

The number of subjects completing pre- and post-training trials varied
from 38 to 100; an average of 83 completed most tests. Though their occupations varied over a wide range, practically all were professional men or
desk-bound white-collar workers.

All testing was done between 7:00 p.m. and 10:00 p.m. Subjects were
instructed to participate in a typical daily routine, but not to eat anything
after 5:00 p.m. and to report to the laboratory at the appointed time, dressed
in gym clothing.

An especially equipped, comfortable, air conditioned, one-room laboratory
was utilized for testing eight subjects per evening. All Cameron Heartometer
tests (2, 3, 4) were administered and scored by the writer, using only
one instrument. The Maximum Chest Minus Abdominal Girth and Cureton Flexibility Tests (5), Cureton's Adipose Tissue Test (5), the vital
capacity test (3), and Cureton's Progressive Pulse Ratio Test (2) were
administered by specially trained laboratory assistants. All tests were administered and scored as directed in the references cited.

Immediately upon reporting to the laboratory each subject was seated
and given approximately 15 minutes of quiet paper work in the form of
a questionnaire. A brief statement designed to explain laboratory procedure
and put subjects at ease was made before beginning the tests. Following
the quiet period, and in the order of his arrival, each subject was given
a Heartometer test consisting of (1) sitting, quiet, diastolic and systolic blood
pressures, and a 30 second, resting brachial pulse wave tracing; (2) a post-
exercise, 20-second, sitting, brachial pulse wave tracing, followed by sitting
diastolic and systolic blood pressures. Post-exercise recording was done immediately after the subject has stepped 30 steps per minute on a 17 inch
bench. After recovery, each subject completed skinfold, flexibility, and vital
capacity tests and then sat quietly to talk or read until he was ready to begin
the Progressive Pulse Ratio Test. This test was administered in the prescribed manner except that by using four especially designed pulse counters[1]

---

[1]Pulse Counter, Model 6702 No. 712, Model 1010 Pulse Transducer, Biocom, Inc., 95522
W. Jefferson Blvd., Culver City, California 90230.

the time required to give the test was reduced considerably. All conditions for post-training tests were made as identical as possible to those prevailing at the time of pre-training tests.

After completing the initial round of tests and presenting evidence of medical approval for participation, each subject was assigned to a class meeting on Mondays, Wednesdays and Fridays at an hour best suited to his daily schedule. All classes were limited to a maximum of 15 men; no one was enrolled after the second week. A specially trained instructor was assigned to each class. The work of the instructors was supervised and coordinated to assure reasonable similarity in content and progression of the workouts.

Instructors led rather than directed the workouts. Subjects followed their instructor but were free to regulate their level of participation by dropping in and out of the class activity as they felt necessary. However, continuous movement throughout each workout was required of all even if part of it was only walking. Periodic checks of pulse rate were made to help instructors establish a realistic tempo for each workout, regulate progression in intensity and duration of the workout, and appraise the effort and progress being made by each subject. Subjects were requested to confine their jogging and rhythmical exercising to that done in class, and to limit any additional exercise to activities which they had been doing previously on a regular basis.

The basic principles and content of the training program follow those proposed by Cureton (1) except for the length of the workouts and the emphasis on jogging. For the first four weeks workouts were limited to 30 minutes. After four weeks the workout time was gradually increased to a maximum of 45 minutes and held at this level from the ninth through the thirteenth week. As a means of achieving a higher calorie cost and getting more endurance work into a shorter period of time, more emphasis was placed on jogging than on rhythmical exercises. After a five-minute walking-calisthenic warm-up routine, the workout continued with a walk-jog routine lasting 10 to 15 minutes. This was followed by a five to ten minute period of exercises which varied from session to session to insure both general coverage and periodic concentration on each body segment. Each class period was then closed with a five minute cool-down period of walking and stretching. As the class time period increased and the ability level of the group permitted, the jogging became more continuous and the exercises more rigorous. In general, the jogging was regulated so that a large majority of each class would be capable of jogging one mile non-stop in 12 minutes or less by the end of the eighth week and two miles in 20 minutes or less by the end of the program.

RESULTS

The t-ratio technique was used to determine the significance of the difference between the pre-training and post-training means for all tests.

Data analyses for the Maximum Chest Minus Abdominal Girth (5) and

Cureton Flexibility Tests (5) are presented in Table 1. The data reveal that significant changes in these specific measures of flexibility were achieved under the conditions of this study ($p < .02$ for all tests).

TABLE I

COMPARISON OF PRE- AND POST-TRAINING FLEXIBILITY TEST MEANS

Test	No. Cases	Means Pre-training	Post-Training	Diff.	S.E. Diff.	t	p
Max. Chest minus Abdominal Girth	95	4.37 in.	5.36 in.	.994	.296	3.36	.01
Shoulder Extension	96	11.75 in.	13.19 in.	1.447	.587	2.46	.02
Trunk Extension	96	12.60 in.	14.06 in.	1.464	.545	2.68	.01
Trunk Flexion	98	13.39 in.	12.20 in.	1.190	.448	2.65	.01

Data analyses for the adipose tissue measurements suggested by Cureton (5) are presented in Table 2. The data reveal that a significant reduction in adipose tissue was achieved under the conditions of the study ($p < .05$ for all but one area).

TABLE 2

COMPARISON OF PRE- AND POST-TRAINING ADIPOSE TISSUE TEST MEANS

Test	No. Cases	Means Pre-training	Post-training	Diff.	S. E. Diff.	t	p
Cheeks	85	14.90 mm.	13.87 mm.	-1.03	.52	1.99	.05
Abdomen	84	27.43 mm.	24.82 mm.	-2.61	1.29	2.02	.05
Hips	83	23.80 mm.	20.52 mm.	-3.28	1.23	2.66	.01
Gluteals	84	29.47 mm.	27.07 mm.	-2.41	1.34	1.78	.10
Front Thigh	82	22.85 mm.	19.97 mm.	-2.88	1.08	2.66	.01
Rear Thigh	84	21.71 mm.	18.57 mm.	-3.14	1.08	2.91	.01
Total Score	83	141.63 mm.	122.23 mm.	-19.40	5.57	3.48	.01

Data analyses for the Heartometer measures of cardiovascular fitness identified by Cureton (1, 2, 3, 4) are presented in Table 3. The data reveal that a significant improvement in cardiovascular fitness was achieved under the conditions of the study ($p < .02$ for eight of 12 measures).

Data analyses for the Cureton Progressive Pulse Ratio Test (2) are presented in Tables 4 and 5. The data are further evidence indicating that a significant improvement of cardiovascular fitness was achieved under the conditions of the study ($p < .05$ for 11 of 12 measures).

TABLE 3

COMPARISON OF PRE— AND POST-TRAINING MEANS FOR HEARTOMETER TESTS OF CARDIOVASCULAR FITNESS

Test	No. Cases	Pre-training	Post-training	Diff.	S. E. Diff.	t	p
Pulse wave Area	100	.355 sq. cm.	.460 sq. cm.	.105	.016	6.56	.01
Systolic Amplitude Before Exercise	100	1.330 cm.	1.500 cm.	.170	.052	3.28	.01
Systolic Amplitude After Exercise	84	1.280 cm.	1.610 cm.	.325	.070	4.64	.01
Diastolic Surge	94	.116 cm.	.126 cm.	.010	.013	.77	NS[a]
Ejection Angle	100	13.200 deg.	10.540 deg.	2.660	.711	3.74	.01
Sitting Pulse Rate Before Exercise	91	81 bpm	71 bpm	10.00	1.500	6.66	.01
Sitting Pulse Rate After Exercise	88	123 bpm	110 bpm	13.00	2.82	4.61	.01
Systolic Blood Pressure Before Ex.	91	127 mm. Hg	119 mm. Hg	8.00	2.79	2.87	.01
Systolic Blood Pressure After Ex.	59	157 mm. Hg	160 mm. Hg	3.00	4.08	.73	NS[a]
Diastolic Blood Pressure Before Ex.	91	71 mm. Hg	69 mm. Hg	2.00	1.45	1.38	NS[a]
Diastolic Blood Pressure After Ex.	60	80 mm. Hg	75 mm. Hg	5.00	2.04	2.45	.02
Pulse Pressure Before Exercise	91	54 mm. Hg	52 mm. Hg	2.00	2.36	.84	NS[a]

a = Not significant at .05 level.

Data analyses for the Vital Capacity Residual (3) are presented in Table 6. The data reveal that the subjects did not achieve a significant change in vital capacity residual under the conditions of the study. However, comparison of the residual change of smokers as compared to that of non-smokers

TABLE 4

COMPARISON OF PRE- AND POST-TRAINING MEANS FOR THE CURETON PROGRESSIVE PULSE RATIO TEST

Test	No. Cases	Pre-Training	Post-Training	Diff	S. E. Diff.	t	p
12 Steps Per Minute	75	2.17	2.13	.039	.023	1.69	.10
18 Steps Per minute	94	2.35	2.26	.093	.023	4.04	.01
24 Steps Per Minute	92	2.56	2.43	.130	.032	4.06	.01
30 Steps Per Minute	95	2.82	2.68	.140	.038	3.68	.01
36 Steps Per Minute	37	3.08	2.94	.140	.060	2.33	.05
Average of 5 Ratios	37	2.59	2.41	.180	.039	4.61	.01
Base Pulse Rate	96	77	70	7	1.440	4.85	.01

TABLE 5

**COMPARISON OF PRE- AND POST-TRAINING MEANS FOR
THE CURETON TWO MINUTE CUMULATIVE PULSE COUNT**

Test	No. Cases	Means Pre-Training	Post-Training	Diff	S. E. Diff.	t	p
12 Steps Per Minute	75	162	150	12	3.96	3.03	.01
18 Steps Per Minute	94	179	161	18	4.28	4.20	.01
24 Steps Per Minute	92	196	175	21	4.59	4.57	.01
30 Steps Per Minute	94	220	193	27	4.67	5.76	.01
36 Steps Per Minute	37	247	216	31	6.57	4.71	.01

reveals that the smoker is apparently appreciably more handicapped than the non-smoker in improving the vital capacity residual.

TABLE 6

**COMPARISON OF PRE- AND POST-TRAINING VITAL CAPACITY
RESIDUAL MEANS**

Group	No. Cases	Means Pre-Training	Post-Training	Diff.	S. E. Diff.	t	p
Total	100	63.8 cu. in.	56.8 cu. in.	7.0	6.65	1.00	NS[a]
Non-smokers	72	69.4 cu. in.	53.3 cu. in.	16.1	9.72	1.65	NS[b]
Smokers	28	60.0 cu. in.	60.0 cu. in.	0.0	.00	.00	NS[a]

a = Not significant at .05 level.

b = For two-tailed test and 70 df, t of 2.00 significant at .05 level.

The findings of this study are similar to those of other investigations (2, 3, 4, 6, 7, 8, 9).

CONCLUSIONS

It is concluded that this training group made a significant reduction in adipose tissue and a significant improvement of flexibility and cardiovascular fitness. It appears reasonable to assume that participation in a program of continuous, rhythmical exercises and jogging, 30 to 45 minutes per day, three days per week for three months caused much of this improvement.

REFERENCES

1. Cureton, Thomas K. *Physical fitness and dynamic health.* New York: the Dial Press, Inc., 1965.
2. _____. *The physiological effects of exercise programs on adults.* Springfield, Ill.: Charles C. Thomas, 1969.
3. _____. *Physical fitness appraisal and guidance.* St. Louis: C. B. Mosby Co., 1947.
4. _____. *Physical fitness of champion athletes.* Urbana, Ill.: University of Illinois Press, 1951.
5. _____. *Physical fitness workbook.* Champaign, Ill.: Stipes Publishing Co., 1944.
6. Larson, Leonard A., and others. *Health and fitness in the modern world.* Chicago: The Athletic Institute, 1960.
7. Ontario Heart Foundation. *Proceedings of the international symposium on. physical activity and cardiovascular health.* 247 Davenport Road, Toronto 5, Ontario, Canada.
8. Raab, Wilhelm. *Prevention of ischemic heart disease.* Springfield, Ill.: Charles C. Thomas, 1966.
9. Staley, Seward C., and others. *Exercise and Fitness.* Chicago: The Athletic Institute, 1960. 1960.

EFFECTS OF DIFFERENT TYPES AND AMOUNTS OF TRAINING ON SELECTED FITNESS MEASURES*

B. DON FRANKS

University of Illinois

ABSTRACT

The purpose of the study was to determine the effects of different types (running and individual sports) and amounts (three and five days per week) of training on middle-aged men. Forty-three men, 25-50 years old, were assigned to running or sports groups three to five days per week for five months. The men were tested every seven weeks at rest, during and after mental arithmetic and a sub-maximal ergometer ride. The men were also tested prior to and at the conclusion of training on selected tests of pulmonary function, motor fitness and manifest anxiety. Although there were slight advantages for the running and five-day-per-week groups, these main effects were less pronounced than the interaction between type and amount of training. Sedentary men appeared to adapt more readily to three days of running and calisthenics than five days per week, whereas the improvements made by the three day sports group were inferior to the other groups during the first five months of training.

INTRODUCTION

There is increasing evidence that regular, vigorous physical activity causes many desirable physiological and psychological changes in people and may be important in prevention of some diseases (7, 11). There appears to be increasing support for the need for regular physical activity, yet many of these statements make no differentiation among different types and amounts of activity.

Two practical questions must be raised concerning physical training programs; namely, how much and what kind of physical activity will cause significant improvement in cardiovascular fitness. (A more difficult question, beyond the scope of this study, is how much and what kind of activity are necessary for optimum health.)

An increasing number of men and women are participating in endurance running and calisthenics programs similar to Cureton's program (7) and many studies have confirmed the important changes that can result from such training (6, 7, 11, 12, 13, 19, 20, 22, 24, 26, 29, 32, 34, 35, 49). These programs have caused greater changes in cardiovascular fitness than such activities as golf (23) and weight training (13) in men and vibrating tables and exercycle (ridden passively) in women (32). Many men and women

*Data collected as part of Ph.D. dissertation (18); Sponsor: T. K. Cureton, Jr. The author appreciates valuable assistance received from Dr. Paul Fardy, Larry Gettman, Maurice Jette and Dr. Jack Wiley in training and testing the subjects.

play various games, such as golf, bowling, handball and badminton. On the basis of four energy cost studies (small samples in each), it seems obvious that the relatively low caloric cost of golf (23) and bowling (31) (.055 and .062 Cal/kg/min respectively) make them inefficient methods for making cardiovascular changes; however, the caloric cost of handball (1) and badminton (unpublished data by author) can be classified from moderate to strenuous (.125 to .192 and .186 Cal/kg/min respectively) depending on the level of ability and competition, thus apparently allowing sufficient expenditure of energy to make a contribution to cardiovascular fitness if played vigorously enough and long enough.

Endurance running and calisthenics one or two days per week appear to be inferior to training three or four days per week (6, 26, 35), although the difference between three and five days per week was not as large (24).

PURPOSE

The purpose of this study was to determine the effects of different types and amounts of physical training on selected measures of fitness of middle-aged men; specifically, to determine the differences: (1) between individual sports competition (handball and badminton) and a combination of running and calisthenics; (2) between training three days per week and five days per week; and, (3) in interaction between type and amount of training.

METHOD

Subjects

Fifty-eight men,* 25 to 50 years old, were selected from men beginning in the University of Illinois Adult Physical Fitness Program (see Table 1 for age, height, weight, and occupation of subjects). These men were assigned — primarily on the basis of preference — to the following groups for a five-month training program:

Group A. Running and calisthenics, three days per week (N = 11).
Group B. Running and calisthenics, five days per week (N = 15).
Group C. Handball or badminton singles competition, three days per week (N = 10).
Group D. Handball or badminton singles competition, five days per week (N = 7).
Group E. Non-training control group (N = 15).

Training Programs

The running and calisthenics groups used Cureton's first twelve low and middle gear lessons (lessons four and seven were omitted because of the equipment involved) (7). Both groups (A and B) spent two weeks on each lesson. The individual sports groups (C and D) played in handball or badminton round robin tournaments three or five days per week. All

---

*Sixty-seven men were contacted originally; 61 completed the first testing period; three dropped out because of family sickness or time involved; five were allowed to change groups within the first two weeks to fit their schedule.

groups spent approximately 40 minutes per work-out in their training and had approximately 80% attendance.

Variables

Time components of the left ventricle (3, 4, 21, 36, 41, 48). The following time components of the left ventricle were determined from simul-

TABLE I

INFORMATION ON SUBJECTS

SUBJECT	AGE (years)	HEIGHT (inches)	WEIGHT (pounds)	OCCUPATION
Group A (Running and calisthenics, 3 days per week)				
PBR	41	71	205	Technician
RCA	50	74	210	Business
ADE	26	73	190	Minister
SFO	27	72	180	Academic
WHU	43	70	215	Business
EJA	35	72	165	Academic
JKR	33	70	217	Academic
DOP	42	68	175	Academic
CPU	33	72	195	Business
AWO	32	72	155	Technician
RZI	49	65	175	Academic
Mean	37	71	188	
Group B (Running and calisthenics, 5 days per week)				
JCA	46	68	145	Lawyer
CED	47	71	180	Missionary
HFA	45	73	250	Technician
PFR	40	70	195	Academic
DGO	50	67	141	Academic
MHE	26	73	178	Academic
JLA	32	65	145	Academic
KLO	26	68	170	Business
RMA	33	68	150	Technician
CMA	42	67	128	Academic
RMU	27	73	240	Academic
JMY	42	70	161	Technician
DSC	36	73	192	Academic
GVD	25	70	160	Academic
DWI	27	72	153	Academic
Mean	36	70	174	

Table 1 (Continued)

SUBJECT	AGE (years)	HEIGHT (inches)	WEIGHT (pounds)	OCCUPATION
Group C (Handball or badminton, 3 days per week)				
MBL	31	72	210	Business
DCO	36	70	175	Academic
CFI	33	69	213	Academic
RFO	33	68	180	Academic
CHU	30	71	165	Academic
SHU	25	70	172	Academic
CLA	31	76	235	Business
SMC	32	73	185	Business
WMO	35	75	210	Academic
HTH	25	72	175	Academic
Mean	31	72	173	
Group D (Handball or badminton, 5 days per week)				
CBE	26	72	200	Academic
PPU	28	68	170	Academic
WSA	27	68	184	Academic
BST	33	68	176	Academic
PSW	25	70	155	Academic
RSV	27	79	250	Business
DWA	26	70	182	Academic
Mean	27	70	173	
Group E (Control, no physical training program)				
GBL	34	70	182	Business
RDE	26	70	168	Technician
EDE	48	68	190	Business
RFI	46	74	163	Academic
GFO	48	64	134	Academic
JKA	26	76	150	Technician
RKE	29	69	160	Business
FKR	27	70	180	Academic
JLO	35	66	152	Business
ALU	31	69	172	Technician
CPO	41	69	165	Business
RST	50	70	185	Business
SSW	25	71	165	Academic
BTO	25	73	185	Technician
HLI	33	68	151	Academic
Mean	35	70	166	

taneously recorded carotid pulse wave, phonocardiogram and electrocardiogram (lead II) on the Sanborn Four-Channel Polyviso Cardiette Model 64A,
with paper speed of 5 cm. per second (see Figures 1 and 2). The mean, in
seconds, of intervals from five successive cycles was used in each condition.
Cycle time (CT), time for one complete cardiac cycle, measured from R to R'
    (ECG).
Diastole (33), time from end of ejection to onset of excitation, measured
    from the second heart sound (S_2) to Q (ECG).

FIGURE I
Left ventricular intervals

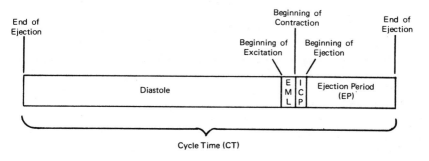

FIGURE 2
SIMULTANEOUS RECORDING OF CAROTID PULSE WAVE, PHONOCARDIOGRAM AND ELECTROCARDIOGRAM

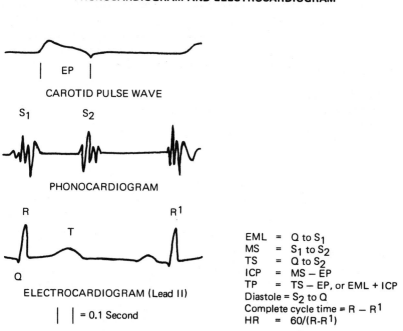

EML = Q to S_1
MS = S_1 to S_2
TS = Q to S_2
ICP = MS − EP
TP = TS − EP, or EML + ICP
Diastole = S_2 to Q
Complete cycle time = R − R^1
HR = 60/(R-R^1)

Electromechanical lag (EML) (27), time from onset of excitation to onset
  of contraction, measured from Q to first heart sound (S_1) (28).

Ejection period (EP) (46), time from onset to end of ejection, as measured
  from onset of steep ascent to nadir of dicrotic notch on carotid pulse
  wave.

Mechanical systole (MS) (47), time from onset of contraction to end of
  ejection, measured from S_1 to S_2.

Total systole (TS) (47), time from onset of excitation to end of ejection,
  measured from Q to S_2.

Isovolumetric contraction period (ICP) (40), time from onset of contraction
  to onset of ejection, measured by MS − EP.

Tension period (TP) (17), time from onset of excitation to onset of ejection, measured by EML + ICP, or TS − EP.

The men were tested at 0 (T-1), 7 (T-2), 14 (T-3) and 21 weeks of training (T-4).

Brachial pulse wave. The following measures were determined from the
Cameron Heartometer (8):

Systolic amplitude.

Area under the curve.

Obliquity angle.

Rest to work ratio.

Fatigue ratio.

Blood pressure. The systolic, diastolic and pulse pressures were also determined from the heartometer (8).

Pulmonary function. Vital capacity residual (8) and breath holding after a
one minute step test (30 steps per minute, 18″ bench) (8) were administered
at T-1 and T-4.

Motor fitness. The following battery of motor fitness measures were administered in the University of Illinois Physical Fitness Research Laboratory
prior to and at the conclusion of the training (9, 10):

Trunk extension backward.

Trunk flexion forward.

Cureton's 4-item dynamometer strength test.

Total strength per pound of body weight.

Illinois progressive balance beam test.

Illinois agility run.

Larson's composite score of chinning, vertical jump and dipping.

Manifest anxiety. The items from the Pittsburgh revision (2) of the
Taylor Manifest Anxiety Scale (44) and the Marlow-Crowne Social Desirability Scale (5) were assigned positions at random in a "Biological Inventory"
which was administered at T-1 and T-4.

Testing Procedure

The motor fitness and pulmonary function tests were administered at
T-1 and T-4 using the standard procedures of the University of Illinois Physi-

cal Fitness Research Laboratory. The cardiovascular tests were administered at T-1, T-2, T-3 and T-4 in the University of Illinois Environmental Laboratory (temperature = 75° F. and humidity = 50%) early in the morning (6:00 to 9:00 A.M.). The subjects were instructed to eat and drink nothing after dinner the night preceding their test, get the usual amount of sleep, and do only the minimum of physical activity before arriving to be tested. The testing schedule is found in Table 2.

TABLE 2

TESTING SCHEDULE FOR CARDIOVASCULAR MEASURES AT REST, DURING MENTAL ARITHMETIC AND POST EXERCISE

MINUTES	CONDITIONS	ACTIVITY	RECORDINGS
0 - 15		Rest	——O——
15 - 17	1. Rest	Lying	3-channel heartograph
18 - 19	2. Mental arithmetic	Work 1st problem*	3-channel
19 - 20	3. Mental arithmetic	Work 2nd problem**(37)	3-channel
21½ - 23	4. 1½' recovery	Lying	3-channel heartograph
25 - 27	5. 5' recovery	Lying	3-channel heartograph
28 - 33	5' warm-up	Bicycle ergometer 2000 ft. lbs./min. 40 r.p.m.	——O——
33 - 36	3' rest	Sit on bicycle	Heart rate
36 - 41	5' ride	Bicycle ergometer 4500 ft. lbs./min.	Heart rate each minute
42½ - 44	6. 1½' post exercise	Lying	3-channel heartograph
46 - 48	7. 5' post exercise	Lying	3-channel heartograph
51 - 53	8. 10' post exercise	Lying	3-channel heartograph

*T-1 and T-3: $\dfrac{(29 \times 37) - 17}{3}$ T-2 and T-4: $\dfrac{(13 \times 49) + 51}{11}$

** $\dfrac{\begin{aligned}(&7 \times 13)\\ +&(23 - 17)\\ +&(56 - 15)\\ +&(6 \times 27)\end{aligned}}{\text{Sum} \times 7}$ $-7\,[(6 \times 13) + (17 - 23) - (57 - 15) \\ -(3 \times 26)]$

Statistical Procedure

The reliability coefficients were determined, using the control group, by test-retest with the testing periods being seven weeks apart for the cardiovascular measures and five months apart for the other measures (corresponding to the time interval between testing periods).

A factor analysis, using varimax (orthogonal) rotation (30), was computed on the resting cardiovascular, ride heart rates, pulmonary, motor fitness, manifest anxiety and social desirability measures on T-1. The tests with the highest loading on each factor were used for additional analyses. A repeated measures analysis of variance was used across conditions on the cardiovascular measures, and only those conditions that were independent from the others were used in the analyses.

A two-way analysis of covariance (14) on the four training groups was used at T-2, T-3 and T-4 (with the T-1 measures being used as covariates) to determine the significantly different changes caused by different types and amounts of training (.10 level).

RESULTS

The reliability coefficients are found in Table 3. Table 4 contains the factor loadings and the list of 18 tests used to represent the factors is found in Table 5.

TABLE 3
RELIABILITY COEFFICIENTS

VARIABLE		RELIABILITY COEFFICIENT			
Cardiovascular*	Rest	Mental 1	Arithmetic 2	Post 1½'	Exercise 5'
Systolic amplitude	.61			.55	.62
Systolic blood pressure	.88			.91	.84
Diastolic blood pressure	.78			.79	.81
Mechanical systole	.83	.74	.78	.85	.64
Electromechanical lag	.84	.82	.85	.72	.82
Isovolumetric contraction period	.66	.70	.60	.69	.42
Diastole	.93	.92	.94	.84	.89
			MINUTES		
Ergometer ride* 0	1	2	3	4	5
Heart rate .67	.74	.87	.86	.83	.82

Motor Fitness, Social Desirability, and Manifest Anxiety**

Breath holding	.75	III. agility run	.82
Trunk extension	.52	Vital capacity res.	.89
Trunk flexion	.77	Weight	.97
Strength/lb.	.87	Social desirability	.92
Balance	.27	Manifest anxiety	.71
Chin-Dip-VJ	.67		

*N = 19; testing periods six weeks apart.
**N = 15; testing periods five months apart.

TABLE 4

FACTOR LOADINGS

VARIABLE	FACTOR								
	1	2	3	4	5	6	7	8	9
Systolic amp.	-.03	-.09	.09	-.94	-.04	.09	.02	.02	-.01
Obliquity ang.	-.09	.00	-.05	.80	.16	.07	.14	-.08	-.27
Rest/work	.85	-.24	.01	.06	.07	-.01	.08	-.07	.05
Fatique ratio	.34	-.08	-.25	.63	.01	.22	.12	.05	-.23
Systolic BP	-.12	.00	-.13	-.06	.11	.03	.09	.11	.84
Diastolic BP	-.17	.12	-.32	.23	.02	.03	.13	-.08	.03
Pulse pressure	.03	-.11	.15	-.26	.09	.00	-.02	.17	.85
Area	.64	-.25	-.04	-.51	-.10	.17	.09	.06	-.04
Mech. systole	.51	-.36	.00	.00	.04	.71	.17	.01	.04
Total systole	.56	-.36	-.01	.06	.05	.64	.18	.00	.04
EML	.17	-.08	.00	.09	.07	-.01	-.02	.01	.03
Eject. period	.49	-.26	.07	-.02	.04	.71	-.34	.03	.03
ICP	.04	-.17	-.13	.03	.00	.00	.91	-.02	.02
Tension per.	.16	-.22	-.12	.10	.05	-.01	.84	-.01	.05
R-R'	.90	-.26	.12	.03	-.05	.17	.03	.04	-.03
Heart rate	-.90	.26	-.12	-.02	.05	-.20	-.03	-.04	.03
Diastole	.92	-.23	.14	.03	-.07	.07	.01	.04	-.04
Ride HR, 0'	-.50	.42	-.03	.10	.15	-.46	.09	.18	.23
Ride HR, 1'	-.30	.78	.13	.05	.01	-.19	-.02	-.02	.03
Ride HR, 2'	-.24	.92	-.04	.05	-.04	-.10	-.10	-.06	-.06
Ride HR, 3'	-.21	.94	-.01	.02	.02	-.09	-.08	-.01	-.06
Ride HR, 4'	-.20	.93	.00	.00	-.04	-.07	-.09	.00	-.01
Ride HR, 5'	-.24	.93	-.02	.02	-.03	-.06	-.08	.00	.01
Breath holding	.01	-.10	.19	.01	.10	.03	.05	-.02	-.01
Trunk extension	.06	.04	.00	.03	.08	.06	.02	.01	-.08
Trunk flexion	.17	-.05	-.13	.04	.15	-.12	.05	-.15	.16
Total strength	-.01	-.10	.01	.03	.37	-.02	.04	.87	.17
St./lb.	.07	.05	.31	-.12	-.13	.02	-.08	.88	.09
Balance	-.02	-.11	.05	-.19	.01	.09	-.15	-.03	-.15
Vert. jump	-.01	-.03	.68	-.09	.39	-.04	-.13	.25	.06
Chins	.07	.10	.85	-.08	-.27	.14	-.10	.05	-.07
Dips	.17	-.09	.82	-.01	-.28	-.10	.09	.01	-.03
C-D-VJ	.05	-.02	.92	-.13	-.03	-.01	-.12	.15	-.01
Agility run	-.18	.05	-.70	.02	-.33	-.15	.04	.01	-.13
Vital cap.	.01	-.01	.26	-.09	-.14	-.15	.04	.04	-.05
Age	.03	-.18	-.54	-.13	-.32	.25	.29	-.08	-.11
Height	-.07	.00	-.04	.10	.92	.07	-.01	.10	.10
Weight	-.08	-.13	-.36	.21	.65	-.10	.16	.10	.08
Soc. des.	-.05	.21	-.06	.01	-.08	-.04	-.01	-.01	.07
Manifest anx.	.28	-.13	-.01	.00	-.03	.15	.01	.04	-.06

Table 4 (Continued)

VARIABLE	FACTOR									
	10	11	12	13	14	15	16	17	18	19
SA	-.04	-.12	.07	.04	-.08	-.10	-.09	-.05	.06	.03
OA	.12	-.05	-.02	.13	-.05	-.17	.10	-.03	.22	.07
R/W	-.14	.08	.05	-.08	.12	-.06	-.08	-.01	-.04	-.22
F.R.	-.15	.34	.02	-.15	-.08	.05	.13	-.14	-.13	-.03
SBP	.01	.40	-.07	.07	-.08	.00	.14	-.01	.10	.00
DBP	-.01	.86	-.06	.06	-.03	.00	.09	.07	.08	-.01
PP	.02	-.34	-.01	.02	-.05	-.01	.06	-.06	.04	.01
Area	-.05	-.05	.18	-.06	-.11	-.04	.11	-.11	.13	.03
MS	-.18	.05	-.13	-.04	.06	.02	-.05	.12	-.03	-.01
TS	.20	.04	-.04	-.05	.07	.08	-.07	.13	-.12	.01
EML	.90	-.02	.17	-.07	.08	.17	-.05	-.01	-.19	.01
EP	-.02	.00	-.10	-.05	.06	.03	-.10	.12	-.08	.00
ICP	-.30	.08	-.05	.02	-.01	-.02	.11	.01	.09	-.01
TP	.39	.06	.08	-.04	.05	.10	.07	.01	-.06	.00
R-R'	.13	-.09	.00	.00	.01	.05	.02	.14	.05	.05
HR	-.11	.08	.04	.02	.01	-.02	-.03	-.06	-.04	-.06
Diastole	.11	-.10	.01	.02	.00	.04	.03	.14	.07	.05
Ride HR, 0'	-.16	-.07	.07	-.01	.05	.14	.03	-.08	-.11	.28
HR, 1'	.04	-.05	.09	-.05	.18	-.03	-.08	-.01	.04	.34
HR, 2'	.06	.04	.02	.03	.06	-.06	.03	-.02	.00	.10
HR, 3'	-.03	.02	-.01	.05	-.03	-.03	.06	-.06	-.03	-.06
HR, 4'	-.05	.03	-.03	.12	-.06	-.02	.02	-.03	-.03	-.11
HR, 5'	-.10	.06	-.04	.09	-.01	.00	.05	-.02	-.02	-.09
Breath hold.	.16	.00	.11	-.06	.01	.93	-.01	.00	.10	-.01
Trunk ext.	.07	-.03	.04	.01	.97	.01	.03	-.06	-.12	.01
Trunk flex.	-.31	.08	-.03	-.06	-.18	.16	.03	-.06	.79	-.02
Tot. st.	.04	-.06	-.15	.07	.03	.00	.03	-.06	-.08	.07
St./lb.	-.02	-.01	.17	-.08	-.01	-.02	.00	.10	-.05	-.04
Balance	.05	-.08	.14	-.07	-.03	.01	-.92	-.04	-.03	-.01
VJ	.06	.00	.10	.07	.02	-.14	.12	-.09	-.13	.40
Chins	.04	-.03	.09	.00	-.05	.13	-.02	.06	.01	-.21
Dips	-.08	-.23	.12	.04	.05	.17	-.02	.09	.08	.02
C-D-VJ	.03	-.09	.15	.00	-.05	.06	.03	.00	-.08	.17
Agility run	-.02	.01	.10	.31	-.07	.07	.16	.20	.04	.20
Vit. cap.	.21	-.05	.85	-.01	.07	.12	-.15	-.03	-.02	.03
Age	.17	.18	.15	.07	-.13	-.09	.24	.00	.35	.00
Height	.04	.02	-.03	-.16	.06	.14	-.04	.03	.12	-.03
Weight	.06	.04	-.42	.20	.06	-.04	.07	-.12	-.02	.14
Soc. des.	-.07	.04	-.03	.93	.01	-.07	.06	-.15	-.03	.00
Man. anxiety	.00	.05	-.02	-.16	-.07	.00	.04	.90	-.04	-.01

The results of the analysis of variance across conditions on some of the cardiovascular variables has been reported (21). In general, the measures taken during the second arithmetic problem were not different from those taken during the first; the measures taken after the problems and ten minutes post exercise were not significantly different from resting measures; thus the eight testing conditions were reduced to rest, during the first problem, 1½ and 5 minutes post exercise.

The results of training (comparison of four training groups with non-training control group) have been reported (19, 20). In general, after five months of training, the training groups had made significantly greater improvements in resting and post-exercise cardiovascular fitness measures than the control group.

TABLE 5
ORTHOGONAL FACTORS

Factor	Test with Highest Loading	Tentative Name	Factor Loading	Per Cent Variance
Group Factors				
1	Diastole	Ventricular diastole (resting phase of cardiac cycle)	.92	13.4
2	Ride Heart Rate	Heart rate during work	.93	12.8
3	Chin-Dip-VJ	Muscular power and endurance	.92	10.4
4	Systolic Amp.	Force of ventricular contraction	-.94	6.2
5	Height	Body composition	.92	5.2
6	Mechanical	Ventricular systole (working phase of the cardiac cycle)	.70	5.0
7	Isovolumetric cont. period	Sympathetic tone of autonomic nervous system	.91	5.0
8	Strength/lb.	Static strength	.88	4.5
9	Systolic blood pressure	Maximum blood pressure	.85	4.5
Specific Factors				
10	Electromechanical lag		.90	3.7
11	Diastolic blood pressure		.86	3.3
12	Vital capacity residual		.85	3.0
13	Social desirability		.93	2.9
14	Trunk extension		.97	2.9
15	Breath holding		.93	2.9
16	Balance		-.92	2.8
17	Manifest anxiety		.90	2.7
18	Trunk flexion		.79	2.6
Total				93.8

The means and standard deviations for all groups at all testing periods are in Table 6. The adjusted F ratios from the analysis of covariance are in Table 7.

TABLE 6
MEANS IN RAW SCORES AND STANDARD SCORES

Group*	T-1, Oct. Raw Score	T-1, Oct. Standard Score	T-2, Dec. Raw Score	T-2, Dec. Standard Score	T-3, Feb. Raw Score	T-3, Feb. Standard Score	T-4, April Raw Score	T-4, April Standard Score
Rest								
Systolic amplitude (cm.)								
A	1.05	47	1.22	58	1.36	68	1.32	66
B	1.21	58	1.42	73	1.39	71	1.51	79
C	1.09	49	1.17	55	1.31	65	1.22	58
D	1.00	43	1.34	67	1.34	67	1.29	63
E	1.10	50	1.16	54	1.16	54	1.22	58
Systolic blood pressure (mm. Hg)								
A	119	43	114	53	114	53	113	55
B	115	52	112	57	113	55	111	58
C	116	50	114	53	111	58	111	58
D	116	50	117	48	113	55	112	57
E	114	53	111	58	109	62	115	52
Diastolic blood pressure (mm. Hg)								
A	78	46	72	56	72	56	73	54
B	74	52	68	64	70	60	70	60
C	74	52	69	62	71	58	70	60
D	74	52	68	64	68	64	66	68
E	75	50	74	52	74	52	74	52
Mechanical systole (sec.)								
A	.345	53	.337	48	.357	63	.362	68
B	.345	53	.339	49	.355	62	.354	61
C	.336	47	.353	60	.350	58	.347	55
D	.332	43	.334	45	.350	58	.352	59
E	.340	50	.339	49	.346	54	.343	52

*Group A, Running and calisthenics, 3 days per week.
Group B, Running and calisthenics, 5 days per week.
Group C, Handball or badminton competition, 3 days per week.
Group D, Handball or badminton competition, 5 days per week.
Group E, Control with no physical activity above normal.

Table 6 (Continued)

Group*	T-1, Oct. Raw Score	T-1, Oct. Standard Score	T-2, Dec. Raw Score	T-2, Dec. Standard Score	T-3, Feb. Raw Score	T-3, Feb. Standard Score	T-4, April Raw Score	T-4, April Standard Score
Electromechanical lag (sec.)								
A	.049	53	.048	55	.048	55	.045	60
B	.051	50	.049	53	.048	55	.046·	58
C	.052	48	.049	53	.049	53	.047	57
D	.054	44	.048	55	.051	50	.047	57
E	.050	52	.049	53	.048	55	.047	57
Isovolumetric contraction period (sec.)								
A	.062	56	.051	42	.058	51	.063	58
B	.059	53	.049	38	.053	44	.058	51
C	.056	48	.053	44	.054	46	.058	51
D	.054	46	.048	37	.055	47	.065	60
E	.056	48	.051	41	.052	43	.053	44
Diastole (sec.)								
A	.542	50	.587	56	.667	67	.665	67
B	.587	56	.633	62	.655	65	.655	65
C	.520	47	.631	62	.600	57	.578	54
D	.542	50	.581	55	.560	52	.575	54
E	.542	50	.603	58	.561	52	.513	46
1st Arithmetic Problem								
MS								
A	.329	56	.324	53	.340	62	.343	64
B	.327	55	.321	51	.338	61	.338	61
C	.306	43	.328	55	.339	62	.339	62
D	.304	42	.308	44	.329	56	.335	60
E	.318	50	.322	52	.334	59	.335	60
EML								
A	.043	56	.046	50	.045	52	.042	58
B	.047	48	.046	50	.046	50	.044	54
C	.046	50	.045	52	.048	46	.044	54
D	.048	46	.046	50	.047	48	.043	56
E	.046	50	.046	50	.044	54	.044	54

Table 6 (Continued)

Group	T-1, Oct. Raw Score	T-1, Oct. Standard Score	T-2, Dec. Raw Score	T-2, Dec. Standard Score	T-3, Feb. Raw Score	T-3, Feb. Standard Score	T-4, April Raw Score	T-4, April Standard Score
ICP								
A	.060	57	.049	45	.053	49	.060	57
B	.058	54	.048	44	.049	45	.053	49
C	.049	45	.048	44	.054	50	.061	58
D	.048	44	.047	43	.050	46	.058	54
E	.052	48	.047	43	.052	48	.052	48
Diastole								
A	.380	51	.434	59	.472	65	.491	67
B	.387	52	.425	58	.471	65	.489	67
C	.340	45	.416	57	.490	67	.493	68
D	.378	50	.368	49	.416	57	.421	57
E	.381	51	.442	60	.446	60	.449	61
Ergometer Ride Heart Rate								
HR-5'								
A	135	54	124	67	120	71	114	79
B	139	49	127	63	124	67	119	73
C	140	48	126	64	124	67	120	71
D	137	51	125	66	121	70	119	73
E	139	49	131	59	131	59	135	54
1½' Post Exercise								
SA								
A	1.10	50	1.22	58	1.25	60	1.38	68
B	1.21	57	1.30	63	1.33	65	1.42	71
C	1.01	43	1.16	53	1.18	55	1.19	56
D	1.12	51	1.27	61	1.31	64	1.36	67
E	1.08	48	1.13	51	1.14	52	1.12	51
SBP								
A	129	47	127	50	128	48	123	57
B	129	47	124	55	124	55	122	58
C	127	50	124	55	120	60	122	58
D	125	53	131	43	121	58	124	55
E	125	53	119	62	120	60	122	58

Table 6 (Continued)

Group*	T-1, Oct. Raw Score	T-1, Oct. Standard Score	T-2, Dec. Raw Score	T-2, Dec. Standard Score	T-3, Feb. Raw Score	T-3, Feb. Standard Score	T-4, April Raw Score	T-4, April Standard Score
DBP								
A	79	50	71	66	68	72	70	68
B	77	54	68	72	68	72	68	72
C	78	52	73	62	73	62	72	64
D	80	48	67	74	70	68	68	72
E	80	48	76	56	74	60	75	58
MS								
A	.295	57	.302	60	.309	64	.321	71
B	.282	50	.300	60	.307	63	.318	70
C	.281	49	.303	61	.312	66	.313	67
D	.279	48	.296	57	.306	63	.314	67
E	.277	47	.288	53	.290	54	.282	50
EML								
A	.043	57	.047	50	.047	50	.045	53
B	.047	50	.047	50	.045	53	.044	55
C	.047	50	.049	46	.046	52	.044	55
D	.050	44	.047	50	.049	46	.046	52
E	.049	46	.051	42	.048	48	.045	53
ICP								
A	.035	52	.029	43	.031	46	.039	58
B	.033	49	.029	43	.029	43	.039	58
C	.035	52	.032	47	.037	55	.042	63
D	.037	55	.035	52	.035	52	.048	72
E	.034	50	.030	45	.030	45	.032	47
Diastole								
A	.409	52	.471	62	.498	67	.535	73
B	.397	50	.460	60	.488	65	.519	70
C	.378	47	.419	54	.476	63	.466	62
D	.390	49	.449	59	.510	68	.489	65
E	.406	52	.443	58	.426	55	.387	49
5' Post Exercise								
SA								
A	0.99	42	1.12	57	1.17	61	1.22	64
B	1.15	59	1.32	72	1.31	72	1.38	77
C	1.02	49	1.03	50	1.13	58	1.07	53
D	1.01	48	1.04	51	1.30	71	1.30	71
E	0.97	45	1.01	48	1.04	51	1.09	54

Table 6 (Continued)

Group*	T-1, Oct. Raw Score	T-1, Oct. Standard Score	T-2, Dec. Raw Score	T-2, Dec. Standard Score	T-3, Feb. Raw Score	T-3, Feb. Standard Score	T-4, April Raw Score	T-4, April Standard Score
SBP								
A	124	40	116	55	118	52	117	53
B	120	48	117	53	115	58	113	62
C	119	50	116	55	115	58	114	60
D	119	50	118	52	114	60	116	55
E	116	55	112	63	111	65	116	55
DBP								
A	80	45	71	63	69	67	72	60
B	76	53	69	68	69	67	67	70
C	77	50	74	57	73	58	72	60
D	78	48	63	78	69	67	70	65
E	77	50	73	58	72	60	74	57
MS								
A	.324	57	.324	57	.335	64	.342	68
B	.314	50	.324	57	.329	60	.339	67
C	.310	47	.317	52	.328	59	.331	61
D	.312	48	.317	52	.333	63	.339	67
E	.312	48	.316	51	.325	57	.314	50
EML								
A	.049	53	.048	55	.050	50	.046	60
B	.049	53	.047	58	.048	55	.046	60
C	.051	48	.051	48	.049	53	.047	58
D	.053	45	.049	53	.051	48	.049	53
E	.051	48	.050	50	.049	53	.046	60
ICP								
A	.046	53	.040	45	.043	49	.051	58
B	.043	49	.039	44	.038	43	.047	54
C	.047	54	.040	45	.045	51	.050	57
D	.048	55	.039	44	.048	55	.054	61
E	.043	49	.039	44	.042	48	.041	46
Diastole								
A	.461	56	.503	62	.557	70	.608	78
B	.425	50	.506	63	.521	65	.576	73
C	.393	45	.441	53	.489	60	.499	62
D	.417	49	.479	58	.549	69	.562	72
E	.437	52	.461	56	.456	55	.412	48

Table 6 (Continued)

Variable	Group A RS	A SS	Group B RS	B SS	Group C RS	C SS	Group D RS	D SS	Group E RS	E SS
Breath Holding (seconds)										
T-1	14.8	47	14.2	45	17.1	55	16.3	52	16.4	53
T-4	18.0	58	18.5	60	18.1	58	16.6	58	16.7	58
Trunk Extension (inches)										
T-1	11.2	40	13.2	49	15.5	58	16.3	61	13.3	49
T-4	14.9	55	16.4	62	16.6	63	17.7	67	14.2	53
Trunk Flexion (inches)										
T-1	13.8	41	10.8	55	11.2	53	9.8	59	12.0	49
T-4	12.8	45	9.9	58	11.4	52	11.9	49	12.6	46
Strength/lb. (total strength/body weight)										
T-1	4.46	41	5.39	58	5.21	55	4.28	38	5.06	52
T-4	5.42	58	5.65	63	5.38	58	5.09	53	5.54	61
Balance (total score on progressive balance beam test)										
T-1	16	48	17	52	18	55	15	45	16	48
T-4	16	48	17	52	22	70	20	62	16	52
Chins-Dips-Vertical Jump (Larson's composite score)										
T-1	189	41	215	49	229	53	252	49	230	53
T-4	201	45	210	47	212	48	259	60	211	48
Vital Capacity Residual (difference with norms for surface area)										
T-1	-64	39	-27	51	-36	48	-25	52	-49	43
T-4	-54	42	-15	55	-32	50	-15	55	-13	56
Social Desirability (Marlowe-Crowne Scale)										
T-1	17.5	50	15.6	55	15.4	55	18.7	47	19.1	45
T-4	18.5	48	16.8	52	16.5	53	18.9	46	18.0	49
Manifest Anxiety (Pittsburgh revision of Taylor Manifest Anxiety Scale)										
T-1	6.5	45	7.6	41	3.1	60	3.7	57	4.9	52
T-4	4.5	54	7.5	41	3.8	57	4.6	53	4.4	55

FIGURE 7

SIGNIFICANT EFFECTS OF DIFFERENT TYPES AND AMOUNTS OF TRAINING*
ADJUSTED F RATIOS

Variable	T-2, 7 Weeks Type	Amount	TxA	T-3, 14 Weeks Type	Amount	TxA	T-4, 21 Weeks Type	Amount	TxA
Rest									
SA	–	5.47 (5)**	–	–	–	–	3.27 (R)**	2.78 (5)	–
SBP	2.20 (R)	–	–	–	–	–	–	–	–
DBP	–	–	–	–	–	2.34 (5S)	3.24 (S)	2.41 (5)	2.16 (5S)
MS	2.73 (S)	–	1.98 (3S)	–	–	–	–	–	2.30 (3R5S)
EML	–	–	–	–	–	–	–	–	–
ICP	–	–	–	–	–	–	–	–	7.14 (5S)
Diastole	–	–	1.79 (3S)	2.81 (R)	1.87 (3)	–	2.58 (R)	–	–
During Mental Arithmetic									
MS	–	3.41 (3)	2.21 (3S)	–	–	–	–	–	–
EML	–	–	–	–	–	–	–	–	–
ICP	–	–	–	1.87 (S)	1.77 (3)	–	4.68 (S)	1.85 (3)	–
Diastole	1.40 (R)	2.25 (3)	–	–	1.70 (3)	1.48 (5R3S)	–	2.70 (3)	2.14 (5R3S)
Work Heart Rate***	–	–	–	–	–	–	–	–	–

*Significantly different changes determined by two-way analysis of covariance, using T-1 data as covariates. $F = 1.36$, $p < .10$.

**Indicates the group(s) that made greatest improvement; R = running and calisthenics groups; S = handball and badminton groups; 3 = 3 day per week groups; 5 = 5 day per week groups.

***Taken during last minute of five minute ergometer ride, 4500 ft lbs/min; at 40 rpm.

Variable	Type	Amount	TxA	Type	Amount	TxA	Type	Amount	TxA
1½' Post Exercise									
SA	–	–	–	–	–	–	1.71 (R)	–	–
SBP	3.85 (R)	–	6.10 (5R3S)	–	–	–	2.35 (R)	–	–
DBP	–	4.37 (5)	1.65 (5S)	–	–	1.68 (5S)	–	3.64 (5)	2.96 (5S)
MS	–	–	–	–	–	–	–	–	–
EML	–	–	–	1.46 (S)	–	3.52 (3R5S)	–	–	–
ICP	3.06 (S)	–	–	4.92 (S)	–	–	5.47 (S)	1.67 (5)	–
Diastole	–	–	–	–	–	–	–	–	–
5' Post Exercise									
SA	6.68 (R)	–	–	–	2.00 (5)	–	1.73 (R)	6.10 (5)	1.47 (3R 5S)
SBP	3.16 (R)	1.42 (3)	–	–	–	–	–	–	–
DBP	–	6.98 (5)	12.30 (5S)	1.56(R)	–	4.89 (3R5S)	–	2.01 (5)	–
MS	–	–	–	–	–	–	–	–	–
EML	2.77 (S)	2.63 (3)	–	–	–	2.03 (3R5S)	–	–	–
ICP	–	–	–	4.95 (S)	–	2.09 (3R5S)	–	–	–
Diastole	–	–	–	–	–	–	–	–	–
Other									
V. Cap. Res.							–	1.78 (5)	–
Breath Hold.							5.32 (R)	–	–
Trunk Ext.							–	–	–
Trunk Flex.							9.13 (R)	–	3.25 (-5S)
Strength/lb.							–	–	–
Balance							7.98 (S)	–	–
C-D-VJ							–	–	2.24 (3R5S)
Weight							–	–	–
Social Desirability							–	–	–
Manifest Anxiety							1.41 (R)	2.93 (3)	1.73 (3R)

DISCUSSION

Looking at the changes within this sample, the running groups made more improvement than the other groups in resting and post-exercise diastole, breath holding, trunk extension and trunk flexion.

There were almost no differences among the four training groups on the improvement in the heart rate during the five minute ergometer ride; all groups making much more reduction than the control group.

The three day per week running group and five day handball group made slight improvement on C-D-VJ while the other groups decreased slightly. These two groups also made more improvement than the other groups on strength per pound, DBP and MS. It appeared that five days of running and calisthenics per week were too strenuous for middle-aged men just starting a physical training program, and these measures may reflect less ability to adapt to the work than the three day running group. Three days of handball didn't seem to be enough activity to show as much improvement in the systolic amplitude of the brachial pulse wave, DBP, MS and strength.

The five day per week handball group made greater gains in the ICP than any other group. The handball groups were also better on balance, although this must be viewed with some caution because of the low reliability of balance in this study.

The three day running group had the largest change in manifest anxiety with a mean reduction of two points on a 20 point scale. There was a slight increase in the handball groups (who started lower), virtually no change in the five day running group (who started with the highest mean value) and a slight decrease in the control group. The main difference on manifest anxiety appeared to be that the three day running and calisthenics training had more effect than the five day program in the first few months of training.

The resting blood pressure levels were stable for the control group and both SBP and DBP were reduced in all training groups. The post-exercise levels were lower for all training groups except the five day handball group's SBP was reduced less than the control group.

There has been some question regarding the effects of training on the autonomic nervous system. If heart rate is used as an indicator, then physical training increases the parasympathetic level. If the systolic amplitude of the brachial pulse wave is used as an indicator, then the sympathetic level increases. Some investigators have concluded that training increases both the parasympathetic and sympathetic levels and have emphasized the importance of the balance between the two. Raab has advocated using the isovolumetric contraction period as an indicator of the sympathetic level of the autonomic nervous system at the heart (36-39). He has reported that training increases this interval, thus adding protection against emotional over-stimulation of the autonomic nervous system (36). Cureton has found that short, hard training shortened this interval. This study confirms both these findings. Except for the control group and three day handball group (both of which had slight reductions), there were sharp reductions in the resting ICP at T-2, with increases at T-3 and T-4, so that the resting ICP was longer after five months of training. A possible explanation of this would be that it is an indication of adaptation to the training. If the work is too hard and the person is unable to adapt to the work, then it does cause an over-stimulation of the sympathetic nervous system and this stress is indicated by a shortening of the ICP. As adaptation to the training takes place after the first few weeks of training, then the increased ability to adapt to stress is indicated by a longer ICP. Physical training could be compared to the stress syndrome described by Selye. The alarm reaction to exercise is quite pronounced in the shortening of the ICP. If the training is too hard, this alarm reaction continues to be reflected by a shortened ICP. As there is adaptation to the training and increased ability to withstand stress, indicated by a longer ICP, there results increased resistance to diseases caused by over-stimulation of the autonomic nervous system and/or the inability to adapt to stress.

CONCLUSIONS

Within the scope of this study, it is concluded that after five months of training, running and calisthenics caused significantly greater improvement in resting and post-exercise systolic amplitude of the brachial pulse wave and left ventricular diastole, breath holding, trunk flexion, and manifest anxiety than handball competition.

The handball competition caused significantly greater improvements than running and calisthenics in resting diastolic blood pressure, the left ventricular isovolumetric contraction period during mental arithmetic and post exercise, and balance.

Five days of training caused significantly greater improvements in resting and post-exercise SA of BPW and DBP, post-exercise ICP, and vital capacity residual than three days of training per week. Three days per week caused significantly greater increases than five days per week in ICP and diastole during mental arithmetic and manifest anxiety.

There was a significant interaction between type and amount of training on resting and post-exercise DBP, resting MS and ICP, diastole during mental arithmetic, trunk flexion, C-D-VJ, and manifest anxiety. All these were caused by relatively more improvement by three day running and five day handball except diastole during mental arithmetic.

REFERENCES

1. Banister, E. W., and others. The caloric cost of playing handball. *Res. Quart.* 35: 236-40, 1964.
2. Bendig, A. W. The development of a short form of the manifest anxiety scale. *J. Consult. Psychol.* 20: 384, 1956.
3. Blumberger, K. Die Wirkungen des peripherischen Kreislaufs auf die zeitliche Dynamik des Herzens beim Menschen. *Vhdlgn. d. dtsch. Ges f. Kreislaufforschg.* 22: 79, 1956.
4. Blumberger, K. and Meiners, S. Studies of cardiac dynamics. In A. A. Luisada (Ed.), *Cardiology and encyclopedia of the cardiovascular system*, Part 4, Vol. II. New York: McGraw-Hill, 1959.
5. Crowne, D. P. and Marlowe, D. A new scale of social desirability independent of psychopathology. *J. Consult. Psychol.*, 24: 349-54, 1960.
6. Cundiff, D. E. *Training changes in the sympatho-adrenal system determined by cardiac cycle hemodynamics, oxygen intake and eosinopenia.* Doctoral dissertation (microcarded), University of Illinois, 1966.
7. Cureton, T. K., Jr. *Physical fitness and dynamic health.* New York: Dial Press, 1965.
8. _____. *Physical fitness appraisal and guidance.* St. Louis: C. V. Mosby Co., 1947.
9. _____. *Physical fitness of champion athletes.* Urbana: University of Illinois Press, 1951.
10. _____. *Physical fitness workbook.* Champaign: Stipes Co., 1944.

11. _____. *The physiological effects of exercise programs on adults.* Springfield, Ill.: C. C. Thomas, 1969.
12. _____. The relative value of various exercise programs to protect adult human subjects from degenerative heart disease. In W. Raab (Ed.), *Prevention of ischemic heart disease.* Springfield, Ill.: C. C. Thomas, 1966.
13. DuToit, S. F. *Running and weight training effects upon cardiac cycle.* Doctoral dissertation (microcarded), University of Illinois, 1966.
14. Edwards, A. L. *Statistical methods for the behavioral sciences.* New York: Holt, Rinehart and Winston, 1964.
15. Fardy, P. S. *The effects of soccer training and detraining upon selected cardiac and metabolic measures.* Doctoral dissertation (microcarded), University of Illinois, 1967.
16. Fascenelli, F. W. and Lamb, L. E. Biomedical monitoring during dynamic stress testing: III. maximum exercise tolerance, ergometer. *Aerospace Med.* 37: 928-35, 1966.
17. Frank, M. N. and Kinlaw, W. B. Indirect measurement of isovolumetric contraction time and tension period in normal subjects. *Am. J. Cardiol.* 10: 800-806, 1962.
18. Franks, B. D. *Effects of training on cardiac intervals and other fitness measures.* Doctoral dissertation (microcarded), University of Illinois, 1967.
19. _____. Effects of training on selected cardiovascular parameters. *Oregon AHPER J.* 2: 13-15, 1968.
20. _____, and Cureton, T. K., Jr. Effects of training on cardiac intervals. *Proceedings of the NCPEAM* 71: 86- 91, 1968.
21. _____, and Cureton, T. K., Jr. Orthogonal factors of cardiac intervals and their response to stress. *Res. Quart.* 39: 524-32, 1968.
22. _____, and Franks, E. B. Effects of physical training on the reduction of stuttering. *J. of Speech and Hearing Res.* 11: 767-76, 1968.
23. Getchell, L. H., Jr. *An analysis of the effects of a season of golf on selected cardiovascular, metabolic, and muscular fitness on middle-aged men; and the caloric cost of golf.* Doctoral dissertation (microcarded), University of Illinois, 1965.
24. Gettman, L. R. *Effects of different amounts of training on cardiovascular and motor fitness of men.* Master's thesis, University of Illinois, 1967.
25. Goldstein, I. M., and others. Influences of exercise and autonomic tone on the duration of left ventricular isometric contraction. *Cir.* 24: 942, 1961.
26. Greninger, L. O. *Effects of frequency of running on the progressive pulse ratio and other cardio-respiratory measures of men.* Master's thesis, University of Illinois, 1967.
27. Harrison, T. R., and others. The relation of age to the duration of contraction, ejection, and relaxation of the normal human heart. *Am. Heart J.* 67: 189-99, 1964.
28. Hyman, A. S. The Q-first heart sound interval in athletes at rest and after exercise. *J. Sp. Med. and Phy. Fit.* 4: 199-203, 1964.
29. Jette, M. J. *Progressive physical training on anxiety in middle-aged men.* Master's thesis, University of Illinois, 1967.
30. Kaiser, H. F. The varimax criterion for analytic rotation in factor analysis. *Psychometrika* 23: 187-200, 1958.
31. Kachadorian, W. A. *An energy cost study of bowling.* Master's thesis, University of Illinois, 1966.
32. Métivier, J. G. *The effects of five different physical exercise programs on the blood serum cholesterol of adult women.* Doctoral dissertation (microcarded), University of Illinois, 1960.
33. Nazarov, I. L. and Muiichuk, Y. I. Influence of body position on phases of cardiac cycle in healthy subjects. *Terapevicheskii Arkhiv.* 37: 106, 1965.
34. Plowman, S. A. *The effects of progressive physical training on cardiovascular intervals under conditions of heat and cold stress.* Master's thesis, University of Illinois, 1966.
35. Pollock, M. L. *Effects of frequency of training on working capacity, body composition, and circulo-respiratory measures.* Doctoral dissertation (microcarded), University of Illinois, 1967.

36. Raab, W. Training, physical inactivity and the cardiac dynamic cycle. *J. Sp. Med. and Phy. Fit.* 6: 38-47, 1966.
37. _____, and Krzywanek, H. J. Cardiovascular sympathetic tone and stress response related to personality patterns and exercise habits. *Am. J. Cardiol.* 16: 42-53, 1965.
38. _____, and others. Adrenergic and cholinergic influences on the dynamic cycle of the normal human heart. *Cardiologia* 33: 351-64, 1958.
39. _____, and others. Cardiac adrenergic preponderance due to lack of physical exercise and its pathogenic implications. *Am. J. Cardiol.* 5: 300-29, 1960.
40. Rushmer, R. F. Anatomy and physiology of ventricular function. *Physiological Review* 36: 400-25, 1956.
41. Shkhvatsabaya, Y. K. Investigation of the length of phases of the cardiac cycle during muscular exercise. *Kardiologiya* 4: 62, 1964 (translated from Russian by Sandor Molnar, University of Illinois, 1967).
42. Sloniger, E. L. *The relationship of stress indicators to pre-ejection cardiac intervals.* Doctoral dissertation (microcarded), University of Illinois, 1966.
43. Stern, B. E. *The effects of frequency of exposure to training to endurance performance and selected cardiovascular fitness tests.* Master's thesis, University of Illinois, 1963.
44. Taylor, J. A. A personality scale of manifest anxiety. *J. of Abnormal and Soc. Psychol.* 48: 285-90, 1953.
45. Weissler, A. M., and others. Observations on the delayed heart sounds in mitral stenosis and hypertension. *Cir.* 13: 165-68, 1958.
46. Weissler, A. M., and others. Relationships between left ventricular ejection time, stroke volume, and heart rate in normal individuals and patients with cardiovascular disease. *Am. Heart J.* 63: 367-76, 1961.
47. Weissler, A. M., *et al.* The effects of Deslanoside on the duration of ventricular systole in man. *Am. J. Cardiol.* 15: 153-61, 1965.
48. Wiggers, C. J. Studies on the consecutive phases of the cardiac cycle, 1. the duration of the consecutive phases of the cardiac cycle and the criteria for their precise determination. *Am. J. Physiol.* 56: 439-59, 1922.
49. Wiley, J. F. *Effects of training with and without wheat germ oil on cardiac intervals and other fitness measures of middle-aged men.* Doctoral dissertation (microcarded), University of Illinois, 1968.
50. _____; Molnar, S.; and Franks, B. D. Time components of the left ventricle during work. *New Zealand J. of Physical Education* to be published November, 1969.

EFFECTS OF FREQUENCY OF TRAINING ON SERUM LIPIDS, CARDIOVASCULAR FUNCTION AND BODY COMPOSITION[1]

MICHAEL L. POLLOCK

JAMES TIFFANY
Wake Forest University

LARRY GETTMEN
Kent State University

RICHARD JANEWAY

HUGH B. LOFLAND
*Bowman Gray
School of Medicine*

ABSTRACT

The purpose of this investigation was to determine the effects of frequency of training on serum cholesterol and triglycerides, cardiovascular function, and body composition. Thirteen volunteer men, between 30-47 years of age were randomly assigned to two experimental groups. Group I exercised two days/week, and Group II, four days/week for 16 weeks. Training periods were 30 minutes in duration and consisted of continuous walking, jogging, or running. A control group of seven sedentary men was also tested.

The seven sedentary controls remained constant in all variables during the 16 week control period. During the same time period, both experimental groups improved significantly in all rest and recovery heart rate response values.

Systolic blood pressure reductions occurred mainly in the latter stages of recovery. Experimental groups significantly decreased their two mile run times. Body weight remained constant for both experimental groups. Reductions in percent fat and total skinfold fat were found in Group II, but no significant differences were found for Group I. A significant reduction in gluteal girth was found in Group II.

Inter-group analyses showed that improvements in cardiovascular functions and body composition were directly proportional to frequency of training. No significant differences in serum lipid concentrations were found between groups.

INTRODUCTION

This is the second in a series of investigations dealing with the effects of frequency of training on certain physiological parameters of adult men.

[1] Supported by the research and Publication Fund, Wake Forest University and by United States Public Health Service Grant, NB 06655.
The authors wish to acknowledge Drs. Henry Miller and James Yopp, Department of Medicine, Bowman Gray School of Medicine, for initial cardiovascular appraisal of subjects; Drs. Howard Jemison and Mary Taylor, and Mrs. Ida Johnson, University Health Service, Wake Forest University, for assistance in drawing blood samples; and, Mrs. Ruth Gagne, Dietetics Department, North Carolina Baptist Hospital, for help in analyzing diet records.

161

The initial study (24), conducted at the University of Illinois in 1966-67, concluded that training effects are derived in proportion to frequency of participation. More specifically, the four day/week group improved significantly more in almost all cardiovascular and body composition variables than did the two day/week group. Although the two day/week regiment elicited a significant cardiopulmonary response to training, it had little or no effect on body composition. The body composition results for the four day program were inconclusive because Group I (two days/week) was less fat initially; thus probably allowed less room for improvement. Also, although the men were asked to keep their dietary habits constant, objective records were not kept.

Serum hyperlipemia, particularly cholesterol and triglyceride concentrations, have been isolated as risk factors in coronary heart disease (1, 3). Evidence indicates conflicting results regarding the reduction of serum cholesterol as a result of physical training (9, 13, 15, 20, 25, 26). Most of the controversy appears to revolve around adequate dietary control and varied intensities of training regimens. Diet, total calories, and the ratio of fat intake to total calories has a marked effect on serum lipid concentrations (2, 4); thus, strict dietary records are necessary for a clearer interpretation of training effects. Recent investigations have found no significant serum cholesterol reductions with physical training when diet and body weight remained constant (15, 16).

Holloszy (15) and Carlson (5) found serum triglyceride reductions with physical training when diet remained constant. The former investigator trained men from 30-40 minutes per day, 3-5 days/week, but did not differentiate training effects with frequency of participation. Therefore, because of the lack of dietary records and the possible bias of Group I in their initial skinfold fat measures; and the importance of further quantification of training and its effect on serum lipids and cardiovascular function; a re-evaluation was deemed necessary.

PURPOSE

The purpose of this investigation was to determine the effects of frequency of training on serum concentrations of cholesterol and triglyceride, cardiovascular function, and body composition.

METHODS AND PROCEDURES

Thirteen volunteer men between 30 and 47 years of age (mean age 36.7) were assigned at random to one of two experimental groups. Group I exercised two days/week and Group II four days/week for 16 weeks, with both groups being tested at the beginning (T_1), middle (T_2) and end (T_3) of the program. Heart rate and blood pressure response to a standard treadmill run (STD-TMR), selected body composition and anthropometric measures, two mile running time, and serum concentrations of cholesterol and triglycerides were determined.

A control group (Group III) of seven adult men of the same age range was tested in body composition, and serum lipids at the beginning (T_1) and end (T_3) of a 16-week control period.

Prior to initial treadmill testing, each subject was given an exercise EKG evaluation (8) and two practice TMR orientation sessions. On treadmill test day, each subject reported to the laboratory prior to 10:00 a.m. in the post-absorptive state. Resting heart rate and blood pressure were determined after the subject sat quietly for 15 minutes. Body composition and anthropometric measures were determined and then the STD-TMR was performed.

The STD-TMR consisted of a five minute run at six mph, 5.0% grade followed by a 10 minute recovery period. Heart rates were determined by the palpation technique, with blood pressure being assessed with a standard mercury syphygomanometer. Terminal heart rates were assessed bts/10 sec immediately upon cessation of exercise and were completed prior to 0:15 of recovery. All other recovery heart rates were observed the last 30 seconds of each minute, i.e., 0:30-1:00, 1:30-2:00 . . . 9:30-10:00. Heart rate values from 5-10 minutes were averaged and reported as recovery six.

Terminal blood pressure was recorded from 0:30-1:00 minute of recovery with subsequent determination at three and ten minutes of recovery.

The two mile run was administered on a quarter mile track during the 5th, 11th and 15th week of training.

Body composition analysis included gross body weight and six skinfold fat measures obtained from the right side of the body by a Lange skinfold fat caliper (chest, axilla, triceps, abdominal, supra-iliac, and front thigh). Landmarks and suggested techniques outlined by the Committee on Nutritional Anthropometry were followed (17). Body density was predicted by Pascale's formula (22) and percent fat from body density by Grande's equation reported by Brozek and Henschel (7). The following girth measures were determined with a Lufkin steel cm tape: chest expansion, abdominal, gluteal, and thigh. Common anatomical landmarks and techniques outlined by Cureton (12) were used.

The mean of three serum lipid determinations taken on three separate days at T_1 and T_3 and a single determination at T_2 were used in the results of this investigation. Subjects reported to the laboratory early in the morning after a 12 hour fast, and approximately 15 ml of blood was drawn from the antecubital vein. Because of the influence of physical activity on the lipids (15), no training took place during the weeks of initial and final testing. The mid-test was preceded by a 24 hour restraint from training.

Serum concentrations of cholesterol were analyzed by the automated procedure of Block, *et al.* (6), and of triglycerides by the method of Lofland (18) as modified by Timms (27).

Three-day diet recalls, including two weekdays and one weekend day, were recorded and calculated for estimations of total kilocalories (Kcal) and grams of carbohydrate, protein, and saturated and unsaturated fat (11). Forms and techniques suggested by the Bureau of Nutrition, Department of Health, The City of New York and the Dietetics Department, North Carolina Baptist Hospital, Winston-Salem, North Carolina, were used. Prior to the investigation, subjects were given orientation and directions for estimation of diet by the head dietician, North Carolina Baptist Hospital. Also, subjects were asked to keep their diets as constant as possible during the 16 week training period.

The training regimen consisted of approximately 30 minutes of interval training with a gradual increase in intensity with adaptation. The first four weeks of training was conducted at a low Kcal of work level to allow for initial adjustments to training. After this time, the men were divided into sub-groups according to specific abilities. Energy expenditure of training sessions was estimated by means of time-motion analysis (23), with daily records of pace and amount of time spent running and walking being recorded for each subject. These values were averaged for each group and then converted to Kcal of energy expenditure by tables outlined by Morehouse and Miller (19).

Statistical procedures included the use of the t test for differences between paired observations for within group analysis, and the analysis of covariance for between group treatments. Test-retest reliability coefficients were determined by the Pearson Product Moment Technique. The .05 level of significance was used for this investigation.

RESULTS

Energy Expenditure of the Training Regimens

The energy expenditure of training programs for weeks 1, 4, 8, 11 and 15 are shown in Table 1. These results show similar patterns of training

Table 1

TIME-MOTION ANALYSIS OF TRAINING

Week	Average Total Kcal		Total Minutes		Average Kcal per minutes	
	I	II	I	II	I	II
1	203.2	213.5	24.8	29.7	8.2	7.9
4	241.4	271.8	28.1	30.8	8.6	8.8
8	319.5	336.6	30.5	32.6	10.5	10.4
11	353.1	338.5	33.4	33.0	10.6	10.3
15	332.4	351.8	30.4	32.4	10.9	10.9

for both experimental groups. Thus, it may be concluded that the results of this study reflect differences in frequency of exercise and not progression, intensity or duration.

Reliability

Test-retest reliability coefficients for heart rate and blood pressure ranged from .80 at rest to .93 during recovery from the STD-TMR. Body composi-

TABLE 2

RESTING HEART RATE AND BLOOD PRESSURE
CHANGES WITH FREQUENCY OF TRAINING

Group	Variable	T_1		T_2		T_3	
		X	SD	X	SD	X	SD
I (n=7)	Heart rate (bts/min)	67.1	6.41	60.8**	6.66	59.4**	8.4
	B.P. Systolic	119.6	6.90	122.6	4.11	114.0**	4.50
	Diastolic (mm Hg)	75.6	5.99	76.7	5.05	72.6	3.40
II (n=6)	Heart rate (bts/min	67.5	10.8	59.3**	6.6	56.2**	6.8
	B.P. Systolic	117.5	6.18	115.7	8.33	114.2	6.82
	Diastolic (mm Hg	77.7	6.71	77.0	6.41	76.0	4.73

** P less than .01 .

TABLE 3

POST EXERCISE BLOOD PRESSURE CHANGES WITH FREQUENCY OF TRAINING

Group	Unit		T_1		T_2		T_3	
			X	SD	X	SD	X	SD
I (n=7)	Terminal	SBP	186.8	17.1	197.8	35.5	194.4	23.2
		DBP	75.0	12.9	73.8	12.4	72.6	11.8
	3 min	SBP	176.3	19.8	164.7*	30.2	160.3*	32.3
		DBP	74.3	10.5	74.6	12.0	72.7	8.78
	10 min	SBP	128.1	13.6	120.4**	11.2	116.6**	9.34
		DBP	75.7	8.19	74.4	4.39	74.4	7.99
II (n=6)	Terminal	SBP	179.5	22.6	186.7	26.8	193.3	31.4
		DBP	75.5	9.54	72.7	10.3	72.0	6.57
	3 min	SBP	166.2	16.7	154.3	24.5	152.5	17.7
		DBP	77.3	8.16	73.5	9.46	75.0	5.76
	10 min	SBP	124.5	11.9	114.5	10.5	114.0*	6.03
		DBP	78.0	5.62	77.3	11.0	76.3	6.12

* P less than .05.
** P less than .01.

tion and anthropometric measures had coefficients above .90, while serum concentrations of cholesterol was .85 and triglyceride .89. These values are consistent with those observed by other investigators. The reproducibility of the cholesterol determination for replicate analyses was six mg/100 ml (one standard deviation); for triglycerides it was 9.5 mg/100 ml (one standard deviation).

STD-TMR & Related Variables

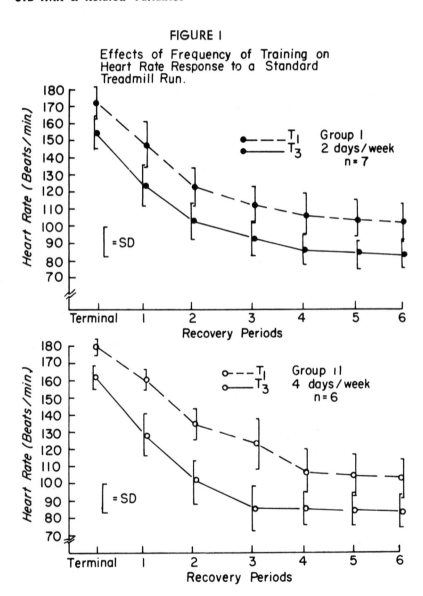

FIGURE I

Effects of Frequency of Training on Heart Rate Response to a Standard Treadmill Run.

Heart rate and blood pressure results for rest are outlined in Table 2 and for post exercise in Table 3 and Figure 1. Heart rate showed a consistently significant decrease at rest and during recovery for both experimental groups from T_1-T_2 and T_1-T_3, and T_2-T_3. Exceptions were

TABLE 4

TWO-MILE RUN CHANGES WITH FREQUENCY OF TRAINING

Group	Unit	T_1 X	SD	T_2 X	SD	T_3 X	SD
I (n=6)	min:	18:42	2:03	17:31**	2:21	16:56**+	1:44
	sec	1,120.7	128.7	1,051.3**	141.3	1,016.5**+	104.8
II (n=6)	min:	18:39	1:14	16:56**	1:02	16:11**+	0:48
	sec	1,117.8	73.9	1,015.8**	61.5	971.0**+	47.8

** P less than .01
+ significant between T_2 - T_3

TABLE 5

BODY COMPOSITION CHANGES WITH FREQUENCY OF TRAINING

Group	Variable	T_1 X	SD	T_2 X	SD	T_3 X	SD
I (n=5)	Weight (Kg)	80.6	12.2	80.2	11.4	79.8	11.3
	Skinfolds (mm)	152.0	31.5	149.2	30.5	146.4	31.0
	% Fat (skinfolds)	22.8	2.8	22.4	3.3	23.2	3.3
	Fat-Free Wgt. (Kg)	62.0	7.4	62.0	6.4	61.5	6.4
II (n=6)	Weight (Kg)	79.4	7.3	79.3	7.3	78.5*	7.2
	Skin folds (mm)	125.7	26.9	117.3	35.8	104.7**+	30.0
	% Fat	20.7	4.7	18.7**	3.5	17.4**+	3.5
	Fat-Free Wgt. (Kg)	62.8	7.39	64.6*	7.55	64.7*	7.57
III (n=6)	Weight (Kg)	81.1	12.9			80.1	11.9
	Skinfolds (mm)	103.7	36.68			108.5	40.6
	% Fat	18.1	4.4			17.5	4.1
	Fat-Free Wgt. (Kg)	66.0	7.75			65.9	8.34

* P less than .05
** P less than .01
+ significant from T_2 - T_3

noted from T_2 - T_3 for resting and terminal values for Group I. Between group analysis showed that Group II improved significantly more than Group 1 from T_1 - T_3 for recovery periods 2, 3 and 5.

Systolic blood pressure reduced significantly from T_1 - T_3 for Group I at rest and during the 3rd and 10th minute of recovery (see Tables 2 and 3). Group II's reduced from T_1 - T_3 during the 10th minute of recovery. No significant diastolic blood pressure changes or between group differences were noted (see Tables 2 and 3).

Two Mile Run

Groups I and II showed significantly consistent improvements in two-mile run times with weeks of training. Table 4 shows Group I improved 104.1 sec and Group II 146.8 sec. Between group differences were found from T_1 - T_3.

TABLE 6

ANTHROPOMETRIC CHANGES WITH FREQUENCY OF TRAINING

Group	Variable	T_1 X	SD	T_2 X	SD	T_3 X	SD
I (n=5)	Chest Expansion (inches)	2.22	.76	2.56	.60	2.71*	.79
	Abdominal	33.3	3.84	33.0	3.28	33.1	2.96
	Gluteal	38.4	1.60	38.2	1.48	38.2	1.52
	Thigh	22.0	.76	22.4	.79	22.3	.98
	Calf	14.4	.55	14.5	.36	14.4	.43
II (n=6)	Chest Expansion (inches)	2.66	.77	2.85	.97	3.12	.81
	Abdominal	33.6	2.49	32.5*	1.90	32.5	1.73
	Gluteal	35.2	7.25	34.8*	7.30	34.4**+	7.39
	Thigh	20.6	3.70	21.0*	3.85	20.8	4.00
	Calf	15.2	2.45	15.1	1.99	15.0	1.59

* P less than .05
** P less than .01
\+ significant from T_2 - T_3 at .05

Body Composition and Anthropometric Measures

Body composition and anthropometric changes were not found for Groups I and III, except for chest expansion from T_1-T_3 for Group I (see Tables 5 and 6). Group II showed consistent reductions in total skinfold fat, percent fat, total body weight, and gluteal girth; and increases in total fat-free weight (FFW). Total body weight showed no significant differences between groups, but Group II improved more in skinfold fat, percent fat, gluteal girth, and FFW from T_1-T_3. Differences from T_1-T_2 were found in % fat and FFW.

Diet and Serum Lipids

Table 7 shows serum cholesterol and triglyceride values for Group III remained constant throughout their control period. Groups I and II's serum triglyceride concentration decreased significantly from T_1-T_3, with cholesterol reflecting a significant reduction for both experimental groups from T_1-T_2, but not from T_1-T_3. A comparison of experimental groups showed no between group differences. Table 7A shows individual serum lipid data for all groups.

TABLE 7

CHOLESTEROL AND TRIGLYCERIDE CHANGES WITH FREQUENCY OF TRAINING

Group	Variable	T_1 X	SD	T_2 X	SD	T_3 X	SD
I (n=5)	Cholesterol (mg/100 ml)	192.2	13.2	172.2*	17.7	170.4	11.2
	Triglyceride (mg/100 ml)	80.0	30.1	70.2	18.9	67.6**	11.3
II (n=6)	Cholesterol (mg/100 ml)	208.2	22.7	197.8*	19.9	198.5	31.1
	Triglyceride (mg/100 ml)	92.8	24.6	96.0	35.8	79.7**	13.1
III (n=7)	Cholesterol (mg/100 ml)	172.7	35.2			181.1	33.6
	Triglyceride (mg/100 ml)	116.3	43.5			117.2	51.9

* P less than .05 from T_1 - T_2 only.
** P less than .01

TABLE 7A
Individual Body Weight, Serum Cholesterol and Triglyceride Values

Subject	Age (Yr.)	Weight (Kg)		Cholesterol (mg/100ml)		Triglyceride (mg/100ml)	
		T_1	T_3	T_1	T_3	T_1	T_3
D.B.	35	76.6	76.3	207	165	75	68
J.M	37	84.8	83.8	185	190	55	53
T.M.	38	69.1	68.6	174	169	61	73
J.R.	31	72.8	72.8	202	163	75	70
S.T.	36	99.8	97.4	193	165	134	74
		Group II					
H.B.	37	72.7	72.1	202	216	95	82
W.B.	33	91.0	89.5	229	205	123	95
J.D.	47	75.9	75.9	174	158	119	92
L.E.	34	86.1	85.1	204	170	84	69
B.G.	37	74.5	71.8	202	202	60	87
A.L.	36	76.3	76.7	238	201	91	66
		Group III					
D.B.	41	64.7	65.7	200	201	210	213
C.B.	33	98.2	94.8	161	177	77	96
S.F.	42	91.4	90.4	229	215	105	127
O.C.	33	69.5	68.0	164	156	123	91
K.H.	33	78.4	78.0	196	186	141	138
G.P.	35	85.5	85.2	145	145	61	50
M.S.	31	77.3	76.7	124	147	56	59

TABLE 8
Three-Day Diet Records

Group	Variable	T_1		T_2		T_3	
		X	SD	X	SD	X	SD
I (n=5)	Total Calories	2,435	339.7	2,539	231.6	2,513	318.8
	Carbohydrate (gm)	225.4	36.0	254.8	56.0	255.8	92.6
	Protein (gm)	98.4	5.85	104.2	26.1	88.0	43.0
	Fat (Sat) (gm)	48.2	27.9	63.8	26.6	48.2	17.4
	Fat (Un sat)	64.4	9.31	68.0	14.1	48.2*	21.6
II (n=6)	Total Calories	2,372	438.8	2,300	385.5	2,404	288.0
	Carbohydrate (gm)	251.0	23.4	271.8	54.5	238.3*	48.5
	Protein (gm)	92.7	21.1	87.0	14.5	107.8	25.0
	Fat (Sat) (gm)	48.3	13.5	50.8	10.6	60.2*	6.36
	Fat (Un sat)	59.3	17.1	49.5	12.9	49.8	17.8

* P less than .05 between T_2 and T_3 only.

During the 16 weeks of training, total calories and grams of protein remained constant for all groups. Group I had a reduction in grams of unsaturated fat from T_2 - T_3 and Group II a decrease in carbohydrate and an increase in saturated fat from T_2 - T_3 (see Table 8). There were no between group differences in diet found from the dietary survey analyzed in this investigation.

FIGURE 2

Effects of Frequency of Training on
Resting Heart Rate

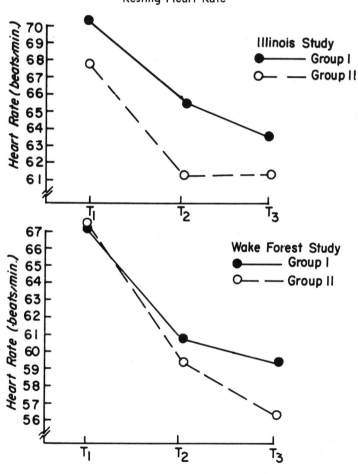

DISCUSSION

Working capacity and cardiovascular function results agree quite well with the pattern of improvement observed in the original investigation (24).

Figures 2, 3, and 4 show the effects of frequency of training on resting heart rate, heart rate response to a STD-TMR, and two mile run time for both the Illinois and Wake Forest studies.

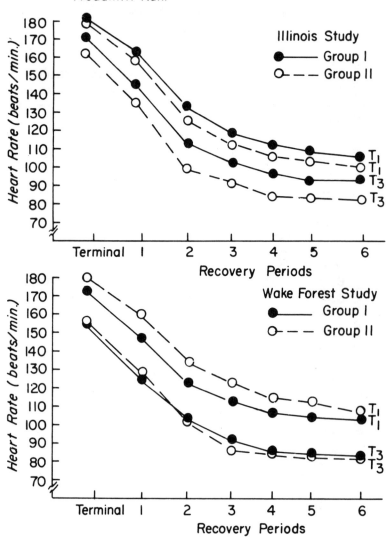

FIGURE 3

Effects of Frequency of Training on Heart Rate Response to a Standard Treadmill Run.

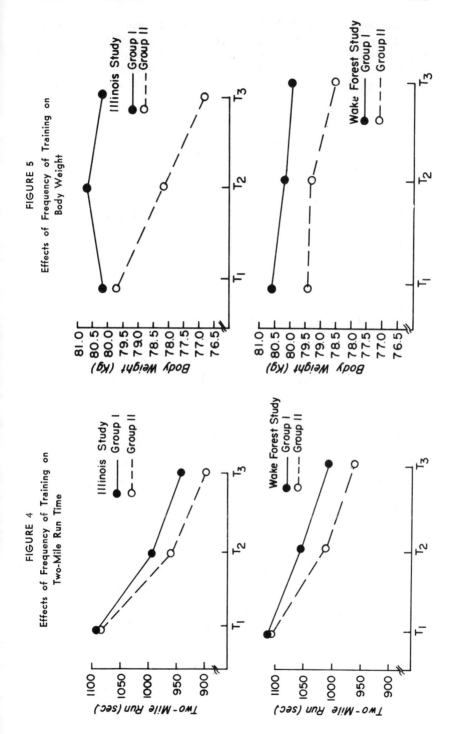

FIGURE 5

Effects of Frequency of Training on
Body Weight

FIGURE 4

Effects of Frequency of Training on
Two-Mile Run Time

Body composition results for both investigations are represented in Figures 5 - 8. These data also follow similar patterns with weeks of training. However, in the latter study the magnitude of total body weight loss for Group II was less. This plus the significant fat loss would appear to account for the increased FFW for Group II in the Wake Forest Study. In the latter

FIGURE 6

Effects of Training on Skinfold Fat

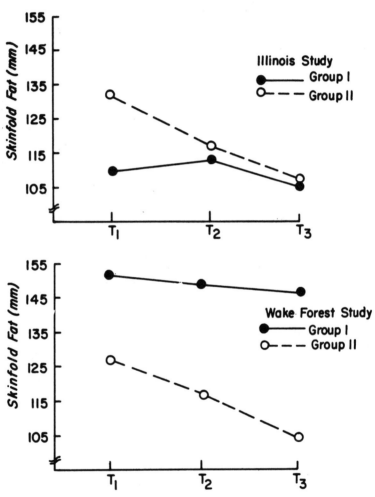

investigation, Group II's lower initial fat and body weight values could account for some of these inter-study differences. One of the criticisms of the Illinois study was that initially Group II was fatter than Group I; thus the significant fat loss by the former was possibly biased. In the latter investigation, Group I was fatter initially, and the same pattern of improvement evolved, i.e., Group II significantly reduced in fat while Group I remained

FIGURE 7

Effects of Frequency of Training on Percent Fat

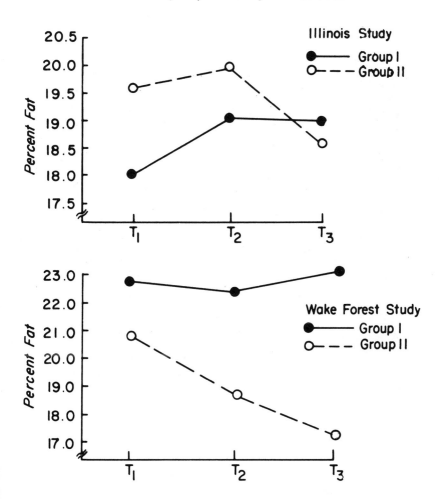

constant. With the added dietary control in the latter investigation, group differences in body composition in respect to frequency of training were substantiated.

Serum cholesterol concentrations were lower for both experimental groups, but the difference was not significant. These conclusions agree with most other investigators whose subject's total body weight and diet remained nearly constant (15, 26). An initial drop $(T_1 - T_2)$ in cholesterol with training was noted for both experimental groups and has been reported elsewhere. This

Figure 8

Effects of Frequency of Training on Fat _ Free Weight

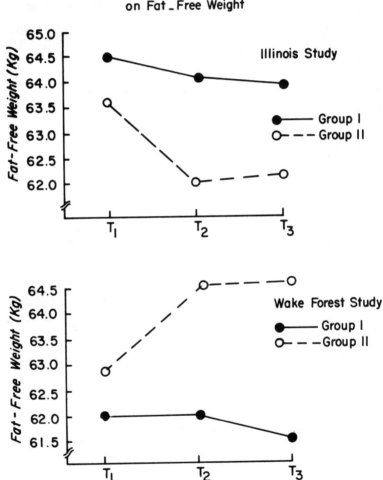

could be attributed to seasonal variation (20), individual daily variations, or early transient effects (10, 14, 15) of the training regimen. The mechanism for this transient reduction in serum cholesterol is often associated with weight loss and usually stops when weight loss terminates. This does not appear to be the case in this investigation, because fluctuations in body weight were small and had no consistent relationship with cholesterol reductions or gains (see Table 7A). Also, the control group's serum lipid values did not decrease. Although this T_1 - T_2 phenomenon cannot be entirely explained, it must be remembered that the long range effect (T_1 - T_3) was non-significant. Also, it is the opinion of the authors that serum cholesterol concentrations changes of this magnitude (11-22mg/100ml) are small relative to the precision of analysis and daily individual variations. Whether or not serum lipid concentrations that are considered well within normal range, initially, can be altered significantly with a more intense regimen, i.e., high Kcal expenditure, or one that is conducted for many more months or years, is not known.

A significant reduction in serum triglycerides was found with training which is in agreement with previous investigations (5, 14, 15).

An important finding evolving from the initial investigation was that between group differences were noted mainly at T_3, i.e., after 20 weeks of training. If the study had been concluded at T_2, 10 weeks, differences between groups would not have been found. The present investigation duplicated these findings, and thus suggests that care must be taken in not developing premature inferences from studies of lesser duration.

SUMMARY AND CONCLUSION

The effects of frequency of training, consisting of 30 minutes of jogging two or four days/week, on serum lipids, cardiovascular function and body composition were studied in middle-aged men. The results of the 16 week training regimen reflected the following conclusions.

1. Adult men participating in endurance training of two or four days/week improve significantly in cardiovascular fitness and serum triglyceride concentrations.
2. Endurance training two days/week is not sufficient to elicit a change in body composition, while a four day/week program significantly improves this variable.
3. The effects of training two or four days/week showed no between group differences in serum lipid concentrations.
4. Most between group differences occurred only after 16 weeks of training; thus suggesting the length of a training regimen as important in affecting optimal changes.

REFERENCES

1. Adlersberg, D.; Schaefner, L.; Steinberg, A.; and Wang, C. Age, sex, serum lipids, and coronary atherosclerosis. *JAMA.* 162: 619-21, 1956.
2. Ahrens, D.; Blankenhorn; and Tsaltas. Effect on human serum lipids of substituting plant for animal fat in the diet. *Proc. Society Exper. Bio. and Med.* 86: 872-78, 1954.

3. Albrink, M.; Meigs, J.; and Man, E. Serum lipids, hypertension, and coronary artery disease. *Amer. J. Med.* 31: 4-23, 1961.
4. Antonis, A. and Bersohn, I. The influence of diet on serum triglycerides. *Lancet.* 2: 3-9, 1961.
5. Blix, G. (ed.) *Nutrition and physical activity.* Stockholm: Almquist and Wiksells, 1967.
6. Block, W.; Jarrett, J., Jr.; and Levine, J. An improved automated determination of serum total cholesterol with a single color reagent. *Clin. Chem.* 12: 681-89, 1966.
7. Brozek, J. and Henschel, A. *Techniques for measuring body composition.* Washington, D.C.: National Academy of Science, National Research Council, 1961.
8. Bruce, R., and others. Exercise testing in adult normal subjects and cardiac patients. *Pediatrics.* 32: 742, 1963.
9. Campbell, D. Influence of several physical activities on serum cholesterol concentrations in young men. *J. Lip. Res.* 6: 478-80, 1965.
10. Cardwell, A. and others. Weight reduction and serum cholesterol levels. *Am. J. Clin. Nutrition.* 12: 401, 1963.
11. Church, C. and Church H. *Food values of portions commonly used.* Philadelphia: J. B. Lippincott Co., 1966.
12. Cureton, T. *Physical fitness workbook.* Champaign: Stipes Publishing Co., 1944.
13. Golding, L. Effects of physical training upon total serum cholesterol levels. *Res. Quart.* 32: 499-505, 1961.
14. Hoffman, A.; Nelson, W.; and Goss, Frank. Effects of an exercise program on plasma lipids of senior air force officers. *Amer. J. Cardio.* 20: 516-524, 1967.
15. Holloszy, J.; Skinner, J.; Toro, G.; and Cureton, T. Effect of a six month program of endurance exercise on serum lipids of middle-aged men. *Amer. J. Cardio.* 14: 753-60, 1964.
16. Johnson, T.; Wang, H.; Shim, R.; Liu, B.; and Hall A. The influence of exercise on serum cholesterol, phospholipids and electrophoretic serum protein patterns in college swimmers. *Fed. Proc.* 18: 77, 1959.
17. Keys, A. (Chairman). Recommendations concerning body measurements for the characterization of nutritional status. *Human Biol.* 28: 111, 1956.
18. Lofland, H. A semiautomated procedure for the determination of triglycerides in serum. *Anal. Biochem.* 9: 393-400, 1964.
19. Morehouse, L., and Miller, A. *Physiology of Exercise.* St. Louis: The C. V. Mosby Co., 1963.
20. Naughton, J. and McCoy, J. Observations on the relationship of physical activity to the serum cholesterol concentration of healthy men and cardiac patients. *J. Chron. Dis.* 19: 727-33, 1966.
21. Olsen, R. Obesity as a nutritional disorder. *Fed. Proc.* 18: 58, 1959.
22. Pascale, L., and others. Correlation between thickness of skinfolds and body density in 88 soldiers. *Human Biol.* 28: 165, 1956.
23. Pollock, M. Quantification of training through time-motion analysis. *The Physical Educator.* 25: 156, 1968.
24. Pollock, M., Greninger, L., and Cureton, T. K. Effects of frequency of training on working capacity, cardiovascular function, and body composition. *Sci. Med. Spts.* in press.
25. Rochelle, R. Blood plasma cholesterol changes during a physical training program. *Res. Quart.* 32: 538, 1961.
26. Taylor, H.; Anderson, J.; and Keys, A. Effects of serum lipids of 1,300 calories of daily walking. *Fed. Proc.* 16: 128, 1957.
27. Timms, A., and others. Modification of Lofland's colorimetric semiautomated serum triglyceride determination, assessed by an enzymatic glycerol determination. *J. Lipid Res.* 9: 675-80, 1968.

THE EFFECTS OF PROGRESSIVE ENDURANCE TRAINING AND VOLUNTARY DIETARY RESTRICTION ON PHYSIQUE AND METABOLIC VARIABLES IN MARKEDLY OBESE SUBJECTS

RONALD G. KNOWLTON
Southern Illinois University

HERBERT WEBER
East State Stroudsburg College

ABSTRACT

The purpose of this study was to investigate the effects of 10 weeks progressive training and voluntary diet restriction using markedly obese subjects on physique variables related to fat deposition and metabolic variables related to aerobic efficiency and acid-base balance of capillary blood. Eighteen experimental and five control subjects were utilized. Measurements included subcutaneous fat-folds, predicted percent body fat and girth measures. Responses. in Cardiovascular Fitness Components I, II, and III were obtained including pH, P_{CO_2} and base excess of capillary blood in recovery. Diet records were obtained and analyzed for all experimental subjects. Tests of significance at .05 level of significance included t tests for correlated means, analysis of variance for trend, and chi-square. Graphical and regression analyses were also employed. Significant alterations in physique. were noted as well as in variables related to metabolic potential which were reflected in acid base control systems. Evidence was presented to support independent influences of weight loss and training on criterion measures. A large subject variability about linear trend lines was noted in the majority of variables.

INTRODUCTION

It is presently recognized that physical education can benefit students with organic and·neuromuscular defects. Specialized programs have now been extended to include the markedly obese student who is functionally normal. Experiments with animals and also human beings under clinical supervision have provided significant data to substantiate the importance of exercise in programs of weight control. To further establish a rational basis for special phyiscal education for the markedly obese, experimental design should be applied to these individuals participating in adapted activity programs with controlled laboratory procedures for data collection.

PURPOSE

This study was conducted to investigate the effects of 10 weeks progressive training with voluntary diet control on measures of physique, cardiovascular and metabolic variables at rest and after a standardized exertion test. The independent variable was applied within the structure of a regularly scheduled university physical education class.

179

PROCEDURE

Eighteen subjects served as experimentals and five subjects, similar in physique, served as the control group. The experimental group possessed a mean Reciprocal of the Ponderal Index of 11.62, a mean body weight 42 percent in excess of values for normal subjects of similar age and height, and a predicted percentage body fat of 26.8 (23). Seven subjects were tested at the K-40 Low Level Radiation Laboratory at the University of Missouri, Columbia. Values for percentage body fat correlated .95 with values obtained by the Pierson Nomogram (23) although the mean value for the latter technique was seven percent lower than for the radiation technique. Based on a personal history questionnaire, obesity was traced to early childhood for all subjects and in most cases they were children of obese parents. The majority of subjects had attempted unsupervised weight control programs without the inclusion of systematic exercise. Results from the Cortes Self Analysis Personality Test (10) indicated that the subjects were strongly disposed toward endomorphic-mesomorphic personality traits.

Minimal dietary information was presented to the subjects and with all cases major realignment of dietary habits was discouraged. In order to estimate the quantity and quality of caloric intake, three day diet records were obtained and caloric consumption determined as well as an analysis of food distribution over the "Basic 4" food groups.

The training program was conducted for a period of 10 weeks and included approximately 27 sessions. An outline of the progression has been included in Table 1. Progressive rhythmical activities were emphasized

TABLE I
SUMMARY TRAINING PROGRAM*

Week	Training Description
One	10 minutes rhythmical stretching exercises Alternate: jog 200 yards, walk 100 yards; total distance 1 mile
Two	10 minutes rhythmical stretching exercises 2 bouts, 10 repetitions each — sit-ups 2 bouts, 5 repetitions each — push-ups 15 minutes individual speed play
Four	3 mile hike — a vigorous pace with 1 rest stop for 5 minutes
Six	10 minutes rhythmical stretching exercises 3 bouts, 15 repetitions each — sit-ups 3 bouts, 8 repetitions each — push-ups 10 minutes vigorous rope skipping
Eight	10 minutes rhythmical stretching exercises 2 bouts, 25 repetitions each — sit-ups 2 bouts, 10 repetitions each — push-ups 15 minutes continuous run-walk
Ten	10 minutes rhythmical stretching exercises 40 sit-ups 15 push-ups 20 minutes continuous jog

*Not included: 3 test sessions and periods of adapted endurance games.

using body resistant activities with individual variations permitted to account for the variable capacities of the subjects. All experimental subjects were highly motivated and required little external motivation. The group was encouraged to incorporate vigorous activity into their personal lives at each opportunity.

Laboratory measurements were obtained in the Physical Education Research Laboratory, Southern Illinois University, at three junctures in the training. Standardized procedures were utilized to obtain physique measures including subcutaneous fat-folds at representative body sites. Aspects of Cardiovascular Fitness Components I, II, and III (12) were measured in addition to exercise response of capillary pH values. The Astrup-Micro-Glass-Electrode Technique (21) was utilized with values converted to variables of metabolic and respiratory components of acid-base balance by means of the Siggard-Andersen Curve Nomogram (3). A strenuous yet submaximal bicycle ergometer test was selected for exertion responses in order to isolate body weight with its anticipated fluctuation, to provide maximal safety and control, and to provide an adequate stress to aerobic mechanisms with minor localized fatigue in obese subjects. Huesner and Bernauer (17) have pointed to poor correlations between pH drop of antecubital blood and maximal performance in exhaustive treadmill running. Subjects were permitted to undertake the Cooper 12-minute maximum distance test (9) on a voluntary basis.

The .05 level of significance was selected for hypothesis testing. Statistical procedures included *t* tests between correlated means to determine the significant changes within the control and experimental groups, F-ratio to determine longitudinal trends between tests as well as individual variations from group linearity (2), chi-square for nonparametric analysis of dietary composition and changes, and regression analysis to determine interaction between criterion and treatment (20).

RESULTS AND DISCUSSION

Physique and Diet Analysis

Table 2 summarizes physique measures for the control and experimental subjects. While significant changes were absent with the control subjects, 12 items were significantly altered with training and diet in the experimental subjects. Statistically the test of significance was more rigorous for the limited number of control subjects, and the significant experimental changes with one exception reflected the mean weight loss of 13 pounds. In the presence of reduced abdominal girth the gain in abdominal fat is difficult to explain other than the fact that subjects demonstrated a strong abdominal reflex contraction to the skinfold pinch at Test 1. Although sites and procedures were utilized as described by Fletcher (15) and Brozek and Keys (7), reliable measures were difficult to obtain about the torso and where fat accumulations were the greatest.

The training was designed to facilitate catabolism, with additional self-induced calorie restriction observed in the subjects. Figure 1 presents results from three day diet records and suggests that experimentals were consuming slightly in excess of 15 calories per pound of desirable body weight previous to training. In association with increased metabolic activity was a significant reduction in total calories and a significant qualitative shift, chi-square .05, in the distribution of the total calories among the Basic Four food groups. Significant serving reductions existed in all but meat products. Although diet records were dependent upon subject cooperation and understanding, it would appear that the diet trend was from foods high in carbohydrate and fat toward those high in protein. Other investigators have noted dietary adjustments to accompany vigorous activity in animals (11) and human beings (22).

Cardiovascular Responses: Components I, II, III

Data concerning cardiovascular fitness have been summarized in Table 3. No significance was noted in control group measures although several absolute differences were equivalent to significant changes with experimental data. Control group responses to the exertion test were nearly identical

TABLE 2
ANTHROPOMETRIC SUMMARY — AVERAGE VALUES

Control Subjects N = 5				Experimental Subjects N = 18		
Test 1	Test 2	Sig.	Measurement	Test 1	Test 2	Sig.
69.4	69.4	—	1 Height (in.)	68.3	68.0	—
221.0	222.0	—	2 Body Weight (lbs.)	214.0	201.0	.01
146.0	147.0	—	3 Relative Weight (%)	142.00	136.00	.02
25.0	25.0	—	4 Body Fat (%)	26.83	23.50	.01
4.31	4.42	—	5 Neck Fat (mm.)	4.91	4.31	—
1.6	.5	—	6 Chest Fat (mm.)	5.08	4.08	.01
5.0	3.0	—	7 Bicep Fat (mm.)	4.37	3.62	.02
33.2	33.7	—	8 Abdominal Fat (mm.)	19.05	22.60	+.05
11.1	11.0	—	9 Patellar Fat (mm.)	10.35	9.57	.10
24.1	25.6	—	10 Subscapular Fat (mm.)	18.32	19.45	—
15.4	13.7	—	11 Triceps Fat (mm.)	13.51	14.13	—
111.3	111.1	—	12 Chest Girth (cm.)	108.3	105.3	.01
104.5	105.0	—	13 Abdominal Girth (cm.)	104.1	97.3	.01
64.0	64.1	—	14 Thigh Girth (cm.)	64.4	63.1	—
33.9	33.8	—	15 Upper Arm Girth (cm.)	35.6	33.8	.01
41.5	42.2	—	16 Calf Girth (cm.)	41.0	40.0	.02
6.8	6.1	—	17 Difference Chest vs. Abdominal Girth (cm.)	5.31	7.05	.05

throughout the experiment which indicated little training influence derived from repeated exposure to laboratory procedures. It was felt that this consistency reflected the natural advantage of obese subjects in ergometric procedures with body weight suspended.

Although a Component I bradycardia occurred, little training influence was noted in blood pressure measures. It may be that these subjects had

FIGURE I

EXPERIMENTAL 3 DAY DIET ANALYSIS

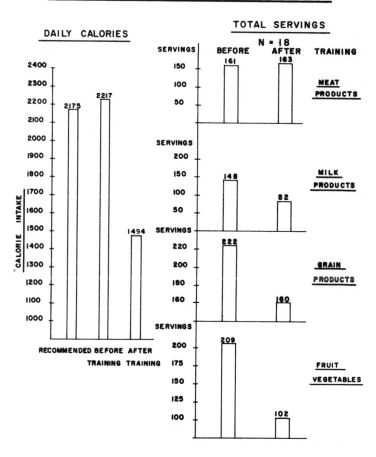

not sufficiently aged to realize the combined influence of adiposity and detraining on the mechanisms supporting blood pressure (19) as before training values did not differ markedly from normal. When pulse rate and systolic blood pressure were combined as an index of metabolic demand on the heart (16), significance was noted throughout. Orthostatic measures were not favorably influenced by the training.

Exertional heart rate responses have been presented in Figure 2. Contrary to the findings of Chiang and others (8), delayed heart rate accelera-

TABLE 3

CARDIOVASCULAR RESPONSES TO TRAINING — MEAN VALUES OF COMPONENTS I, II, AND III

Control Subjects N = 5			Measurement	Experimental Subjects N = 18		
Test 1	Test 3	Sig.	COMPONENT I	Test 1	Test 3	Sig.
77	76	—	1 Heart Rate	71	64	.05
140	134	—	2 Systolic Pressure	131	127	—
82	81	—	3 Diastolic Pressure	72	68	—
58	53	—	4 Pulse Pressure	59	59	—
111	108	—	5 Mean Pressure	102	98	—
10,780	10,184	—	6 Systolic Pressure x Heart Rate	9,301	8,128	.05
			COMPONENT II (Standing)			
89	93	—	1 Heart Rate	84	78	—
143	135	—	2 Systolic Pressure	128	122	.05
99	102	—	3 Diastolic Pressure	87	84	—
44	33	—	4 Pulse Pressure	41	38	—
121	119	—	5 Mean Pressure	107	103	—
12,727	12,555	—	6 Systolic Pressure x Heart Rate	10,752	9,516	.05
12	17	—	7 Orthostatic Δ Heart Rate	13	14	—
-13	-19	—	8 Orthostatic Δ Pulse Pressure	-17	-22	.01
10	10	—	9 Orthostatic Δ Mean Pressure	+3	+6	—
			COMPONENT III (900 KPM/MIN — 6 MIN)			
153	157	—	1 Mean Heart Rate	150	137	.01
166	163	—	2 Terminal Heart Rate	163	147	.01
2.67	2.74	—	3 V_{O_2} Max Predicted (cc/min)	2.75	3.39	.01
27	27	—	4 V_{O_2} Max Predicted (cc/kg)	29	36	.01
111	114	—	5 5th Minute Recov. Heart Rate	104	88	.01

FIGURE 2
PULSE CHANGE (A) REST TO WORK
900 KPM / MINUTE ; (B) WORK TO RECOVERY

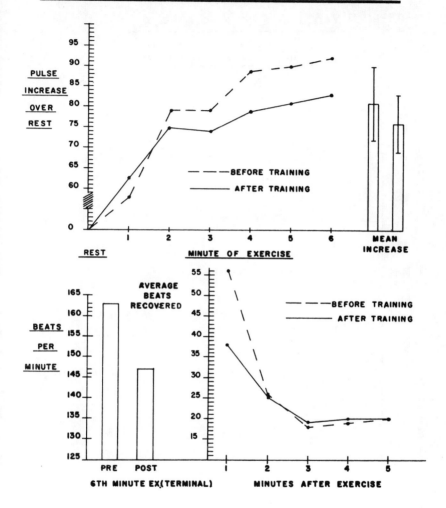

FIGURE 3
REGRESSION ANALYSIS

$$Y = a_o u + a_2 X_2 + a_3 X_3 + a_4 X_4 + a_6 X_5$$

A— PREDICTED MAXIMUM OXYGEN INTAKE

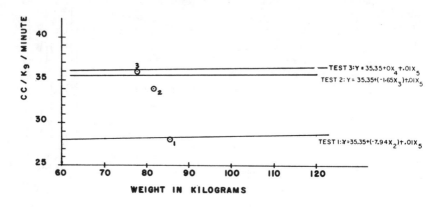

B — PREDICTED MEAN RECOVERY HEART RATE

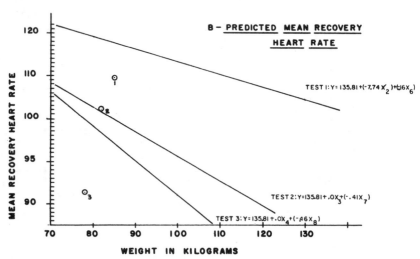

tion was not indicated but rather the training effect became dominant only in the later phases of exertion. The finding was consistent with a homeostatic definition of cardio-respiratory fitness and resulted from a greater ability to control the anaerobic stimuli to exercise pulse rate. When pulse rate data was applied to the Astrand Nomogram (4), significant increases in aerobic power were recorded. A consistent dynamic influence on metabolic potential was observed in that percentage improvement in Vo_2 max expressed in cc/kg/min ($+22\%$) and distance covered in the Cooper 12 minute test ($+21\%$) were nearly identical. The physiologic principle that correlates pulse rate recovery with the degree of exercise displacement (1) was applicable to these subjects (Fig. 3,B). Based on the number of beats recovered from terminal exercise divided by elapsed recovery time, after minute two of recovery a pattern was presented suggestive of genetic influences rather than training adaptations.

Regression analysis was employed to test the interaction of predicted Vo_2 maximum and mean recovery heart rate with body weight. Within the interest range of these subjects no interaction was noted which indicates the main effect to have resulted from training rather than weight reduction.

TABLE 4
MEAN VALUES ACID BASE – VARIABLES CAPILLARY BLOOD

Measurement	Rest Experimentals	Controls	After Exercise Experimentals	Controls
Actual pH				
Before Training	7.374	7.394	7.321	7.334
After Training	7.372	7.389	7.329	7.322
P_{CO_2} (mmHg)				
Before Training	41.6	41.4	34.2	39.2
After Training	40.5	43.5	35.8	39.9
Standard Bicarbonate (MEQ/L Plasma)				
Before Training	23.26	28.0	18.49	20.16
After Training	23.18	26.0	19.14	20.10
Base Excess (MEQ/L Blood)				
Before Training	-.77	0.0	-7.43	-5.50
After Training	-1.30	-1.20	-6.54	-5.50
Total CO_2 (MEQ/L Plasma)				
Before Training	25.56	25.65	18.30	21.22
After Training	24.61	27.80	18.90	21.84
Buffer Base (MEQ/L Blood)				
Before Training	47.30	50.52	42.01	44.58
After Training	48.76	53.06	44.11	44.64

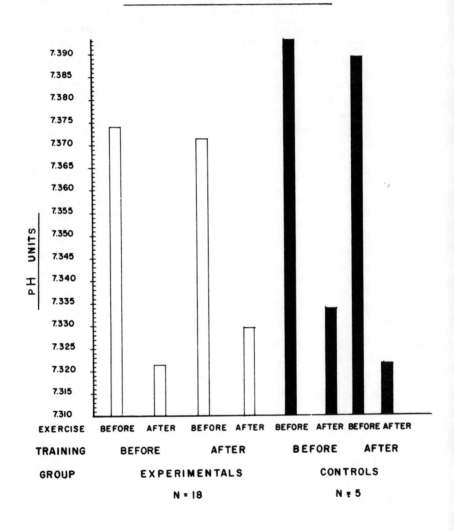

FIGURE 4

CAPILLARY BLOOD

This was the intended purpose in selection of the Ergometer test. The line of best fit, Figure 3, relates degree of training to the elapse of time of the experiment which was reduced between tests two and three. Dots have been placed on A and B which represent the course of training for a subject. Reduction of weight is associated with an increase in predicted maximal oxygen intake and a decrease in the mean recovery heart rate. Heavier subjects reacted no differently than lighter subjects to the exercise training.

Capillary Acid Base Measures

Modern techniques of blood pH determination have shown capillary samples as acceptable standards with the normal range between 7.37 and 7.43 (6). Deviations from normal result either by the metabolic gain of a strong acid and loss of bicarbonate or a respiratory reduction in alveolar ventilation. An uncomplicated exercise response would exemplify a partially compensated metabolic acidosis since both pH and $[HCO_3\text{-}]$ are reduced with associated hypocapnea (18, 26, 27). In any event it is necessary to determine pH, $[HCO_3\text{-}]$, and Pco_2 in order to fully understand the acid-base balance mechanisms in exercise as the bicarbonate and Pco_2 can vary independently of pH (3).

Table 4 presents acid-base measures for all subjects and indicates rest values to be within the expected normal range.

Exertion brought significant acidosis to all subjects both before and after the period of training.

This suggests the exertion to have been of adequate quality to require utilization of anaerobic metabolic pathways. The fall in standard bicarbonate was considered to be proportional to the accumulation of lactic acid. Exercise values were obtained approximately five minutes after the bicycle test in order to permit equilibrium of lactic acid throughout the body water.

Figure 5 presents the respiratory and metabolic components of acid-base balance plotted against pH values for control and experimental subjects.

The slight depreciation of alkali reserve in experimental subjects may be related to the reduction of citrus fruit consumption and its associated alkalinizing effect on the blood and altered metabolic pathways associated with significant catabolism in obese subjects (14). These as well as the Pco_2 value at rest were not significantly altered for either subject group during the experiment.

It is clearly evidenced that the accumulation of acidosis cannot be explained by an excess of CO_2 in the experimental subjects. Shropshire (25) has explained the mechanism accounting for lactate increase in the presence of oxygen deficiency. In view of the accumulated acidosis present in control subjects resulting from exercise, it was postulated that this group lacked the ability to mobilize and divert blood buffers as required as well as an insensitivity leading to hypoventilation of the alveoli. A vital capacity of 81 percent of predicted values supported the later view.

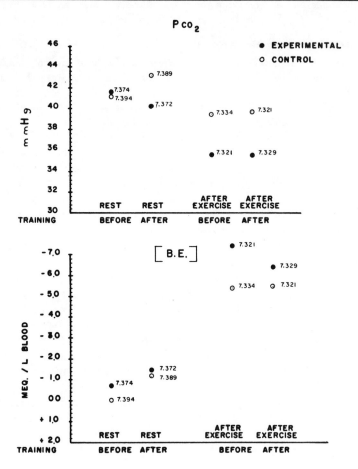

FIGURE 5

ACID BASE VALUES

CAPILLARY BLOOD WITH $_pH$ VALUES INDICATED

The experimental subjects displayed the expected sequence resulting from increased energy metabolism. Available base was mobilized to buffer lactic acid which eventuated in increased ventilation of the alveoli. Training made little variation in respiratory response but acidosis was reduced in response to exercise with reduced expense to the buffer systems of whole blood. This was in accordance with the findings of Robinson and Harmon (24) using submaximal tests on highly competent distance runners. In light of resting acid-base values, it was concluded that the influence of training on acid-base balance was a response to the increased oxidative potential which permitted more complete utilization of organic food products.

Trend Analysis

The results obtained from F-ratios calculated to determine group linearity in trend supported significance tests of correlated means. Forty-eight experimental variables showed significance when the total series of tests was used and not just the start and end point of training. There was less evidence of a group tendency to fluctuate about the linear trend line as 25 variables were able to survive this test at .05 level of significance. Although the group slope is significantly different from zero for the subjects, it must be concluded that throughout training it is difficult to assign a slope common to all individuals. This was considered to be a consequence arising from the compounded effect of obesity and detraining which fostered individuality in both the training program and the training effects.

CONCLUSIONS

1. A ten week program of progressive training combined with dietary restriction was adequate to reduce body fat accumulation but not adequate to eliminate significant obesity. It was further noted that significant alteration in the quality and quantity of ingested food was self-imposed and in support of the process of catabolism.

2. A ten week program of progressive physical training brought significant improvement in at least four major components of cardiovascular fitness. Most general of the improvements were those variables dealing with aerobic potential as predicted from both submaximal and maximal exertion tests. Evidence was presented to indicate the training of metabolic potential to be separate from the neutralization of obesity.

3. Evidence was presented which contrasted compensated acidosis in control and experimental subjects. Acid-base control systems responded to training more as reflection of aerobic capacity than an increased buffer-potential of whole blood. The decreased acidosis with training resulted from more complete oxidation of organic foodstuffs rather than increased alkali reserve.

4. The detrained state that apparently accompanies obesity predisposes such subjects susceptible to moderate exposure of physiologic overload. A number of structural and functional measures were significantly altered from training 27 times over a span of ten weeks averaging 30 minutes of

work per training. Although favorable linear group trends were observed in a large number of measures, individual randomness was noted to have occurred. This was interpreted as an intrinsic phenomenon to be encountered in training markedly obese subjects.

REFERENCES

1. Adolph, Edward F. Some physiologic regulations illustrated in exercise. In Warren R. Johnson (Ed.), *Science and medicine of exercise and sports*. New York: Harper & Bros., 1960.
2. Alexander, Howard W. The estimation of reliability when several trials are available. *Psychometrika* 12: 79-99, 1947.
3. Andersen, Siggard O. Blood acid-base alignment nomogram. *The Scand. J. of Clin. Invest.* 15: 211-217, 1963.
4. Åstrand, P. O. *Work tests with the bicycle ergometer*. Varberg, Sweden: Monark.
5. Åstrand, P. O., and others. Blood lactates after prolonged severe exercises. *J. Appl. Physl.* 18: 619-28, 1963.
6. Astrup, P. Ultra-micro methods for determining pH, Pco_2 and standard bicarbonate in capillary blood. Published lecture, Radiometer Corporation, 1958.
7. Brozek, J. and Keys, A. The evaluation of leanness-fatness in man: norms and interrelationships. *Brit. J. Nutr.* 5: 194-206, 1941.
8. Chiang, Benjamin N., and others. Physical characteristics and exercise performance of pedicab and upper socioeconomic classes of middle-aged Chinese men. *Amer. H. J.* 76: 760-68, 1968.
9. Cooper, Kenneth M. *Aerobics*. New York: Bantam Books, 1968.
10. Cortes, John B. and Gah, Florence M. Physique and self-description of temperament. *J. Consult. Psych.* 29: 432-39, 1965.
11. Crews, Eugene L., and others. Weight, food intake and body composition: effects of exercise and protein deficiency. *Amer. J. of Physiol.* 216: 1969.
12. Cureton, Thomas K. The nature of cardiovascular condition in normal humans. *J. Assoc. Phys. Ment. Rehab.* 11: 186-96, 1967.
13. Davenport, Horace W. *The ABC of acid-base chemistry*. Chicago: The University of Chicago Press, 1950.
14. Felig, P., and others. Utilization of metabolic fuels in obese subjects. *Amer. Journ. Clin. Nutr.* 21: 1429-33, 1968.
15. Fletcher, Ronald F. The measurement of total body fat with skinfold calipers. *Clin. Sci.* 22: 333-46, 1962.
16. Hellerstein, Herman K. A new approach to cardiac energy requirement by oxygen consumption and dynamic electrocardiography. *Proc. Third Natl. Conf. on Work Eval. Units*. Washington, D.C., 66-71, 1966.
17. Huesner, William and Bernauer, E. Relationship between level of physical condition and pH of antecubital venous blood. *Journal of Appl. Physl.* 9: 171-75, 1956.
18. Kamm, D. E., and others. Acid-base alterations and renal gluconeogenesis: effect of pH, bicarbonate concentration and Pco_2. *Journ. of Clin. Invest.* 46: 1172-77, 1967.
19. Kannel, W., and others. The relation of adiposity to blood pressure and development of hypertension. *Annls. of Intern. Med.* 67: 48-59, 1967.
20. Kelly, Francis J., and others. *Multiple regression approach*. Carbondale: Southern Illinois University Press, 1969.
21. Maas, A. H. J. and Van Heijst, A. N. P. Comparison of the pH of arterial blood with Astrup's micro glass electrode. *Clin. Chim. Act.* 6: 31-33, 1961.
22. Mayer, Jean. Exercise and weight control. In Warren R. Johnson (Ed.), *Science and medicine of exercise and sports*. New York: Harper & Bros., 1960.
23. Pierson, William R. and Eagle, E. L. Nomogram for estimating body fat, specific gravity and lean body weight from height and weight. *Aerospace Med.* 40: 161-64, 1969.

24. Robinson, S. and Harmon, P. The lactic acid mechanism and certain properties of the blood in relation to training. *Amer. J. Physl.* 132: 757-69, 1941.
25. Shropshire, Spencer, Jr., and others. Changes in acid-base balance induced by 100 percent gradient headward acceleration. *Aerospace Med.* 40: 237-47, 1969.
26. Wasserman, K. Change to anaerobic metabolism during exercise. *Proc. Third Natl. Conf. on Work Eval. Units.* Washington, D.C., 35-46, 1966.
27. _____. Lactate and related acid-base and blood gas changes during constant load and graded exercise. *Canad. Med. Ass. J.* 96: 775-83, 1967.

THE EFFECT OF DYNAMIC PHYSICAL ACTIVITY ON HANDICAPPED UNIVERSITY STUDENTS

KARL G. STOEDEFALKE

BRUNO BALKE

ALLAN J. RYAN

JAMES B. GALE
University of Wisconsin

ABSTRACT

The University of Wisconsin Adapted Physical Education Program is a cooperative effort between the Student Health Services Department and the Department of Physical Education. Students with medically diagnosed abnormalities which range from mild to moderate handicaps are assigned to a special physical education program to meet their individual needs. The student received a functional capacity evaluation (motor driven treadmill or bicycle ergometer) to test his adaptability to increased energy demands. These assessments served as base line measures for prescribing the type and the intensity of physical activity for each student. The attitude of the adapted student toward his handicap as well as his self-esteem were evaluated through an attitude inventory and semantic differential test. The adapted student's program of physical activity consisted of endurance (cardiorespiratory) training and the development of sport or recreational exercise skills. Specific therapeutic type exercises necessary to alleviate physical deficiencies became an integral part of the student's program. However, such therapeutic exercise was considered remedial and was performed by the student before or after the scheduled class time. Re-evaluation of the students occurred during the 16th week of each semester, including a medical examination and the re-evaluation of the student's functional capacity. Based on a population of 92 subjects using descriptive and inferential statistics the following results were obtained. Physiological changes — Significant improvement in work capacity; lowered heart rates and arterial blood pressures during sub-maximal work intensities. Surprising physical skills were acquired. Psychological — The student's self esteem improved and the handicap was not perceived as debilitating to the subject after the course as it had been prior to participation.

INTRODUCTION

Adapted physical education is a common offering in college and university physical education programs. The disabled university student is medically identified as an individual who, as a result of a physical problem, is not acceptable for a basic physical education program. Activity of a social recreational nature which minimize the chance of injury is recommended.

When the student meets the course time requirement a grade is submitted and the physical education commitment is fulfilled. Hopefully, the student has gained knowledge of his limitations, developed a sport skill, and has learned something about human motion. But, is he physically educated? Can a semester of darts, shuffleboard, deck tennis or archery provide the foundation for a physically active life? Semi-active activities tend to be the rule rather than the exception in adapted physical education classes. The lack of sufficiently vigorous physical activity in adapted programs often rests with the physical educators' fear of legal reprisal in the event of accident or injury, and activities with placebo characteristics are made attractive to parents, administrators, and physicians. Actually, the handicapped student deserves to be treated with more professional efficiency.

It was the purpose of this study to determine the physiological and psychological changes made by disabled students engaged in an activity program with medical supervision, with adequate functional evaluation, and dynamic physical activity of an enjoyable nature.

PROCEDURE

Ninety-two University of Wisconsin ambulatory male underclassmen with mild to moderate medical disabilities who ranged in age from 18 to 20 years were assigned to the adapted physical education section of the basic instruction program. The disabilities consisted of a wide variety of medical problems. These were orthopedic in nature, concerned with knees, ankles, feet and shoulders, or with functional and structural problems of the vertebral column as well as with rheumatoid arthritis. Neurological problems were represented by students with cerebral palsy (spastic and athetoid), epilepsy, previous polio, and with traumatic cerebral concussion. Students who had asthma, diabetes, or a nutritional imbalance were also included.

After the student's medical examination a functional capacity test was given. This test involved either walking on a treadmill, riding a bicycle ergometer, a sustained 15 minute run, or using an adjustable stepping device. The subject's arterial blood pressures and heart rates were measured each minute of the walking, cycling or stepping exercise to determine the approach of functional limits for physical work and the amount of work the subject was capable of doing within a physiological margin of safety. Furthermore, this assessment of the student's capacity for circulatory and respiratory adjustment to physical exertion allowed for more individualized treatment of the student during the activity program, with respect to the duration and intensity of certain exercises. The test was stopped in the presence of pain or discomfort or when the heart rate reached 160-180 beats per minute. The test results provided information on the student's capacity to perform physical work as well as establishing the base line measures for subsequent re-evaluation.

If the student had an orthopedic problem, strength measures were taken of the involved and contralateral segments, and exercises were prescribed to improve muscle strength. If the student had asthmatic tendencies additional respiratory data were obtained: namely, vital capacity including inspiratory capacity and expiratory reserve; MVV (max. voluntary vent); and forced expiratory volume.

In conjunction with the Department of Counseling and Behavioral Studies, (4) 28 second semester freshmen subjects were selected to determine whether changes in self-perception occurred as a result of 16 weeks participation in the adapted physical education program. Two instruments were used to measure the student's attitude towards the physical disability: The Handicapped Problems Inventory (7) and a semantic differential test (5).

Physical Activity Program

Class size varied from 6 to 15 students. The physical activity program consisted of two parts. During the first eight weeks, meeting two hours per week for 30 to 40 minutes of sustained physical activity — developmental and strength exercises were emphasized. Students were led through a variety of physical activities which included running, walking, jogging, leaping, jumping, rolling, and crawling with or without sport balls and equipment. Emphasis was placed on sustained physical activity performed by the entire class whenever possible. Each student — according to his handicap, functional capacity, and skill — received constant instruction and direction from the physical educator. At no time did the instructor lead structural calisthenics. Instruction was given while the student was moving.

Students were taught to recognize the signs of fatigue. There was a decrease in the level of activity in the presence of discomfort, excessive perspiration, and labored breathing. During each class session the instructor led activity which elevated the student's heart rate to the range of 120 to 160 beats per minute. An energy expenditure equivalent to approximately 350 calories was the desired goal for each activity session. Periodically, heart rates were measured by the student for a 15 second duration. These measurements served as cues to increase or decrease the intensity of activity. Progress in covering longer distances with increasing velocity, an excellent criterion of cardiovascular capability, was expected to be slow, but attempts were made by the disabled students to develop the capacity to sustain a 20 minute run.

Early in the program, in addition to the walk, jog, run, the students were introduced to different types of sport balls and were eventually taught simple ball games. Medicine balls of six to twelve pounds, as well as soccer, volley, and basketballs were used. These balls were passed, thrown, handed, struck, bounced, or kicked, in single, partner or group exercises. Emphasis was on a continuous and sustained flow of activities in time. Each student received instruction in adapting the activity to suit his condition and was encouraged to experiment with alternatives to produce the desired movement. Emphasis was placed on developing the nondominant or nonpreferred hand or lower extremity. Low organized and simple ball games were enjoyed by the students. Rules for such ball games were frequently altered or waived to ensure the most efficient participation and the optimum competitive spirit of the students.

After eight weeks of sustained activity, a satisfactory level of improved capacity had developed, and a variety of recreational activities were introduced. These included tennis, handball, volleyball, pit volleyball, paddleball, badminton, squash racquets, and golf. Students with post-concussion syndrome or cervical vertebrae involvement, wore hockey or baseball helmets to minimize the possibility of injury to head and neck.

Throughout the semester, a Friday swim was an integral part of the program. The nonswimmer was carefully introduced to water, the beginning swimmer was given the opportunity for working on skill proficiency, and the proficient swimmer was required to increase endurance capacity by swimming for distance. In working with medicinally controlled epileptics the swimming instructor to pupil ratio was at the 1:1 or 1:2 level.

During the last week of the semester each student was retested in the laboratory. Functional capacity assessments were made and the students were medically re-examined.

RESULTS

Treadmill Performance

The results of the Progressive Treadmill Test (1) were as follows: functional limitations, considered to interfere with adequate oxygen supply, were encountered at 12.8 minutes, on the average (range: 7 to 25 minutes). The oxygen demand for this work intensity involved was 33.6 ml/kg per minute. This performance was classified as "fair" and rates according to the Progressive Treadmill Test norms published by Howell and others (3) at the 35 standard score level.

After 16 weeks of physical activity in the Adaptive Physical Education Program the T_2 mean walking time was 15.3 minutes and the mean oxygen demand for this work load was 37.59 ml/kg/min. This is classified as an "average" performance on the Progressive Treadmill Test (1) and is rated at the 50 standard score level on the Howell college norms (3).

The difference in the T_1 to T_2 mean value shows an increase of 3.97 ml O_2/kg/min. The standard error of difference of the group means was calculated at 1.068 and a $\underline{t}$ of 3.72 with 91 degrees of freedom was significant at the .01 level. Initially, this group of handicapped students tended to be below non-disabled contemporaries in the ability to perform aerobic work, but it is apparent that significant changes in aerobic capacity occurred with dynamic physical activity programs of a single semester duration.

Figure 1 shows a heart rate pattern common to any group of subjects; namely, that as the work load increases the heart rate slowly increases in a more or less rectilinear manner. As an individual increases his aerobic power, treadmill performance time increases and heart rates are significantly lowered. Significant differences between T_1 and T_2 at the .01 level were found at rest and during the first 11 minutes of the Progressive Treadmill

Test. Recovery heart rates were reduced significantly, at the .05 level, during the second and third minute post exercise.

Mean arterial blood pressures are shown in Figure 2. Significant changes between T_1 and T_2 in systolic and diastolic blood pressures occurred during the first 12 minutes of the Progressive Treadmill Test. It is suggested that the lack of significant differences in the latter stages of the test could be attributed to fewer subjects walking at grades in excess of 15%.

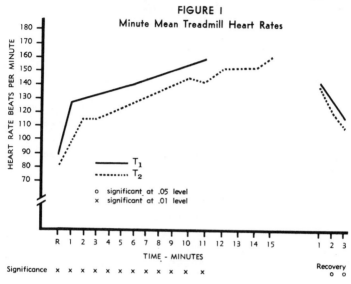

FIGURE I
Minute Mean Treadmill Heart Rates

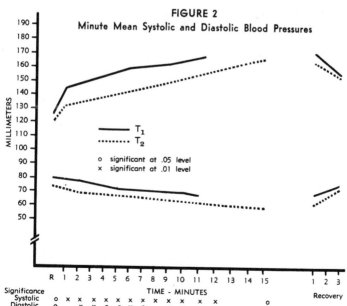

FIGURE 2
Minute Mean Systolic and Diastolic Blood Pressures

Psychological Testing

The Wright Handicap Problems Inventory (HPI) and a semantic differential test were used to determine the psychological changes. During the spring semester (1967) 28 students took part in this investigation. Five did not complete the tests because of the "pressures of academic classes." Two significant changes were observed in the semantic differential test: The first concept "Me as I really am" rated higher in the post-exercise than in the pre-exercise testing. This result indicated that the student thought more of himself and thereby elevated his self-concept and a positive change occurred. Secondly, as was expected "Me as I would like to be," rated lower in the post test because thinking more highly of himself, the ideal person was less far away. Therefore, the student's self concept was closer to his ideal in the post testing session that at the onset of the program and a significant t value resulted.

The results of the HPI indicated a significant difference in only one hypothesis which related to "personal" items. High scores on this item are related to an exaggeration of the effects of the disability and low scores indicate denial of the disability or a realistic attitude toward a minor disabling condition. Since the subjects were all mild to moderately impaired it appears that checking fewer items on the post test reflected an objective or realistic approach to the disabling condition.

CONCLUSIONS

Within the limitations of this study, it is concluded that disabled university students who engaged in a medically supervised, progressive, vigorous physical activity program which stressed enjoyable, sustained human motion made the following changes:

1. Increased aerobic capacity.
2. Lowered progressive treadmill test heart rates and arterial blood pressures.
3. Significant improvements in self esteem.
4. Acquisition of sport and recreation skills.

REFERENCES

1. Balke, B. and Ware, R. W. An experimental study of physical fitness of Air Force personnel. *U.S. Armed Forces Med. J.* 10: 675-88, 1959.
2. Cornell, F. G. *The essentials of educational statistics.* New York: John Wiley and Sons, Inc. 1956.
3. Howell, M. L., and others. Progressive treadmill test norms for college males. *Res. Quart.* 35: 322-25, 1964.
4. Johnson, D. M. *Changes in self perceptions of mildly handicapped freshmen students participating in an adaptive physical education program.* Unpublished Master's thesis, University of Wisconsin, 1957.
5. Osgood, C. E., and others. *The measurement of meaning.* Urbana: University of Illinois Press, 1957.
6. Ryan, A. J., and others. The Wisconsin program in adaptive physical education. *J. of Amer. College Health Assoc.* 15: 351-56, 1967.
7. Wright, G. Manual: *The handicap problems inventory.* Purdue Research Foundation, 1960.

EFFECTS OF PREPUBERTAL EXERCISE ON BODY COMPOSITION*

W. D. VAN HUSS

W. W. HEUSNER

O. MICKELSEN
Michigan State University

ABSTRACT

One-hundred-eighty male albino rats (Sprague-Dawley) were used in this investigation of the effects of pre-pubertal physical training. At 30 days of age, each animal was assigned to one of three initial treatment groups: sedentary, voluntary exercise, or voluntary plus forced exercise. The pre-pubertal experimental period, in which the voluntary-forced exercise rats were forced to swim 30 min. daily, lasted 35 days. Following training, some of the animals from each group were sacrificed. The remaining animals then were placed in voluntary cages for 160 days. Again, some of the animals from each group were sacrificed. The remaining animals in each group were divided into two subgroups: one half reverted back to their original experimental condition, the other half received the forced swimming regimen for 35 days. Following the second training period, several animals from each of the subgroups were sacrificed. The other animals were retained to old age in voluntary cages. The forced-exercise animals at puberty had lower body weights, shorter tibias, lower relative fat and greater relative protein, ash and moisture than the controls ($p < .05$). However, the absolute protein, ash, and moisture values were lower in the forced-exercise animals. The absolute body composition values, when considered with the shorter bone lengths in the trained animals, indicate that forced exercise during pre-puberty resulted in smaller animals. At 160 days post-puberty, the relative body composition values were not significantly different.

INTRODUCTION

Currently, activity programs for children range from free play to highly intensive regimens of endurance or power training for competition. The existence of such a great diversity of programs warrants considerable study of the implications of imposing various exercise-induced stresses upon children.

Although extensive knowledge already exists concerning the effects of acute and chronic exercise (15, 29), the continuum of physical activity often has been mistakenly regarded as a single entity. Investigators have used many types and intensities of exercise, with different age groups, in such a way that it is difficult to integrate and interpret the results of various studies other than in general terms. In particular, there is a dearth of evidence con-

*Supported by NIH Grant HD 00963.

201

cerning the residual anatomic and physiologic effects of specific pre-pubertal exercise programs. Knowledge of these effects is needed to ensure proper planning of physical activities for young children.

This study was undertaken to determine the residual effects of forced swimming and voluntary running, during the pre-pubertal period, upon body composition and long-bone growth. In order to achieve precise direct measures, male albino rats were used as subjects for this investigation. The limitations inherent in obtaining body composition measures in humans are well recognized (2, 19). Several indirect techniques for estimating the composition of the human body are available, but direct chemical analyses provide the most accurate procedures for arriving at the absolute and relative amounts of any body component.

LITERATURE REVIEW

Exercise and Body Composition

As compared to sedentary subjects of the same age and sex, physically active adults have higher body densities reflecting greater proportions of lean body mass (21). Subcutaneous fat decreases in adolescents and young adults as a result of various types of training, i.e., swimming, wrestling, basketball, gymnastics, and hockey (12, 13, 21). Lean body mass has been found to increase with gymnastic (21) and strength training programs with increases up to 40% in the latter (3). Parizkova found physical activity to be one of the most important factors influencing body composition. She concluded that, at all ages, the influence of physical activity is to change the relative proportions of lean body mass and fat (21).

Body weight alone does not accurately reflect body composition changes due to physical activity as there often is a shift in the various body components as evidenced by altered girth measures. However, during physical training, a change in body weight usually reflects a loss in fat which may be accompanied by an increase in muscle mass (21).

Animal studies, in which body composition has been done, support the human investigations. Higher relative protein and lower relative fat values have been found in trained than in untrained animals. In addition, the relative ash and moisture values were higher (14) and bone densities were greater in the trained animals (26). In most of the studies involving endurance activity, the trained animals' body weights were lower than those of the control animals (4, 8, 14, 20). Both Edgerton and Carrow found the muscle sizes to be smaller in endurance-trained animals, with the weight of the triceps surae highly correlated ($r = .87$) with body weight (4, 8).

Parizkova found the usual differences in body fat, but no differences in body weight, between three groups of animals. One experimental group was restrained; a second experimental group was forced to run on a treadmill; the control group lived in communal cages (22).

Exercise and Linear Bone Growth

There is no agreement in the reports on the effects of exercise on bone growth. Actually, the conclusions arrived at by different investigators range all the way from increased to retarded bone growth associated with physical activity.

The work supporting the concept that exercise stimulates bone growth has been summarized by Rarick (24) who concluded that an undefined minimum of muscular activity is essential for normal bone growth. Increased bone growth associated with exercise was reported by Donaldson (7). However, the bones of immobilized limbs are longer and thinner than are those of contralateral control limbs. With immobilization, there is histologic evidence of increased growth at the epiphysis (29). Some investigators suggest that immobilization protects the epiphysis from pressure and thus facilitates increased bone growth.

A number of investigators have reported that the linear growth of long bones in rats was impaired as a result of both voluntary and forced exercise (17, 23, 27). A similar result was observed in junior high school boys. Those competing in athletics showed an impairment in growth (9, 25), as shown by a 0.37 inch decrement in height over a six-month period (9), when compared with non-athletes. Japanese children engaged in heavy labor were short of stature (16). This was associated primarily with short legs. The epiphysis of the lower end of the femur and at both ends of the tibia and fibula showed early closure. This viewpoint is supported by the well-controlled work of Henrichson and Storey (11) who found that compression applied across the epiphyseal cartilage for 40 days caused a mean impairment of 2 mm in linear growth of the tibia of rats. Likewise, in chickens reared in a centrifuge, the long bones were significantly shortened (28).

FIGURE I
EXPERIMENTAL DESIGN OF PREPUBERTAL EXERCISE STUDY

Phase	1	2	Sacrificed	3	Sacrificed	4	Sacrificed	5	Sacrificed
Days	6	35		160		35		236	
Exercise	Vol[1] (180)[2]	None (50)	(10)	Vol	(10)	None (10) / Forced (20)	(10)	Vol / Vol	(10) / (10)
		Vol (50)	(10)	Vol	(10)	Vol (10) / Forced (20)	(10)	Vol / Vol	(10) / (10)
		Forced (50)	(10)	Vol	(10)	Vol (10) / Forced (20)	(10)	Vol / Vol	(10) / (10)

[1]Vol = Voluntary activity (the rats had constant access to an exercise wheel).

[2]Figures in ( ) represent numbers of animals. The 30 rats showing greatest deviation in activity during the last 4 days of Phase 1 were discarded.

It appears that Steinhaus' conclusion, after reviewing the literature (29), that the pressure effect of exercise stimulates the epiphyses of bones and results in increased linear growth up to an optimal length but excessive and prolonged pressure retards bone growth, is still quite plausible.

METHODS

One-hundred-eighty male Sprague Dawley rats, 25 days old born on the same day were placed in voluntary exercise cages for 7 days. On the basis of the last 4 days of voluntary activity, the 30 animals showing the greatest deviations in activity, low or high, were discarded from the study (phase 1). The remaining 150 animals were matched into 50 trios, according to voluntary activity level, and randomly assigned within trios to one of three initial treatment groups: sedentary, voluntary-exercise, or forced-exercise.

The design shown in Fig. 1 was replicated four times through phase 4 with male animals and once with females. The design was extended through phase 5 only once. The design, laboratory conditions and animal strain were held constant in the replications. This was necessary to obtain a sufficient number of cases where certain measures precluded obtaining others. For example, bone length measures and body composition could not be measured directly on the same animals. Thus, the numbers of cases are different in the various analyses.

In phase 2 which lasted 35 days, animals in the sedentary group were allowed no exercise other than that available in their individual 10 x 8 x 7 inch cages. The rats in the voluntary-exercise group were allowed to run at will in individual 14-inch diameter exercise wheels attached to their living quarters. Each animal in the forced-exercise group could run at will in a voluntary-exercise wheel attached to its cage and also was forced to swim 30 minutes daily in an individual tank of water (35-37°C) with a weight equal to 2 percent of its body weight attached to its tail.

At the end of the initial treatment period (phase 2) when all animals were postpubertal, 10 trios were sacrificed. This represented 10 animals from each group. The remaining 120 animals were placed in voluntary-exercise cages for 160 days (phase 3). At the end of the 160-day voluntary-activity phase, 10 more trios were sacrificed. The 30 remaining trios were randomly divided into two groups as follows: (a) The animals in 10 trios were returned to their initial treatments with the exception of the 10 animals in the forced-exercise group which were maintained in voluntary-exercise cages. (b) Each of the animals in the remaining 20 trios was forced to swim 30 minutes daily with a weight equal to 2 percent of its body weight attached to its tail during phase 4 which lasted for 35 days. At this time the animals in 10 of the trios, which were exercised in phase 4, were sacrificed. The animals in the remaining 20 trios were maintained in voluntary exercise cages for 236 days (phase 5), at which time all of the surviving animals were sacrificed.

After sacrifice by ether anesthesia, the heart, kidneys, spleen, adrenals, liver and testes of each animal were removed and weighed. In most cases, evisceration was completed, the carcass placed in a plastic bag and frozen for subsequent body composition analysis as described by Mickelsen and Anderson (18).

Following phase 2 the right tibia of ten animals from each group was dissected out and the bone length measured by vernier calipers.

Animals in all groups were fed the same prepared ration[1] *ad libitum* and were given free access to water. All rats were handled daily. The lights in the animal room were on for 12 hours and off for 12 hours. Room temperature was maintained between 78 and 83°F.

The data were statistically analyzed using standard t and analysis of variance procedures. The Tukey test was used to determine the significance of difference between means following analysis of variance.

RESULTS
Phase 2

Pre-pubertal exercise impaired the growth of rats. This was evident in the heavier body weights and larger amounts of protein in the bodies of the sedentary animals (Table 1). Mean body and carcass weights of the sedentary animals were significantly heavier than those of the voluntary- and

TABLE I
Body Composition: Phase 2

	Group Means			"F" Value	Signif-icance	Mean Comparison (Tukey)		
	Sedentary (N=20)	Voluntary (N=20)	Forced (N=19)			S vs V	S vs F	V vs F
Body Wt. (gms)	352	310	300	25.4	S	S	S	N
Carcass Wt. (gms)[1]	259	224	217	31.0	S	S	S	N
Carcass Components in %								
Water	64.3	65.7	66.0	21.3	S	S	S	N
Fat	8.5	6.2	5.6	28.3	S	S	S	N
Protein	21.8	22.2	22.4	5.0	S	N	S	N
Ash	4.0	4.3	4.4	25.2	S	S	S	N
In Grams								
Water	166.6	147.4	143.0	24.0	S	S	S	N
Fat	22.0	13.9	12.3	40.5	S	S	S	N
Protein	56.5	49.8	48.6	23.5	S	S	S	N
Ash	10.3	9.8	9.5	3.3	S	N	S	N

S = Significant, $F_{.05}$ = 3.17; N = Not Significant

[1] Carcass weight = Body weight - weight of visceral contents

[1] The percentage composition of this grain ration was: ground corn, 60.7; soybean meal (50% protein), 28.0; alfalfa meal (17% protein), 2.0; fish meal (12.5% protein), 2.5; dried whey (67% lactose), 2.5; limestone (38% Ca), 1.6; dicalcium phosphate (18.5% P, 22-25% Ca), 1.75; iodized salt, 0.5. Supplementary minerals, vitamins and antibiotics were added to provide per kilogram of feed: (in mg) Mn, 121, Fe, 95; Cu 7; Zn, 4; I_2, 4; Co, 2; Choline chloride, 400; Ca pantothenate, 6; riboflavin, 3; niacin, 33; menadione, 2; DL-methionine, 500; penicillin, 2; streptomycin, 8; arsenilic acid, 968; (in ug) vitamin B_{12}, 7; (in international units) vitamin A, 8010; vitamin D_2, 750; vitamin E, 5 (Alpha Tocopherol Powder, Nutritional Biochemicals Corporation, Cleveland).

forced-exercise animals. The relative body components for the two exercised groups were all significantly different from the sedentary group in the expected directions. These results are similar to the earlier observations of Jones, *et al.* (14) and Parizkova (20). Since swimming with 2% of the body weight is but a mild endurance exercise for young animals, the lack of significance between the forced and voluntary groups is not disturbing. In previous work we observed a reduction in voluntary activity when prepubertal rats were forced to exercise. Thus, unless the forced exercise is quite rigorous voluntary and forced-exercise groups tend to be similar.

The absolute body composition results were surprising. In every measure, the values for the sedentary animals were significantly higher. On the basis of *a priori* reasoning one would anticipate that exercise should have enhanced the synthesis of protein and with that increase the total amount of moisture and ash in the carcass. However, these data indicate that exercise significantly impaired protein synthesis and probably the overall growth of the animal.

Two procedures were followed to check these results and their interpretation. In the next replication, following phase 2, the tibias were dissected and their lengths measured by vernier calipers. The tibias in the sedentary animals (Fig. 2) were significantly longer than those of the forced-exercise

FIGURE 2

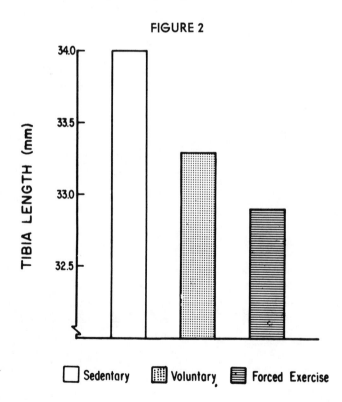

□ Sedentary   ▦ Voluntary   ▤ Forced Exercise

animals ($F = 8.37$; S vs F — Sig.). This was replicated at a later date using female animals from which the femur was dissected and measured. The results were the same ($F = 3.43$; $p = .05$ with S vs F — Sig.) with the

TABLE 2

(Data from Jones et al. Am. J. Physiol. 207:460, 1964)

	Group Means			"F"	Signif-	Mean Comparison (Tukey)		
	Sedentary (N=22)	Exercise (N=20)	Diet (N=22)	Value	icance	D vs E	D vs S	E vs S
Body Wt. (gms)	476	421	422					
Carcass Wt. (gms)	416	364	368	10.6	S	N	S	S
Carcass Components in %								
Water	56.8	62.5	56.6					
Fat	20.4	12.5	21.0					
Protein	18.2	19.8	17.7					
Ash	3.5	4.0	3.6					
In Grams								
Water	235.2	227.7	207.9	7.8	S	S	S	N
Fat	85.6	45.7	77.2	25.2	S	S	N	S
Protein	75.3	72.1	65.2	7.7	S	S	S	N
Ash	14.6	14.3	13.2					

S = Significant, $F_{.05} = 3.15$; N = Not Significant

mean length of the femurs 31.1 and 31.7 mm, respectively, for the forced and sedentary groups (1).

Confirmation of the impairment of growth by physical activity comes from a previous study carried out in this laboratory with 91 day old male Sprague Dawley rats. When the data of that study (14) were recalculated, absolute reductions were found in the amount of protein, water, ash and fat content of the carcasses of the exercised rats as compared with their sedentary controls (Table 2). Although forced exercise did not start in this earlier study until postpuberty and continued with a progressively more intense swimming regimen, body composition data are similar in both studies. In the earlier study, the trend for body components was in the same direction as in the present study, but the moisture and protein values for the sedentary and exercised groups were not significantly different (Table 2). It is interesting, however, that about 80% of the 50 gm carcass weight difference between the exercised and sedentary groups was due to fat.

TABLE 3

Organ Weights: End of Phase 2

	Sedentary (N=20)	Voluntary (N=20)	Forced (N=19)	"F" Value	Significance	S vs V	S vs F	V vs F
	Group Means					*Mean Comparison (Tukey)*		
Relative Weights								
Adrenals ($\times 10^{-3}$)	13.0	16.0	17.4	17.2	S	S	S	N
Heart ($\times 10^{-2}$)	32.6	33.5	35.3	6.1	S	N	S	N
Kidneys ($\times 10^{-2}$)	68.6	69.4	68.2	0.6	N	—	—	—
Spleen ($\times 10^{-2}$)	21.4	21.6	21.9	0.3	N	—	—	—
Testes ($\times 10^{-2}$)	97.5	109.1	113.2	19.0	S	S	S	N
Liver ($\times 10^{-1}$)	45.5	43.6	42.9	1.3	N	—	—	—
Absolute Weight (gms)								
Adrenals ($\times 10^{-2}$)	4.57	4.91	5.20	3.9	S	N	S	N
Heart	1.16	1.04	1.06	7.3	S	S	S	N
Kidneys	2.41	2.15	2.05	17.3	S	S	S	N
Spleen ($\times 10^{-1}$)	7.55	6.69	6.56	6.4	S	S	S	N
Testes	3.42	3.37	3.39	0.2	N	—	—	—
Liver	16.02	13.60	12.91	9.9	S	S	S	N

S = Significant, F $_{.05}$ = 3.17; N = Not Significant

The body composition results in the current investigation (as well as in the Jones, *et al.* data) are in agreement with Parizkova's recent work (20, 22). The body-weight values and bone-length results, however, are different. The discrepancy is likely due to the fact that the sedentary animals in the current study were housed individually whereas Parizkova housed her sedentary animals either in communal cages, where there was considerable physical activity, or in restraining cages, which impose a stress known to affect body weight. The conditions of communal living and restraint in her two control groups could well have affected both the bone growth and total body weight results without distorting body composition data. The results of the current investigation are also contradictory to one of Donaldson's studies (7) but support Price-Jones (23) and Slonaker's (27) results.

The relative and absolute organ weight data for these animals are presented in Table 3. The results were as expected and are similar to other data of this type (1, 10, 17).

Phase 3

The initial treatment period was followed by a period of 160 days of voluntary exercise for all animals. At the end of that voluntary-exercise period, body weights and protein content of the exercised animals were restored to levels equal to those in the sedentary animals (Table 4). Although the differences were not significant, the voluntary and forced-exercise animals had less body fat than the controls.

Although body weight comparisons in Table 4 were not significant, a further analysis was possible on body weight since three additional replications with male animals were completed. This raised the number of cases, for this variable to 39. These means, which are not presented elsewhere in

TABLE 4
Body Composition: End of Phase 2

| | Group Means | | | "F" Value |
	Sedentary (N=10)	Voluntary (N=10)	Forced (N=10)	
Body Wt. (gms)	502	533	490	1.3
Carcass Wt. (gms)	381	407	377	2.4
Carcass Wt. in %				
Water	62.0	62.8	62.3	0.8
Fat	10.1	9.3	9.5	0.5
Protein	23.1	23.5	23.2	2.2
Ash	4.4	4.2	4.6	1.7
In Grams				
Water	235.9	255.4	234.8	3.0
Fat	38.5	37.7	35.9	0.3
Protein	87.7	95.3	87.4	3.7*
Ash	16.9	17.2	17.3	0.1

*Significant, $F_{.05}$ = 3.37; V > S, V > F

TABLE 5
Relative Organ Weights: Before and After Phase 4

							Analysis of Variance		
Treatment I:	Sedentary[1]	Sedentary	Voluntary[1]	Voluntary	Forced[1]	Forced			Groups x Test
Treatment II:		Forced		Forced		Forced	Groups	Test	
			Means as % of Body Weight						
Organs:									
Heart ($\times 10^{-2}$)	28.2	30.3	28.3	32.2	28.6	31.9	7.50*	111.67*	61.67*
Liver ($\times 10^{-1}$)	32.0	31.8	32.3	28.3	31.5	32.0	1.36	2.57	7.00*
Adrenals ($\times 10^{-3}$)	11.93	13.75	11.88	13.86	11.31	14.58	0.28	21.99*	13.22*
Spleen ($\times 10^{-2}$)	14.9	15.8	14.2	14.5	15.3	14.5	1.08	0.00	1.76
Testes ($\times 10^{-2}$)	76.4	79.2	71.6	76.0	72.9	80.0	1.01	4.05*	3.17
Kidneys ($\times 10^{-2}$)	58.9	66.9	60.7	65.7	60.9	65.0	0.16	8.40*	9.20*
N	10	7	10	7	10	11	—	—	—

*P = .05
[1] From sacrifice prior to phase 4

tabular form, were 500 gms for the sedentary group, 514 gms for the voluntary-exercise group and 482 gms for the forced-exercise group. The differences between all groups were significantly different ($F = 63.00$; $V > S > F$). The highest absolute protein weight shown in Table 4 is a reflection of the body weight of the voluntary-exercise group. Although the voluntary-exercise group weighed more and had more protein, there were no differences in the relative protein concentrations. It is clear, however, that the large differences in body composition present following phase 2 were not evident after 160 days of voluntary activity.

The relative organ weights after 160 days of voluntary activity showed no significant differences (Table 5) (all F values < 0.7). Furthermore, none of the differences in absolute weights were significant. Thus the differences in adrenal, heart, and testes weights observed following phase 2 were not evident 160 days later.

Phase 4

Forced exercise (swimming) in the second treatment period increased the relative size of the heart, adrenals, testes and kidneys (Table 5). The increase in heart size as a result of the enforced exercise was greater in the original voluntary- and forced-exercise groups than in the original sedentary group. The significant group x test interaction reflects different responses in heart hypertrophy of the groups in phase 4. Forced exercise resulted in an enlargement of the adrenal glands in all groups, with the group that

TABLE 6

Body Composition: End of Phase 5 (498 days of age)

Group Designations*	S-S (N=8)	S-F (N=6)	V-V (N=6)	V-F (N=5)	F-V (N=8)	F-F (N=5)	F*** Value
Body Wt. (gms)	560	550	590**	530**	555	570	0.56
Carcass Wt. (gms)	440	426	450**	405**	436	433	0.22
Carcass Components in %							
Water	56.4**	59.4**	56.4	58.2	58.2	58.9	0.60
Fat	17.1**	13.6**	17.3	15.3	15.2	15.1	0.43
Protein	21.5	21.8	21.5	21.5	22.0	21.5	0.49
Ash	4.4	4.6	4.2	4.5	4.3	3.9	0.19
In Grams							
Water	248.0	252.2	252.4**	237.0**	254.0	255.1	0.20
Fat	75.4	59.0	80.2	63.2	66.8	65.2	0.49
Protein	94.6	92.6	96.4**	87.7**	96.0	92.8	0.13
Ash	19.3	19.4	18.7	18.5	18.6	17.1	0.23

*S-S The first letter indicates the treatment in the phase 2 and the second letter the treatment in phase 4.

**Statistically significant, "t" comparisons between groups having the same prepubertal experimental treatment.

***F value reflects comparison of the S-S, V-V, and F-V groups not exercised in phase 4.

had been exposed to forced exercise in phase 2 showing the greatest enlargement. Here again the group responses were significantly different. Forced exercise after 160 days of voluntary activity produced larger testes in all groups. As a result of the exercise in phase 4 the kidneys increased in size in all groups. However, the groups responded differently with the greatest hypertrophy in the animals that were sedentary in phase 2 and least in the animals forced to exercise in phase 2. The changes in the size of the adrenals, heart, and testes in the second period of exercise follow the general pattern of the changes seen after phase 2 (Table 2).

Phase 5

The body composition results for all groups in the first replication are presented in Table 6. The animals were sacrificed 236 days following phase 4 at 498 days of age. During this time all animals were housed in individual voluntary exercise cages.

Forced exercise during phase 4 maintained body fat lower and moisture higher in the rats that initially were sedentary (Table 6). Comparable changes in body composition occurred in the groups that were initially subjected to voluntary or forced exercise, but, in these cases, the differences were insignificant. The significant absolute moisture and protein values are a reflection of the body weight difference between the two original voluntary groups. All three groups forced to exercise during phase 4 showed lower mean

TABLE 7

			Group Means				F**
Group Designations	S-S (N=8)	S-F (N=6)	V-V (N=6)	V-F (N=5)	F-V (N=8)	F-F (N=5)	Value
Body Weight	560	550	590*	530*	555	570	0.56
Relative Weights							
Adrenals (x10^{-3})	8.0	10.0	9.1	11.4	10.6	11.9	2.13
Heart (x10^{-2})	30.0	31.0	27.2	31.9	29.3	30.2	0.67
Kidneys (x10^{-2})	59.6	62.9	57.2	65.7	60.0	62.2	0.30
Spleen (x10^{-2})	14.9	17.0	15.0*	20.3*	16.7	19.0	1.18
Testes (x10^{-2})	66.5	66.5	66.0	66.2	72.2	64.2	0.97
Liver (x10^{-1})	32.9	34.5	33.2	37.6	33.0	35.8	0.21
Absolute Weights (gms)							
Adrenals (x10^{-2})	4.97	5.47	5.36	6.05	5.86	6.79	1.41
Heart	1.68	1.71	1.60	1.69	1.62	1.72	0.33
Kidneys	3.35	3.46	3.37	3.48	3.34	3.55	0.02
Spleen (x10^{-1})	8.36	9.33	8.63	10.74	9.22	10.92	0.71
Testes	3.71	3.64	3.77	3.49	3.95	3.71	0.75
Liver	18.41	18.98	19.56	19.91	18.31	20.42	0.44

*P = .05 for t-values between groups having the same original treatment.

**F value reflects comparison of the S-S, V-V, and F-V groups not forced to exercise in phase 4.

carcass weights, but only the difference between the two original voluntary groups was statistically significant. However, the relative protein values are the same for all groups suggesting that absolute protein levels are fairly closely related to carcass weight.

Although the numbers of animals are small, the statistically significant data (i.e. relative moisture and fat in the original sedentary groups and carcass weight in the original voluntary groups) and the consistency of pattern found in the non-significant data indicate that the animals exercised as adults weighed less, were less fat, and also had less absolute protein.

An analysis of variance was run between the three groups (S-S, V-V, and F-V) not forced to exercise during phase 4. There were no statistically significant differences between these groups. However, since the numbers of cases were quite small, conclusions as to whether pre-pubertal exercise has residual effects on body composition must await further research. Since the mean values were consistently in the hypothesized direction (i.e. higher relative moisture and protein, and lower relative fat in the exercised animals), it appears the problem is worth pursuing further.

The relative and absolute mean values for organ weights are presented in Table 7. The three groups forced to exercise in phase 4 were each compared with the group having the same original treatment. Although two t comparisons were significant, body weight and relative spleen weight in the two original voluntary groups, these were only two of 39 total comparisons, and conclusions are not warranted.

Analyses of variance were run on the mean relative and absolute organ weights for the three groups not forced to exercise in phase 4. No conclusions can be drawn from these data as none of the F values were statistically significant and the number of cases quite small. Although some patterns do seem evident in the mean values, conclusions as to whether pre-pubertal exercise has residual effects upon organ sizes must await further investigation.

SUMMARY

One-hundred-fifty male albino rats (Sprague-Dawley strain) were used in each replication of this investigation of the effects of pre-pubertal physical training. At 32 days of age, each animal was assigned to one of three initial treatment groups: sedentary, voluntary exercise, or voluntary plus forced exercise. The pre-pubertal exercise period, in which one group of rats was forced to swim 30 minutes daily, another group permitted voluntary exercise, and the third kept sedentary, lasted 35 days. Following this, some of the animals from each group were sacrificed. The remaining animals then were placed in voluntary activity cages for 160 days. Again, at the end of that period some animals from each group were sacrificed. The remaining animals in each group were divided into two subgroups: one half reverted back to their original experimental condition (except that those original forced-exercise animals were maintained in voluntary-exercise cages), the other half received the forced swimming regimen for 35 days. Following the second training period, several animals from each of the subgroups were sacrificed. The other animals were retained to old age (498 days of age) in voluntary cages.

The forced-exercise animals at puberty had lower body weights, shorter tibias, lower relative fat and greater relative protein, ash and moisture contents than the controls (p = .05). However, the absolute protein, ash, and moisture values were significantly lower in the forced-exercise animals. The absolute body composition values, when considered with the shorter bone lengths in the trained animals, indicate that forced exercise during prepuberty resulted in smaller animals.

When the rats in the various groups were permitted to exercise voluntarily for 160 days following puberty, there was no difference in concentration of body components. As a result of phase 4 significant residual effects of pre-pubertal exercise were noted in that adrenal weights were significantly greater in the animals previously forced to exercise. The increase in kidney weight was greater in the sedentary animals than in the forced exercise animals. Change in heart size was also significant with the least change in sedentary and the greatest in the voluntary exercise animals.

In the old age (498 days of age) no significant differences were found which could be attributed to exercise in phases 2 and 4. The consistency in pattern of the mean values, when considered with the small number of cases used, indicates that further investigation for longitudinal residual effects of exercise is warranted.

REFERENCES

1. Blaustein, S.; Heusner, W. W.; and Van Huss, W. D. "The effects of pre-pubertal exercise upon the growth of long bones in the female rat." (paper in preparation).
2. Brozek, J. (Ed.). *Human Body Composition.* New York: Pergamon Press, 1965.
3. *Body Composition in Animals and Man.* Washington: National Academy of Sciences. Publication 1598, 1968, p. 129.
4. Carrow, R. E.; Brown, R. E.; and Van Huss, W. D. "Fiber sizes and capillary to fiber ratios in skeletal muscle of exercised rats." *Anat. Rec.* 159: 33, 1967.
5. Dickerson, J. W. T. and Widdowson, E. M. "Chemical changes in skeletal muscle during development." *Biochem. J.* 74: 247, 1960.
6. Donaldson, H. H. "On the effects of exercise beginning at different ages on the weight of musculature and of several organs of the albino rat. *Am. J. Anat.* 53: 403, 1933.
7. Donaldson, H. H. "Summary of data for the effects of exercise on the organ weights of the albino rat: comparison with similar data from the dog." *Am. J. Anat.* 56: 57, 1935.
8. Edgerton, R. "Histochemical changes in rat skeletal muscle after exercise." Ph. D. Thesis, Michigan State University, 1968.
9. Fait, H. F. "The physiological effects of strenuous activity upon the immature child." *FIEP Bulletin,* 26: 28, 1956.
10. Hatai, S. "On the influence of exercise on the growth of organs of the albino rat." *Anat. Rec.* 9: 647, 1915.
11. Henrichson, G. J. and Storey, E. "The effect of force on bone and bones." *Angle Orthodont.* 38: 155, 1968.
12. Jokl, E. "Body composition as criterion of physical fitness." In K. Kato (Ed.) *Proc. Int. Cong. Sp. Sci.,* Tokyo, 1964, p. 322.

13. Jokl, E. "Physical activity and body composition, fitness and fatness." *Ann. N. Y. Acad. Sci.* 110: 778, 1963.
14. Jones, E. M.; Montoye, H. J.; Johnson, P. B.; Martin, M. J. M.; Van Huss, W. D.; and Cederquist, D. "Effects of exercise and food restriction on serum cholesterol and liver lipids." *Am. J. Physiol.* 207: 460, 1964.
15. Kato, K. (Ed.) *Proceedings International Congress Sports Sciences,* Tokyo, 1964.
16. Kato, S. and Ishiko, T. "Obstructed growth of long bones due to excessive labor in remote corners." In Kato, K. (Ed.) *Proc. Int. Cong. Sp. Sci.,* Tokyo, 1964, p. 479.
17. Lamb, D.; Van Huss, W. D.; Carrow, R. E.; Heusner, W. W.; Weber, J.; and Kertzer, R. "Effects of pre-pubertal physical training on growth, voluntary exercise cholesterol, and basal metabolism in rats." *Res. Quart.* 40: 123, March 1969.
18. Mickelsen, O. and Anderson, A. A. "A method for preparing intact animals for carcass analysis." *J. Lab. Clin. Med.* 53: 282, 1959.
19. Moore, F. D. Oleson, K. H.; McMurray, J. D.; Parker, H. V.; Ball, M. R.; and Boyden, C. M. *The Body Cell Mass and Its Supporting Environment: Body Composition in Health and Disease.* Philadelphia: W. B. Saunders, 1963.
20. Parizkova, J. "Fat content and lipoprotinase activity in muscles of male rats with increased or reduced motor activity." *Phys. Bohemoslovaia* 15: 237, 1966.
21. ————. "Impact of age, diet and exercise on man's body composition." *Ann. N. Y. Acad. Sci.* 110: 661, 1963.
22. ————. Personal Communication, 1969.
23. Price-Jones, C. "The effect of exercise on the growth of white rats." *Quart. J. Exp. Physiol.* 16: 61, 1926.
24. Rarick, G. L. "Exercise and growth." In W. Johnson (Ed.) *Science and Medicine of Exercise and Sports.* New York: Harper and Bros., 1960, p. 440.
25. Rowe, F. A. "Growth comparisons of athletes and non-athletes." *Res. Quart.* 4: 108, 1933.
26. Saville, P. D. and Smith, R. "Bone density breaking force and leg muscle mass as functions of weight in bipedal rats." *Am. J. Phys. Anthrop.* 25: 35, 1966.
27. Slonaker, J. R. "The effect of a strictly vegetable diet on the spontaneous activity, the rate of growth and longevity of the albino rat." *Stanford University Publications,* April 2, 1912, pp. 1-52.
28. Smith, A. H. and Kelly, C. F. "Influence of chronic acceleration upon growth and body composition." *Ann. N. Y. Acad. Sci.* 110: 410, 1963.
29. Steinhaus, A. H. "Chronic effects of exercise." *Phys. Rev.* 13: 103, 1933.
30. Van Huss, W. D.; Heusner, W. W.; Weber, J.; Lamb, D.; and Carrow, R. E. "The effects of pre-pubertal forced exercise upon post-puberty physical activity, food consumption, and selected physiological and anatomical parameters." *Proc. 1st. Int. Cong. Psych. of Sp.* 1965, p. 734.

Analysis of Selected
Fitness Measures

THE EFFECT OF VELOCITY CHANGES OF SELECTED HEMODYNAMIC PARAMETERS

ROY D. MOORE
North Carolina A & T State University

PURPOSE

The purpose of this study was to determine the relationships between the velocity of the brachial upstroke and several selected hemodynamic parameters. Also, to investigate the changes in the selected hemodynamic parameters after occluding the brachial artery at 80 and 115 millimeters of mercury of pressure.

REVIEW OF LITERATURE

Studies related to the velocity of the upstroke of the brachial artery as revealed by the pulse wave are very meagre. Cureton (5) reviewed the work done with the Cameron Heartometer to measure energy of the heart as shown by the amplitude of the pulse waves. However, no studies were found that investigated the hemodynamic parameter after the cuff pressure was changed.

PROCEDURE

Thirty women subjects participated in an adult fitness program from February through May of 1968. Each person volunteered for this project; therefore this was considered a select sample. The subjects met on Mondays and Thursdays of each week at 7 p.m. Each person was advised to eat a light meal at least two hours before reporting for the fitness program. The average age of the participants was 39.5 years. The mean height and weight were 63.9 inches and 161.2 pounds respectively. Each subject presented an affidavit to the fitness program director at the beginning of the pre-activity tests. The most frequent answer to a health habit questionnaire was a feeling of fatigue, periodic nervousness and short windedness while participating in physical work. Since these factors require more space and time than this project affords, there was no statistical treatment of the data received on the health-questionnaire. The hemodynamic parameters were measured at the brachial artery. The Cameron Heartometer was used at 80 mm of pressure and again at 115 mm of pressure. The data on each subject as measured by the heartometer was the average of three different recordings. Hence, there was no other reliability test administered. Curves were made to show the changes in selected measures between February and May. Multiple prediction analyses were used to ascertain the contribution of the measured factors to velocity of stroke volume as measured by systolic amplitude.

RESULTS

The restriction of the brachial artery at pressures of 80 and 115 millimeters of mercury revealed that no definite trend could be established relative to the selected hemodynamic parameters that were investigated.

The correlation matrix revealed that at 80 mm of pressure there is a significant relationship between velocity of the upstroke and dicrotic notch (.538), diastolic amplitude (.542), diastolic surge (.430), angle of obliquity (−.642), and systolic amplitude − dicrotic notch (.565). The means of the measures at 80 millimeters showed little change from the measures at 115 millimeters.

Multiple prediction analyses of the data collected at 80 mm and 115 mm of pressure indicated that systolic amplitude, time of systolic amplitude, dicrotic notch − systolic amplitude ratio, and dicrotic notch were the largest contributors to velocity of the upstroke of the brachial pulse wave.

Correlation matrix of the data investigated at 115 millimeters of pressure indicated that higher related parameters with velocity of systolic amplitude were diastolic amplitude and systolic amplitude − dicrotic notch ratio.

Multiple prediction analyses of data collected at 115 mm of pressure revealed that systolic amplitude, time of systolic amplitude, dicrotic notch, and systolic amplitude − dicrotic notch ratio were the largest contributors to velocity of the upstroke of the brachial pulse wave.

TABLE I

MEANS OF STANDARD DEVIATIONS OF VARIABLES AT 80 MM AND 115 MM OF PRESSURE

Variable	Unit	80MM of Pressure		115MM of Pressure	
		Means	SD	Mean	SC
Systolic Amplitude	CM	.49	.23	.49	.26
Time of Systolic Amplitude	Sec.	.21	.07	.17	.06
Velocity	CM/Sec	2.65	1.45	2.94	1.49
Fatigue Ratio	CM	.66	.21	2.67	1.11
Dicrotic Notch	CM	.30	.13	.02	.01
Work/Rest	CM	.86	.40	.08	.02
Diastolic Amplitude	CM	.33	.12	.18	.12
Diastolic Surge	CM	.01	.03	.03	.02
Angle of Obliquity	Degree	36.9	9.14	33.1	5.42
Pulse Rate	Beats	78.8	1.18	79.03	1.24
SA-DN	CM	.19	.16	.29	.21
Height	Inch	63.9	1.98	63.9	1.98
Weight	Lbs.	161.2	35.2	161.2	35.2
Age	Year	39.5	8.82	39.5	8.82

DISCUSSION

Table 1 shows the mean and standard deviation of the measured variables at 80 mm and 115 mm of pressure. Time of systolic amplitude revealed a cuff pressure decrease of .04 seconds which may show arterial elasticity. This is significant to health because reduced cholesterol is proportional to increased elasticity. There was no change in the systolic amplitude (.49

cm). This suggests little change in interventricular pressure from 80 to 115 mm of pressure increase in the cuff around the brachial artery. Velocity showed an increase of .29 centimeters per second which reveals a possible factor of arterial distensibility. A faster transmission of the pulse wave is accompanied by a less distensible artery. However, the difference in the fatigue ratio of 1.01 centimeters shows the work response of the heart to the increased pressure on the brachial artery. Diastolic surge and pulse rate, with increases of .02 cm and .23 beats may not give statistical significance, but may have physiological significance in that there appears to be sympathetic response to cuff pressure changes. The systolic amplitude and dicrotic notch difference increased .10 cm upon the cuff pressure change in the measured variables at either 80 or 115 mm of pressure.

This increase in SA - DN should merit further consideration of this variable as a measure of adaptability to stress of the artery.

TABLE 2

CORRELATIONS OF VELOCITY OF SYSTOLIC AMPLITUDE WITH OTHER VARIABLES AT 80 MM OF PRESSURE

Variable	r	.05	.01
Systolic Amplitude	.711	yes	yes
Time of Systolic Amplitude	-.591	yes	yes
Fatigue Ratio	-.324	no	no
Dicrotic Notch	.528	yes	yes
Work/Rest	.083	no	no
Diastolic Amplitude	.542	yes	yes
Diastolic Surge	.430	yes	no
Angle of Obliquity	-.642	yes	yes
Pulse Rate	.124	no	no
SA - DN	.565	yes	yes
Height	-.080	no	no
Weight	-.451	yes	no
Age	-.085	no	no

.396 - $<$.05 Significance
.505 - $<$.01 Significance

Table 2 shows correlations of the velocity of the systolic amplitude with the measured variables at 80 mm of pressure. Systolic amplitude, dicrotic notch, diastolic amplitude, diastolic surge, and systolic amplitude — dicrotic notch were positively related to velocity at the standard cuff pressure of 80 mm. The angle of obliquity was inversely correlated to velocity of systolic amplitude which may reveal quick myocardial action during ejection of blood from the left ventricle.

Table 3 shows correlations of velocity of systolic amplitude with the measured variables at 115 mm Hg. Three variables, systolic amplitude, diastolic amplitude, and SA - DN difference, were positively correlated with systolic amplitude velocity. The stress imposed by such occlusion of the artery is reflected in blunting of the pulse waves.

Table 4 shows no definite trend established relative to systolic amplitude velocity. Curves were made to show the changes in selected measures between February and May. Multiple prediction analyses were used to ascertain the

TABLE 3

CORRELATIONS OF VELOCITY OF SYSTOLIC AMPLITUDE WITH OTHER VARIABLES AT 115 MM OF PRESSURE

		Significance	
Variable	r	.05	.01
Systolic Amplitude	.766	yes	yes
Time of Systolic Amplitude	-.224	no	no
Fatigue Ratio	-.063	no	no
Dicrotic Notch	.381	no	no
Work/Rest	.131	no	no
Diastolic Amplitude	.468	yes	no
Diastolic Surge	.146	no	no
Angle of Obliquity	-.641	yes	yes
Pulse Rate	.259	no	no
SA - DN	.719	yes	yes
Height	.085	no	no
Weight	-.088	no	no
Age	-.114	no	no

.396 < .05 Significance
.505 < .01 Significance

TABLE 4

INTERCORRELATIONS AT 80 MM OF PRESSURE

	1	2	3	4	5	6	7	8	9	10	11	12	13	14
Systolic Amplitude	1.000													
Systolic Amplitude Time	-.803	1.000												
Systolic Amplitude Velocity	-.253	.361	1.000											
Fatigue $\frac{DE}{AB}$	-.641	.766	-.224	1.000										
Dicrotic Notch	-.152	.011	.095	-.063	1.000									
Work to Rest	-.607	.598	.401	.381	.168	1.000								
Diastolic Amplitude	.085	.117	.264	.131	-.105	.151	1.000							
Diastolic Surge	-.689	.668	.385	.469	.191	.856	.071	1.000						
Angle of Obliquity	-.023	.129	.119	.146	-.156	-.378	.138	-.234	1.000					
Pulse Rate	-.109	.064	-.102	.259	-.184	.112	.472	-.102	-.031	1.000				
Systolic Amplitude - Dicrotic Notch	-.623	.882	.201	.719	-.087	.151	.045	.319	.377	.006	1.000			
Height	-.352	.343	.459	.021	.159	.513	-.221	.423	-.093	-.177	.121	1.000		
Weight	.226	-.341	-.328	-.088	.019	-.018	-.130	-.174	-.075	.335	-.392	-.043	1.000	
Age	.096	-.038	.095	-.114	-.099	.159	-.093	.098	-.287	-.187	-.149	.240	.102	1.000

Significance at .05 level = .396
Significance at .01 level = .505

TABLE 5

INTERCORRELATIONS AT 115 MM OF PRESSURE

	1	2	3	4	5	6	7	8	9	10	11	12	13	14
Obliquity	1.000													
SA	.079	1.000												
T/SA	.712	-.591	1.000											
Velocity	-.421	-.089	-.324	1.000										
DE/AB	.729	-.001	.538	.241	1.000									
DN	.397	.298	.083	-.171	.332	1.000								
W/R	.723	-.008	.542	-.120	.751	.385	1.000							
DA	.606	.059	.430	-.424	.258	.126	.263	1.000						
DS	-.795	-.018	-.642	.116	-.776	-.423	-.625	-.349	1.000					
PR	-.078	-.310	.124	-.275	-.283	.329	-.278	.038	.234	1.000				
SA - DN	.820	.110	.565	-.780	.209	.285	.397	.641	-.487	.118	1.000			
Age	-.000	.094	-.079	-.276	-.314	-.261	-.256	.075	.150	.210	.269	1.000		
Height	.751	-.019	-.045	.612	-.207	-.289	-.308	-.172	.436	-.136	-.477	.103	1.000	
Weight	.107	.188	-.085	.166	.224	.094	.226	.236	-.037	-.165	-.050	-.043	.258	1.000

Significance at .05 level = .396   TABLE 6   Significance at .01 level = .505

CAUSAL ANALYSIS AND MULTIPLE REGRESSION
80 MM OF PRESSURE

Variable	B	B_2	$B^2/_\Sigma B^2$	100
Systolic Amplitude	4.1906	18.4607	.1122	11.22
Time of Systolic Amplitude	-11.9821	143.5492	.8702	87.02
Fatigue Ratio	- .7354	.5408	.0033	.33
Dicrotic Notch	- .8769	.7689	.0041	.41
Work/Rest	- .5173	.2676	.0016	.16
Diastolic Amplitude	.3919	.1536	.0009	.09
Diastolic Surge	1.2001	.1440	.0009	.09
Angle of Obliquity	- .0381	.0015	.0002	.02
Pulse Rate	.0090	.0000	.0000	.00
SA - DN	- .9909	1.0711	.0065	.65
Height	- .0340	.0012	.0001	.01
Weight	- .0023	.0000	.0000	.00
Age	- .0006	.0000	.0000	.00
		$\Sigma = 164.9506$		100.00

R = .977   SE = .460

Prediction Equation: $Y = (a + b, X, + b_2 X_2 + b_3 X_3 - - - - b_n + X_m$

Velocity of SA = 7.92 + 4.19 (SA) - 11.98 (T/SA) - .74 $(\frac{DE}{AB})$ - .88 (DN) - .99 (SA-DN)
          80 MM

contribution of the measured factors to velocity of stroke volume as measured by systolic amplitude.

Table 6 reveals that time of systolic amplitude was the strongest factor contributor to velocity of the ejection phase of the pulse wave.

Table 7 shows that four variables reveal relevancy toward the velocity of systolic amplitude, systolic amplitude (31.08), time of systolic amplitude (25.02), dicrotic notch (22.25), and systolic amplitude - dicrotic difference.

TABLE 7

CAUSAL ANALYSIS AND MULTIPLE REGRESSION
115 MM OF PRESSURE

Variable	B	B^2	$B^2/\Sigma B^2$	100
Systolic Amplitude	18.0795	326.8683	.3108	31.08
Time of Systolic Amplitude	-16.2206	263.1079	.2502	25.02
Fatigue Ratio	- .0006	.0000	.0000	00.00
Dicrotic Notch	-15.2964	233.9799	.2225	22.25
Work/Rest	1.1355	1.2894	.0012	00.12
Diastolic Amplitude	4.5988	25.6490	.0243	02.43
Diastolic Surge	4.9407	24.4105	.0233	02.33
Angle of Obliquity	.0153	.0002	.0000	00.00
Pulse Rate	.0084	.0001	.0000	00.00
Sa = DN	-13.2933	176.5118	.1678	16.78
Height	.0085	.0001	.0000	00.00
Weight	.0679	.0046	.0000	00.00
Age	.0003	.0000	.0000	00.00
		1051.8218		100.00

a = -.3 = 8367;   R = .976;   SE = .480

Prediction Equation: $Y = a + b, x, + b_2 x_2 + b_3 x_3 - b_n x_m$

Velocity of SA = 3.84 + 18.08 (SA) - 16.22 (T/SA) - 15.30 (DN)
115 MM

CONCLUSIONS

1. In order to extradite time and computations that may be necessary in order to measure velocity of the upstroke of the brachial pulse wave, the prediction equations with a multiple correlation (R) of 0.977 with S.E. = .460 follow:

Prediction Equations:

1. 80 millimeters of pressure

   Vel. SA = 7.92 + 4.19 (SA) — 11.98 (T/SA) — .74 (DE) — .88 $\left(\dfrac{DN}{AB}\right)$ — 99 (SA - DN)

2. 115 millimeters of pressure

   Vel. SA = 3.84 + 18.08 (SA) — 16.22 (T/SA) — 15.30 (DN) — 13.29 (SA - DN)

RECOMMENDATIONS

1. A study should seek to determine the relationship between velocity of pulse wave and stroke volume.
2. An investigation should be undertaken which would study the relationship between velocity of pulse wave and resistance to blood flow.

REFERENCES

1. Barron, D. H., "The Pressure Gradient and Pulse in the Vascular System," *Medical Physiology and Biophysics* (Ruch and Fulton, editors). Philadelphia: W. B. Saunders Co., 1941.
2. Brawell, V. C., "The Changes in Form of the Pulse Wave in the Course of Transmission," *Heart,* 12: 23, 1925.

3. Crampton, C. W., "The Gravity Resisting Ability of the Circulation: Its Measurement and Significance," *American Journal of Medical Science,* 75: 721-34, November, 1920.
4. Cureton, T. K., *Physical Fitness Appraisal and Guidance.* St. Louis: C. V. Mosby Co., 1947.
5. Cureton, T. K., "Sympathetic Versus Vagus Influence Upon The Contractile Vigor of the Heart," *The Research Quarterly,* 32: 4, 1961.
6. Finkielman, S., et al., "Hemodynamic Pattern in Essential Hypertension," *Circulation,* 31: 360, 1965.
7. Luisada, A. A., (Ed.), *Cardiovascular Function.* New York: McGraw-Hill Co., 1962.
8. Malcolm, J. E., *Blood Pressure Sounds and Their Meanings.* Springfield, Ill., Charles C. Thomas Publishers, 1947.

MEASUREMENTS OF BODY POTASSIUM BY WHOLE-BODY COUNTING AND ITS APPLICATION TO PHYSICAL EDUCATION RESEARCH[1]

HARVEY F. MURPHY
University of North Carolina at Charlotte

T. G. LOHMAN
University of Illinois

LAWRENCE OSCAI
Washington University

MICHAEL POLLOCK
Wake Forest University

ABSTRACT

Body fat estimates based on underwater weighings compared relatively closely with estimates from body potassium, as measured by ^{40}K counting, for adult men, 25 to 45 years of age, who were not engaged in a physical training regimen. The use of age, weight and gluteal girth in addition to body potassium further increased the precision with which body fat, as estimated from underwater weighing, could be predicted. Body fat estimates from skinfold measurements were not as closely related to body fat estimated from underwater weighing. Considerable differences were found in estimation of the change in fat content associated with physical training programs depending on whether skinfold or body ^{40}K measurements were used to estimate body fatness.

INTRODUCTION

Because of the ease with which body potassium can be estimated in human subjects by whole-body ^{40}K counting, and because body potassium is found mainly in the fat-free body, physical educators have become interested in obtaining estimates of body composition from whole-body counting. Other methods commonly used for estimating body composition are underwater weighing and measuring the thickness of skinfolds. Data from underwater weighing and skinfold thicknesses are used to estimate body density from which body fat and fat-free body can be estimated. This study was conducted to compare body fat content as estimated from whole-body ^{40}K counting with fat content as estimated from underwater weighing and skinfold thicknesses.

PROCEDURE

The data collected for this study was taken from three groups (I, II, and III) and their sub-groups. Group I consisted of 76 adult men ranging

---

[1] A joint project of the Department of Physical Education and the Department of Animal Science, University of Illinois, Urbana, Illinois.

TABLE I

Measures of Body Composition in Group I

	Mean	S.D.
Body weight, kg.	79.9	10.0
Body height, cm.	179.8	6.1
Body density, gm./cc.	1.0567	.0156
Body potassium, gm.	172.6	22.4
Age (yrs.)	32.2	6.3
Gluteal girth, cm.	96.6	5.3
Triceps skinfold, cm.	2.00	0.70
Subscapular skinfold, cm.	2.63	0.98
FFBW kg.	64.69	7.87
Body fat (%)[1]	18.39	6.4

[1]Estimated from body density.

in age from 25 years to 45 years (Table 1). The mean age was 32 years. Fat percentages for the group ranged from 6.07 in a 25-year-old man to 34.800 in a 36-year-old man based on estimates from underwater weighing. Total body weight ranged from 56.8 kg. to 108.2 kg. with a mean of 79.7 kg. All 76 subjects were weighed underwater according to the method described by Murphy (7). Underwater weight was used to estimate body density which was subsequently converted to a percentage of body fatness by a densimetric formula (4.570/Body Density − 4.142) (100.00) from Brozek, *et al.* (1).

On the same day skinfolds were measured with a Lange skinfold caliper at the triceps and subscapular sites. The anatomical measurements for these sites are described by Montague (5). Instructions for measurement by Consolazio, *et al.* (3) were followed. Body density was estimated from skinfold regression equations by Pascale, *et al.* (9) using the following equations.

Body Density = 1.0951 − .00202 (triceps, cm)
Body Density = 1.0896 − .00179 (subscapular, cm).

Immediately following the measurement of skinfolds, a 4π liquid scintillation whole-body counter, described by Twardock, *et al.* (11), was used to measure the naturally-occurring potassium-40 gamma radiation of each subject. Subjects were measured for two consecutive counting periods of three minutes each. One three-minute background count was made before entry of the subject into the counter and after exit of the subject from the counter (a total of 6 minutes). Standards of known ^{40}K activity were counted to measure the efficiency of the counter at each counting session.

The fat-free weight was calculated for each subject by the following equation:

Fat-free weight = $\dfrac{\text{Potassium (gms)}}{2.66 \text{ gms K/kg. fat-free wt.}}$

Where:

$$\text{Potassium (gms)} = \left[\frac{\text{Net CPM of Standard on Date of Calibration}}{\text{Net CPM of Standard on Date of Subject Count}}\right]$$

Net subject
count per minute
(CPM)

$$\frac{\text{Subject detection efficiency}}{100} \text{ (Gamma Ray Disintegrations of K/Min./gm)}$$

Where:

$$\text{Net subject CPM} = \left[{}^{40}\text{K} \frac{\text{Total subject}}{\text{Count}-\text{Bkd ct}} \right] + \left[\text{Bkd. Depression/min.}\right]$$
$$\text{6 min.}$$

Where:

Background Depression = dimunition of background counts per minute because of absorption of background gamma rays by the sample = [6.993 (subject wt., kg.) − 58.5]

Where:

Net CPM on date of calibration = efficiency of instrument on date of calibration as measured by counting standards of known ${}^{40}\text{K}$ activity = 94180.

Where:

Net CPM of Standard on date of subject count = counting efficiency of instrument on date of subject count as measured by counting standards of known ${}^{40}\text{K}$ activity.

Where:

Subject detection efficiency = efficiency of the counter for measuring ${}^{40}\text{K}$ gamma radiation in the subject based on a ${}^{40}\text{K}$ phantom calibration curve by Murphy (7) which related efficiency to height and weight = [23.12% − .0447 (wt., kg.) − .0069 (ht., cm)]

Where:

Gamma ray disintegration of K/min./gm. = 180

Where:

Fat-free weight was calculated assuming 2.66 gm. K/kg. fat-free wt. (4)

To convert kilograms of fat-free weight to a percentage of body fatness, the following equation was used:

$$\frac{\text{Total subject body wt., kg} - \text{subject fat-free wt., kg.}}{\text{Total subject body wt., kg.}} \times 100$$

The estimated body fat percentages by skinfold measurements and ${}^{40}\text{K}$ whole-body counting were compared with the estimated body fat percentages obtained from underwater weighing.

To aid in the comparisons, the Pearson-product moment correlation between the results was computed. Also, the difference between the means for paired observations was calculated and the resulting t ratio was used for statistical significance at the .05 level. The data were placed in sub-groups according to age (years) (A = 25-29, B = 30-34, C = 35-39, and D = 40-45) and subjected to the same statistical treatment. Thirty-two subjects were measured twice by each technique within the same week so that reliability coefficients could be obtained.

Group II consisted of subjects engaged in an exercise training study by Pollock (10). The sub-groups were as follows:

A: A group of 10 adult men ranging in age from 28 to 39 years engaged in an intensive 2 days/week exercise training program for 20 weeks. The mean weight was 80.2 kg. with a range from 70.8 kg. to 98.1 kg.

B: A group of 7 adult men ranging in age from 28 to 39 years engaged in an intensive exercise training program of 4 days/week. The mean weight was 79.7 kg. with a range from 67.5 kg. to 107.9 kg.

C: A control group of 7 adult men ranging in age from 24 ιυ 40 years. The mean weight was 73.8 kg. with a range from 59.8 kg. to 87.7 kg.

D: A group of 14 adult men used for obtaining the reliability coefficients of skinfold and body K measurements. Two measurements for each method were taken one week apart. The age range was 27 to 57 years. The mean weight was 80.2 kg. with a range from 66.6 kg. to 95.4 kg.

Group III was comprised of an exercise training group involved in a training study by Oscai (8). These were 14 adult men ranging in age from 26 to 64 years with a mean age of 37. They ranged in weight from 65.8 kg. to 94.1 kg. and the mean weight was 79.5 kg. They were engaged in a vigorous exercise training program of a minimum of 3 days per week for 16 weeks.

For Groups II and III, the subjects were measured for body ^{40}K and for skinfold axilla, mammilla, and triceps at the beginning (T_1) at the middle (T_2) and at the end (T_3) of the training program. An estimate of body density was calculated from the following regression equation by Pascale, et al. (9):

Body Density = 1.0884868 − .007123 (mid-axilla, cm)
− .004834 (mammilla, cm)
− .005513 (triceps, cm)

TABLE 2

Comparison of Calculated Fat Percentages From Underwater Weighting and ^{40}K Counting

N	Age	Mean % Fat, Underwater Weighing	Mean % Fat, ^{40}K Measurement	r	Required t at .05 level	t ratio
76	25-45	18.29	18.55	.88	1.99	0.46
33	25-29	15.89	16.52	.88	2.03	1.46
17	30-34	16.68	16.65	.93	2.12	0.18
14	35-39	22.20	21.20	.76	2.16	0.87
12	40-45	23.22	23.89	.77	2.20	0.48

16 The linear relationship between the two methods is shown in figure 1.

FIGURE I

The Relationship Between Fat Percentage Calculated from Body Density and Fat Percentages Calculated from Body Potassium

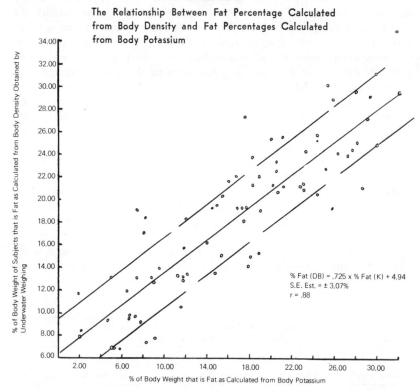

% Fat (DB) = .725 x % Fat (K) + 4.94
S.E. Est. = ± 3.07%
r = .88

The estimate of body density was converted to a percentage of body fatness by the regression equation of Brozek, *et al*. (1) previously described and compared with the estimates of fatness based on body potassium.

RESULTS AND DISCUSSION

Similar results were found for estimates of body fatness by underwater weighing and by whole-body ^{40}K counting (Table 2 and Figure 1).

A multiple correlation of .90 was found by including age, weight, gluteal girth and body potassium in a multiple regression analysis (Table 3). Body fat content was predicted with a standard error of estimate of 2.79%. From the partial regression coefficients (all significant at the .05 level), it was found that, holding body potassium constant, the addition of each kg. of weight, each year of age and each cm. of gluteal girth resulted in .5, .2, and .3 increase in percent body fat. These results suggest that while body K content accounts for much of the variation in body fatness as estimated by body density, other measures of body size in addition to potassium may add further precision to prediction of fat content. The weight of fat-free body was also predicted from the four independent variables. The regression coefficients indicate that, holding body K constant, fat-free body weight decreases with increasing age and gluteal girth.

Both body density and whole-body potassium were measured on two separate occasions within a week for each of 32 subjects to estimate the measurement errors of each method. The reliability coefficients and standard errors of estimate are shown in Table 4. From these results, a coefficient of variation [(standard error of estimate/mean) x 100] of 3.1% was found for body density and 2.8% for body potassium on the basis of one measurement for each method.

A similar study of body fat estimates from underwater weighing and whole-body potassium counting was conducted by Myhre and Kessler (6). Their subjects ranged in age from 15 to 87 years. A correlation coefficient between methods of .87 was obtained. Mean differences between methods in estimated body fat content were statistically significant at the .05 level for all age groups (15-87, 15-17, 18-23, 24-38, 40-48, 50-58, and 60-87). In contrast to the results of Myhre and Kessler where 82 of 100 subjects had higher body fat contents based on body potassium than based on body density, only half of our subjects showed higher body fat contents as estimated from measurement of body potassium. The studies differed in three important aspects: 1) residual lung volumes where estimated by the nitrogen washout method in the study of Myhre and Kessler and from vital capacity measured with a vitalometer in our study; 2) body potassium was estimated from

TABLE 3

**Estimation of Fat Content and Fat-free Body Weight
from Multiple Regression Analysis**

Independent variable	Dependent Variables			
	Percent body fat		Fat-free body weight (kg.)	
	Regression coeff.	Error	Regression coeff.	Error
Body potassium (gm.)	-.259*	.026	.217*	.021
Body weight (kg.)	.527*	.098	.379*	.079
Age (yr.)	.235*	.059	-.157*	.048
Gluteal girth (cm.)	.306*	.149	-.248*	.121
Constant term	-16.0		26.0	
Multiple correlation	.904		.960	
Standard error of estimate	2.79		2.27	

*P < .05

TABLE 4

Reliability Coefficients for Body Density and Potassium

Measurement	r	Standard Error of Estimate
Body density (gm./cc.)	.965	.0047
Body potassium (gm.)	.955	7.1

^{40}K count using a
^{42}K calibration to relate subject detection efficiency to
body weight in their study and a ^{40}K phantom calibration in our study,

TABLE 5

Comparison of Calculated Fat Percentages from
Underwater Weighing and Triceps Skinfolds

N	Age	% Fat Underwater Weighing	% Fat Triceps	r	Required t at .05 level	t ratio
76	25-45	18.28	20.25	.58	1.99	3.00
33	25-29	15.67	20.25	.64	2.03	5.01
17	30-34	16.05	18.70	.64	2.12	1.43
14	35-39	22.26	21.19	.42	2.16	0.82
12	40-45	22.94	22.26	.66	2.20	0.71

TABLE 6

Comparisons of Body Fat Content Derived from
Skinfold and Potassium Measurements

Group and Test Period	% Fat (Skinfold) $\bar{x}$	% Fat (^{40}K) $\bar{x}$	r	t ratio
Group II A (N = 10)				
T_1	16.87	24.34	.74	4.70**
T_2	18.93	21.25	.79	1.42
T_3	18.26	22.40	.86	3.55**
B (N = 7)				
T_1	18.11	23.52	.87	2.88*
T_2	18.76	21.21	.87	1.59
T_3	16.98	21.13	.84	1.83
C (N = 7)				
T_1	17.15	22.47	.83	3.96*
T_3	17.91	23.20	.94	5.91**
D (N = 14)				
T_1	17.49	18.68	.78	0.75
T_2	17.68	20.76	.70	2.37*
Group III (N = 14)				
T_1	21.71	23.72	.73	1.69
T_2	21.29	24.71	.64	2.45*
T_3	19.25	25.02	.84	5.49**

*P < .05
**P < .01

and 3) the subjects of Myhre and Kessler's study were more variable in weight and age.

From a comparison of body fat percentages calculated from the triceps skinfolds and body fat percentages calculated from underwater weights, it was found that less than half of the variation in body fat (underwater weights) was accounted for by the triceps measurement both within age groups and for the total sample (Table 5). In addition, the triceps method significantly (.05 level) overestimated body fat content in two of four age groups. The use of sub-scapular skinfold instead of triceps to estimate body fatness produced an overall correlation of .49 with underwater weighing. All groups reflected statistically different means between methods at the .10 level.

From the comparisons of ^{40}K counting and skinfolds for Groups II and III, different amounts of body fat were found between methods within subgroups (Table 6). In all cases a lower amount of body fat was found based on skinfold measurements. Although the relation between the two methods is comparatively close within each subgroup, the fat content changed significantly between treatments (test period) five times based on skinfold measurement where no significant change was found based on body potassium and three times based on body potassium with no significant change in skinfolds (Table 7). These results indicate that the two methods yield different results in estimating change in body fat associated with physical training programs.

TABLE 7

Change in Body Fat Content Associated with Physical Training

Group II	Test	Change in Fat Content (skinfold)	t Score	Change in Fat Content (^{40}K)	t ratio
A	T_1-T_2	-2.06	-2.15	3.09	3.39**
	T_2-T_3	0.67	1.47	-1.15	-1.22
	T_1-T_3	-1.39	-1.63	1.94	3.74**
B	T_1-T_2	-0.65	-1.27	2.31	2.60*
	T_2-T_3	1.78	4.89**	0.08	0.09
	T_1-T_3	1.13	2.93*	2.39	2.53
C	T_1-T_3	-0.76	-1.27	- .73	- .66
D	T_1-T_2	-0.19	-0.56	-1.08	1.45
Group III					
	T_1-T_2	0.42	6.24**	- .99	-1.21
	T_2-T_3	2.04	5.55**	- .31	-0.31
	T_1-T_3	2.46	6.57**	-1.30	-1.58

*P < .05

**P < .01

REFERENCES

1. Brozek, Josef; Grande, Francisco; Anderson, Joseph T.; and Keys, Ancel. Densiometric analysis of body composition: revision of some quantitative assumptions. In Harold E. Whipple (Ed.), *Body composition, part 1, annals of the New York Academy of Sciences.* 110: 113-140, New York, N. Y.: The Academy, 1963.
2. Buskirk, Elsworth R. Underwater Weighing and Body Density. In Josef Brozek and Austin Henschel (Ed.), *Techniques for measuring body composition.* Washington, D.C.: National Academy of Sciences—National Research Council, 1961.
3. Consolazio, C. Frank; Johnson, Robert E.; and Pecora, Louis J. *Physiological measurements of metabolic functions in man.* New York: McGraw-Hill, 1963.
4. Forbes, G. B. and Lewis, A. M. Total sodium, potassium and chloride in adult man. *J. Clin. Invest.* 35: 596, 1956.
5. Montague, Ashley. *A handbook of anthropometry.* Springfield, Illinois: C. C. Thomas, 1964.
6. Myhre, L. G. and Kessler, W. V. Body density and potassium-40 measurements of body composition as related to age. *J. of Applied Physiology* 21: 1251-55, 1966.
7. Murphy, Harvey F. *A comparison of techniques for estimating the amount of fat in the human body.* Unpublished doctoral dissertation, Univeristy of Illinois, 1967.
8. Oscai, Lawrence. *Effects of training on blood volume.* Unpublished doctoral dissertation, University of Illinois, 1967.
9. Pascale, Luke R.; Grossman, Morton I.; Sloane, Harry S.; and Frankel, Toby. Correlations between thickness of skinfolds and body density in 88 soldiers. *Human Biology* 28: 165-176, 1956.
10. Pollock, Michael L. *Effects of frequency of training on working capacity, body composition, and circulo-respiratory measures.* Unpublished doctoral dissertation, University of Illinois, 1967.
11. Twardock, A. R.; Lohman, T. G.; Smith, G. S.; and Breidenstein, B. C. The Illinois Animal Science Counter: performance characteristics and animal radioactivity measurement procedures. *J. of Animal Science,* 25: 1209-17, 1966.
12. Yuhasz, Michael S. *The effects of sports training on body fat in man with predictions of optimal body weight.* Unpublished doctoral dissertation, University of Illinois, 1955.

DAILY VARIABILITY OF A THREE-MINUTE WORK TEST

ROBERT D. LIVERMAN
Illinois State University

ABSTRACT

This study was designed to investigate variability of the three-minute step test administered on five consecutive days. Thirty-one students at Temple University ranging from 18 to 38 years of age volunteered as subjects for this study. Fifteen males and seven females served as experimental subjects while six males and three females served as control subjects. The experimental subjects were tested on five consecutive days, Monday through Friday. The control subjects were tested on Monday and Friday only. The subjects stepped up and down on an 18 inch bench for three minutes at the rate of 30 trips per minute for the males, and 24 trips per minute for the females. The test score was the sum of three recovery pulse counts. A reliability coefficient of 0.86 for the five test days was estimated from the analysis of variance. The experimental group mean values for the five days of testing demonstrated a progressive decline in the total of the three recovery pulse rates. Dunnett's test showed the mean values at the fourth and fifth days were significantly different from the values at the first day at the .05 level. The analysis of covariance showed that the experimental group did not have a significantly greater change from the first to fifth day than did the control group.

INTRODUCTION

The validity of the results of any study on the effects of a training program on cardiovascular condition as measured by an accepted test depends, partly, on the stability of the test scores. If the test scores are not stable, the measurement of change in the scores from the beginning to the end of the study would not be valid. The common procedure for determining the stability of the test scores is to compute the reliability coefficients by the test-retest method. A high reliability would then indicate that the test scores are stable and any change which takes place is due primarily to the experimental treatment if other factors are accounted for by including a control group.

One factor, however, which is not considered is the effect of becoming familiar with the testing procedures and the test itself. Although the test-retest procedure for determining reliability has been established, it does not take into account possible systematic changes in test scores on succeeding trials. This can be accomplished by the analysis of variance intraclass correlation model, allowing for a trend effect (7). If the trend effect is not subtracted out from the total variance, systematic trial-to-trial variance will affect reliability estimates by tending to lower them (3). It is quite possible that just repeating a test on successive days will result in a systematic change

235

in the test scores due to the subjects becoming familiar with the test and be unrelated to any real change in cardiovascular condition.

In a study of the fatigue effects of taking an efficiency test for college women on five consecutive days, Scott and Matthews (4) concluded that "there is no evidence of lasting or excessively severe fatigue from any of the activities studied." The activities in this study, however, were very simple in nature and very moderate in intensity. In addition the conclusion was based on the close agreement of the test-retest reliabilities for the first day vs. the second day, the second day vs. the third day, the third day vs. the fourth day and the fourth day vs. the fifth day. This procedure did not take into account any systematic effect that might occur due to the repeated tests. That systematic error may occur has been shown in a recent study by Blair and Vincent (1). They found that resting pulse rate before and recovery pulse rates at 30-second intervals during a two-minute period following a six-minute ride on a bicycle ergometer significantly decreased over five days of testing. Young (8), however, found that a four-week program of bench-stepping five-minutes a day five days a week had no significant effect on oxygen up-take, pulse rates and blood pressures taken before, during and after a five-minute ride on a bicycle ergometer. This would support the theory that any systematic change in test scores on repeated trials is due to the subjects' familiarity with the test.

PURPOSE

This study was designed to investigate the variability of the three-minute step test when it is administered on five consecutive days, in terms of 1) the reliability of the test, and 2) the effects of repeated trials. The major concern of the study is the variability of sum of three recovery pulse counts.

PROCEDURES

Thirty-one students at Temple University ranging from 18 to 38 years of age volunteered as subjects for this study. Fifteen males and seven females served as experimental subjects while six males and three females served as control subjects. The subjects were normally active but none were engaged in a training program.

The experimental subjects were tested on five consecutive days, Monday through Friday. The control subjects were tested on Monday and Friday only. The time of the day for the testing was between 7 a.m. and 12 noon. For the test, the subjects stepped up and down on an 18 inch bench for three minutes. The rate for the male subjects was 30 trips per minute as suggested by Van Huss, *et al.* (6). The rate for the female subjects was 24 trips per minute as recommended by Skubic and Hodgkins (5). The test was scored on the basis of the sum of three, 30-second pulse counts taken at one, two, and three minutes following the termination of stepping.

In an attempt to further evaluate the outcome of the test some additional information was collected. Heart rates were recorded at rest and during exercise, and oxygen consumption was measured by the Collins Respirometer at rest, during exercise, and during recovery so that the energy cost of the test could be determined.

The procedure was to have the subjects rest for 10 minutes while the electrodes were being attached and then rest for an additional 10 minutes while resting oxygen intake and heart rate were being recorded. The subjects then stepped for three minutes with oxygen consumption and heart rate being recorded. Immediately following the exercise the recovery oxygen consumption and heart rate were recorded for 10 minutes.

RESULTS AND DISCUSSIONS

The data for the experimental subjects were analyzed by the analysis of variance for repeated measures (7). In addition to the traditional test-retest method, reliability coefficients were estimated from the analysis of variance as suggested by Winer (7). The estimated reliability coefficient is an estimation of the average intercorrelation of all test days and is computed from the analysis of variance information. Dunnett's Test (2) was used to compare the mean values of the first day with the mean values of the following four days. The analysis of covariance was used to determine whether or not the experimental group had a significantly greater change than the control group over the five day period.

The test-retest reliability coefficients and estimated reliability coefficients

TABLE I

**RELIABILITY COEFFICIENTS OF TEST SCORES
FOR THE EXPERIMENTAL GROUP**

N = 22

Variable	Test-Retest T_1 VS T_2	Estimated Reliabilities Avg. Inter Corr.
Resting Heart Rate	.839	.781
Peak Heart Rate	.865	.887
Total of Recovery	.846	.864
Caloric Cost	.650	.504

are shown in Table 1. The total of the three recovery pulse counts demonstrated the least variability in coefficients with an increase from 0.846 for the test-retest method to 0.864 for the estimated coefficient. This would indicate that this measure is reliable and that the reliability is stable over five consecutive days. Except for caloric cost of the exercise, the rest of the measurements studied showed adequate reliabilities for cardiovascular variables. The low reliabilities for the caloric cost of the exercise were probably due to the use of the closed system method rather than the variable itself.

A comparison of the experimental group mean values for the five days of testing showed a progressive decline in the total of the three recovery pulse counts (Figure 1). The mean values for the five days were 166.0, 161.9,

TABLE 2

MEAN SCORES FOR THE FIVE TEST DAYS

Variables	Monday	Tuesday	Wednesday	Thursday	Friday
Resting Heart Rate					
Experimental Group	70.6	70.9	71.2	69.6	69.5
Control Group	71.3				74.3
Exercise-Peak Heart Rate					
Experimental Group	172.9	171.5	172.1	171.3	169.8
Control Group	171.6				171.6
Total of Three Recovery Counts					
Experimental Group	166.0	161.9	161.8	157.9	156.7
Control Group	169.6				168.2
Calorie Cost/Hr./M^2					
Experimental Group	384.5	393.4	378.2	370.4	372.1
Control Group	414.0				401.8

161.8, 157.9 and 156.7, respectively (Table 2). The Dunnett Test showed that the values for the fourth and fifth days were both significantly different at the .05 level from the first day.

In order to determine whether or not the change from Monday to Friday could be attributed to the effects of repeating the test over the five consecutive days, a comparison with the control group was made by analysis of covariance. The results of the analysis showed that the experimental group did not have a significantly greater decrease in the total of the three pulse counts than the control group. This would tend to discount any effect due to the repeated testing. When one considers, however, that the adjusted mean difference of 8.33 beats was just slightly less than the significant decrease of 9.27 beats of the experimental group from Monday to Friday and that the experimental group showed a steady decrease from Monday to Friday, it would appear that the repeated testing does have some systematic rather than random effect on the test scores.

The changes over the five day period for resting heart rate, peak heart rate and caloric cost can be seen in Figures 2 through 4. The analysis of variance for these variables indicated that there were no significant changes. The analysis of covariance also indicated no significant differences between the experimental and control groups in mean changes.

The results would indicate, therefore, that any treatment effect which

FIGURE 1

TOTAL OF THREE RECOVERY PULSE COUNTS — MEAN RAW SCORE CHANGES FROM MONDAY

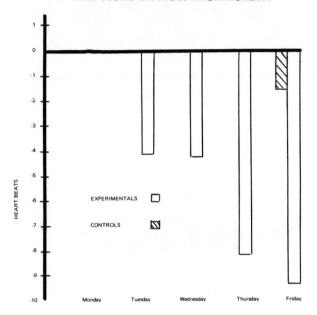

FIGURE 2

RESTING HEART RATE — MEAN RAW SCORE CHANGES FROM MONDAY

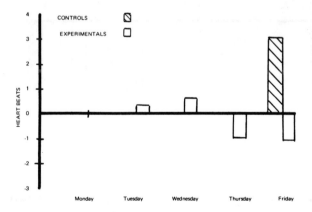

FIGURE 3

PEAK HEART RATE — MEAN RAW SCORE CHANGES FROM MONDAY

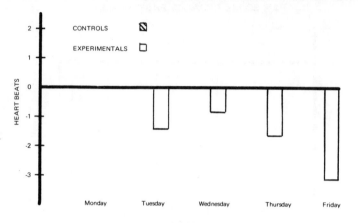

FIGURE 4

CALORIE COST OF THE EXERCISE — MEAN RAW SCORE CHANGES FROM MONDAY

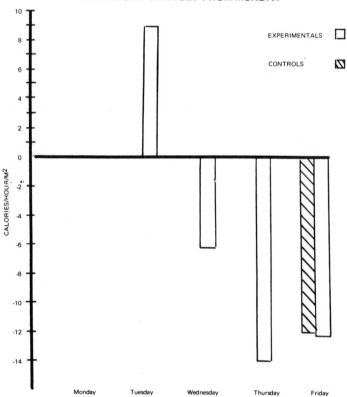

took place was due to the subjects becoming familiar with the test rather than any change in physiological functioning due to training. It would also appear that the most sensitive variable to a systematic change was the total of the three recovery pulse counts.

CONCLUSIONS

Based on the results of this study, the following conclusions have been made:

1. When given on five consecutive days the three-minute step test shows little inter-individual variability in that it has a high estimated reliability.
2. There is considerable intra-individual variability in the test since there is a progressive improvement in the test scores.

REFERENCES

1. Blair, Steven and Vincent, Murray. The effect of laboratory environment on selected cardiovascular parameters. A paper presented at the AAHPER Convention, Boston, April 14, 1969.
2. Edwards, Allen L. *Experimental design in psychological research.* New York: Rinehart and Company, Inc., 1960.
3. Liba, Marie. A trend test as preliminary to reliability estimation. *Res. Quart.* 33: 245-48, 1962.
4. Scott, Gladys and Matthews, Helen. A study of fatigue effects induced by an efficiency test for college women. *Res. Quart.* 20: 134-41, 1949.
5. Skubic, Vera and Hodgkins, Jean. Cardiovascular efficiency test for girls and women. *Res. Quart.* 34: 191-98, 1963.
6. Van Huss, Wayne, and others. *Physical activity in modern living.* Englewood Cliffs, N. J.: Prentice-Hall, Inc., 1960.
7. Winer, B. J. *Statistical principles in experimental design.* New York: McGraw-Hill Book Company, 1962.
8. Young, William P. *The effect of a step-up exercise program upon selected circulo-respiratory functions.* Unpublished master's thesis, East Stroudsburg State College, East Stroudsburg, Pennsylvania, 1965.

PHYSICAL WORKING CAPACITY OF MALES AS ASSESSED BY BICYCLE ERGOMETRY*

EUGENE V. DOROSCHUK

Université Laval

ABSTRACT

After a survey of the methods of evaluating the physical working capacity, the bicycle ergometry techniques according to Holmgren (Wahlund, Sjöstrand), Åstrand, Müller, Holman, Binkhorts and Leowven were selected and compared. An analysis of variance of the work capacities resulting from all tests showed that the differences are large enough to prevent "cross-prediction" of work capacity from one test to another. The relationships between the increases in work-load, heart rate and oxygen consumption on one progressive method using a constant load Lanooy bicycle ($N = 19$) was compared to the same parameters on two progressive work-load tests involving the step test.

INTRODUCTION

Cardio-respiratory fitness measurement is based on studies which evolved from the pioneer work of A. V. Hill and his associates (24-26). The work of Margaria, *et al.* (40), Robinson (50), Taylor (57) and Cureton (19) followed. Tests of cardio-respiratory function, especially in the measurement of oxygen intake and oxygen debt were derived from these studies, as well as others by Åstrand (7), Balke (11), Mitchell, *et al.* (41) and Buskirk and Taylor (17). It is generally accepted that maximal oxygen intake is one of the best measures of an individual's capacity to perform work (8, 51, 58), and an attempt to find a substitute for this measurement is still continuing. A large variety of methods for determining maximal oxygen intake have evolved, although as Buskirk (18) has recently stated, "the term maximal oxygen intake is misleading because 'maximal' can only refer to that value of oxygen intake achieved under specified experimental conditions."

REVIEW OF METHODS OF ASSESSMENT OF WORK CAPACITY

Three methods are currently in widespread use in the assessment of working capacity: (1) treadmill, (2) bicycle ergometer, and (3) step test. There is no best test instrument for the measurement of work capacity. Each test has its advantages and disadvantages — these should be carefully considered before a method is selected.

Treadmill

The treadmill is usually accepted as the best laboratory instrument for measurement of work capacity (e.g., The International Biological Program Manual listed the methods in this order of preference: treadmill, bicycle

*This study was supported in part by a grant from the Fitness and Amateur Sport Directorate, Ottawa, Canada.

243

ergometer, and step test). It presents the subject with a unique experience of walking on a moving belt resulting in more subject apprehension than with the bicycle or step bench; therefore, training to walk on the treadmill is a definite necessity before objective tests can be carried out. Proponents of the use of the treadmill for analysis of work capacity have stated that its advantages include:

1. It is a standard laboratory instrument whose construction principle varies little from laboratory to laboratory.
2. Work can be more exactly reproduced since speed is independent of the subject's efforts (21).
3. A larger mass of muscles and support of the body weight are involved.
4. Walking is a more common activity than cycling.
5. With modern instrumentation, determinations which can be made on the bicycle can usually be made on the treadmill.
6. Hydrostatic changes of blood distribution should be included in evaluation of working capacity.

Bicycle Ergometer

Bicycle ergometry is presently gaining wide acceptance in the measurement of both working capacity and oxygen consumption. An excellent survey of the literature prior to 1948 is given by Wahlund (61). The early work was involved mainly with elucidating the relationships among various physiological variables such as pulse rate, oxygen intake, cardiac output, ventilation, etc. This search for physiological relationships also extended to a search for an ideal bicycle ergometer. Thus, we have various types of bicycles described in the literature, including: (1) friction braked (46, 60, 64), (2) eddy current braked (12, 34, 36), (3) dynamo braked (32, 33), (4) oil pump braked (20), (5) magnetized d-c generator (30), and (6) hyperbolic ergometer (1, 35). Although claims made for bicycle ergometry are reproducibility and universality of results, Lanooy (35) and Aitkins (1) have pointed out the errors in these assumptions. The two main sources of error in bicycle ergometry are from friction and changes of speed. All the principal types of bicycle ergometers suffer from the changes in loading, that follows a change in pedal r.p.m. The Holmgren bicycle (30) is a recent development in which working load is kept constant independent of pedalling rate. Both Lanooy and Aitkins, who have developed accurate constant work rate ergometers, state that r.p.m. must also be constant. A five percent change in speed, common at higher rates of work, would involve more than four percent error for friction and more than eight percent error for electromagnetic brake type machines at 1,000 ft lbs/min.

German Methods — One of the earliest attempts at developing a work capacity test was the work of Müller and Gross-Lordemann (22, 42, 43, 44, 45, 47, 48). A high correlation was shown between logarithmic values of work load and maximal performance. Performance time, according to this method, increases in a predictable way as the work load is lowered. The maximal physical working capacity is then defined as the maximal work intensity for a certain type of work which can be maintained for a certain period of time. Small changes in maximal physical working capacity will correspond to large changes in maximal performance time provided the work intensity is kept constant.

Another early work test, called the Amplitudon Puls Frequenz, was proposed by Lehman and Michailis (37). This test consists of measuring pulse rate and pulse amplitude in response to rapidly increasing load. The working time until the product of these two variables becomes 10,000 is the criterion of working capacity — a longer time indicating a greater capacity. In a comparative study of various tests (23), this test was found to be more highly related to maximal oxygen intake criterion than was Müller's (47) Leistungs-Pulsindex method of steadily increasing work load from 0 to 600 kpm/min during a 10 minute period.

Another method is described by Karrasch and Müller (31) and Nöcker and Böhlau (49). This Arbeitspulsummen (erholungspulssumme, gesamt-pulssumme) consists of various additions of pulse rates during and after a load of 5 kpm/sec for 10 minutes. These methods are compared in two recent studies of work capacity of children and youth by Rutenfranz and his co-workers (52, 53). They conclude that the Leistungspulsindex and Puls-summe method both yield valid and comparable results. They questioned the amplituden-frequenzproduct as a good method for children and stated that the Puls frequenz nach Arbeitsende was least valid of all methods. Working Capacity (PWC 170) of Wahlund (61) is highly related to the Leistungspulsindex, as shown in the following correlation matrix:

TABLE I
Correlation Matrix for Selected Tests of Physical Working Capacity

	2	3	4	5	6
1. LPI	.68	.69	.69	.44	− .47
2. PWC 170		.71	− .61	− .49	.64
3. APS			.86	.66	− .56
4. GPS				·82	− .55
5. EPS					− .30
6. AFP					

Holman (27) described another test which consists of three minute loads of increasing intensities to a total of 24 minutes. Beginning at three mks (9.82 watts = one mks), there is an increase by four mks (two for children) until pulse rate of 180 is reached with continuous oxygen intake and other cardiovascular measures being taken.

Dutch Methods — The Lanooy bicycle ergometer (35) was used by Binkhorts and Leowven (14) for two rapid methods for determination of aerobic capacity. One method consists of continuously increasing the load with work starting at 0 watts and continuing to a point of exhaustion. The second method consists of a continuously increasing load but work is started after a warming-up period with a load at which the pulse rate was 140-150 beats/min and maintained until exhaustion. They concluded that it was possible to measure aerobic capacity in a single session with a continuously increasing load. The continuously increasing load was also used by Bink (13) and Bonjer (15, 16). Bink used "physical working capacity" to refer to the energy expenditure that can be maintained throughout the working time by an individual with a given aerobic capacity. He expressed the relationship between physical working capacity and the logarithm of working time as follows:

$$A = \frac{\log 5700 - \log 5}{3.1} \times a \text{ kcal/min}$$

where
A = physical working capacity in kcal/min
t = working time
a = aerobic capacity in kcal/min

Scandinavian Methods — Three methods of measuring work capacity (referred to by the name of the originator or principal proponent) have evolved. The Anderson method (2) consists of three six-minute loads of increasing intensity. Oxygen intake values are determined for each load. In succeeding tests the loads are increased (i.e., a 300-600-900 kpm series would become a 400-700-1000 kpm) until maximal oxygen intake is reached and the oxygen intake curve levels off. This method requires at least two and sometimes three working sessions, as well as high motivation by the subjects.

The Åstrand-Rhyming work (4, 5, 6, 54) resulted in the development of a nomogram for calculation of aerobic capacity from pulse rate during submaximal work (9). Values of heart rate and oxygen consumption of healthy well-trained men and women, 20-30 years of age, were used for this development. The use of submaximal work on bicycle, treadmill or step test of five to six minutes duration is suggested with best results occurring when heart rate is at steady state between 125 and 170 beats/min. Both Åstrand and his wife have measured maximal oxygen intake directly in their research. In a recent study, I. Åstrand, *et al.* (3) used three work loads — 300, 600, and 900 kpm for seven minutes each with 10 minutes rest between loads. Åstrand and Saltin (10) have compared oxygen consumption in various types of cycling and sports activities. They have also studied (10) the oxygen uptake during the first minutes of heavy muscular exercise concluding that aerobic capacity can be measured in a work test of from a few up to eight minutes duration, the severity of the work determining the actual work time necessary.

A third method was first suggested by Sjöstrand (55) and has been studied extensively by Wahlund (61). The test, as described by Wahlund, consists of work on a Krogh bicycle ergometer at a pedalling rate of approximately 60 r.p.m. The work consists of an uninterrupted series of loads beginning with 300 or 600 kgm/min and increasing at approximately every 6½ minutes by 300 kgm/min until the subject cannot go any longer or until work at 1200 kgm/min is accomplished (although some subjects were tested at 1500 and 1800 kgm/min). Pulse rates were determined for 30 sec from the beginning of the third, fifth and seventh minutes of each load. Ventilation and oxygen consumption were determined for 2½ minutes from the fourth minute of each work load.

With the development of a constant work load bicycle by Holmgren and Mattson (30), work capacity came to be defined as the intensity of work (kgm/min) that is performed at a frequency of 170 beats/min (29). It is obtained by inter- or extrapolation to pulse 170 using the pulse frequency after six minutes at each of two or three loads and the *approximate* linear relationship between pulse frequency and work load. In cases where relative steady state of pulse frequency is not reached in six minutes (i.e., pulse rate increases more than 10 beats) work capacity is obtained by inter- or extrapolation to 160, provided a final pulse frequency of 150 beats/min or more is reached. Holmgren pointed out that patients often could not work up to pulse rates as high as 170.

Linderholm (38) has stated that work capacity is not, as a rule, limited by muscular strength, but by the ability of the body to transport oxygen to the muscles. In normal subjects, cardiac output is the limiting factor for oxygen transport and therefore the major determinant of work capacity. Holmgren (28) has stated that the ability to perform work in a steady state is mainly dependent on the oxygen transport capacity of the body, and it is generally assumed that this is normally limited by circulation and not by lung function (although muscular limitation cannot be excluded). The finding (56) that in younger ages the most usual reason for breaking off the test was fatigue in the legs and in higher ages dyspnea has led to a new interest in the measurement of muscular strength in evaluation of working capacity (59).

Advantages — The proponents of the bicycle ergometer state that its advantages include the following: (61)

1. A practical apparatus, taking up small space and being easy to handle.
2. A large number of muscles are involved.
3. Oxygen consumption is directly related to work load and the mechanical efficiency shows comparatively slight differences.
4. It is possible to make a direct comparison between different subjects at different loads as there are few extra movements not taking part in the production of the work output.
5. Various determinations are easily made during work.
6. Hydrostatic changes of blood distribution may be expected to play a comparatively minor role.

Step Test

The continued use of various step tests is pragmatic evidence of the advantages of this method, which include:

1. It is the cheapest and most practical of all methods of testing working capacity.
2. A larger number of muscles are involved in lifting the whole body than in sitting on a bicycle.
3. Determinations made on treadmills can usually be made on step tests.
4. Hydrostatic changes of blood distribution will play a role as in the treadmill test.

Hettinger and his co-workers (23), in a comparison of several work tests, concluded, "it would seem reasonable to encourage the use of the Harvard step test as a rapid and simple method of assessing physical working capacity." The disrepute into which the Harvard step test has fallen is principally due to the use of recovery pulse rates rather than pulse rates during work as the criteria from which to predict working capacity. When principles of progression similar to those applied to bicycle and treadmill are used, the step test is a valid test of working capacity as Wyndham and his co-workers (62) have shown.

WORK CAPACITY STUDIES

First Problem

The first problem investigated was the comparison of four basic methods to determine whether differences exist. Fifteen subjects aged 13 to 16 were tested on a Monark bicycle using the Åstrand, Sjöstrand, Holman and Balke-Binkhorts-Müller procedures. Each subject was tested a total of nine times with the tests randomly distributed so that practice effects were eliminated from the analysis. The length of the tests varied from four to twenty-four minutes. The Åstrand tests were of six minutes duration using 300, 450 and 600 kpm work loads. The Sjöstrand tests were 18 minutes in length and the loads varied — 150, 300, 450 or 150, 450 and 750 kpm. The Holman procedure started at 0 load and increased each third minute in one test and each fourth minute in the other by increments of 150 kpm. Total time was 24 minutes. The Balke-Binkhorts-Müller procedure consisted of stepwise increases of 150 kpm to a cut-off of 180 beats/min. or fatigue of the legs for the long test and 150, 300, 450 and 600 kpm for the shorter four minute test.

Heart rates were recorded for each minute of work plotted against work load, and the line intra- or extrapolated to heart rate of 170 and 180 to give predicted work capacities at both of these levels.

An analysis of variance shows that there is no significant difference between methods if 180 beats/min. cut-off level is used. This is indicated below in Table 2.

TABLE 2

Source of Variation	Sum of Squares	df	Mean Square	F
Between groups	5275	5	1055	2.00 (N.S.)
Within groups	44514	84	530	
Total	49789	89		

However, when 170 beats/min. is used as a cut-off level, the difference between means is significant at the .05 level.

When inter-method comparisons are envisaged, the 180 beats/min. level seems to be a more adequate point at which predicted work loads should be calculated. At this point there does not appear to be any difference between work tests in which six, four, three or one minute bouts of work are used.

Second Problem

As part of a multiple item fitness battery, the application of the progressive bicycle test with one minute step increases of either 100 or 150 kpm was found to be useful. In general, the test lasts between 8 and 10 minutes before fatigue sets in. The terminal pulse rates range from 160 to 180 and oxygen uptake values are similar to those found when the Sjöstrand test is used (40 ml/min/kg) but lower than those reached on the treadmill (48 ml/min/kg). PWC_{170}'s for 63 untrained young adults between the ages of 19 and 23 averaged 989 kpm on this test. This is similar to that of Swedish army conscripts (1058 kpm) given by Tornvall (59). The PWC of adult business men undergoing regular physical training is slightly higher — 1140 kpm. For trained young men the work capacity value was 1360 kpm. As a short screening method the procedure is effective and efficient (Figure 1).

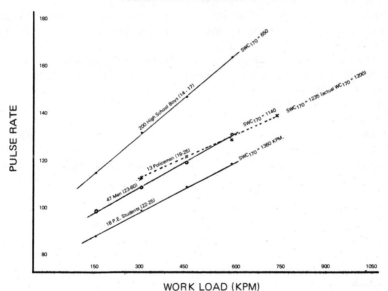

FIGURE I
SUBMAXIMAL WORKING CAPACITY

Third Problem

In an attempt to relate two different methods, e.g., step and bicycle, 63 subjects were given a five minute step test and a progressive bicycle test. Correlation between work capacity and total recovery pulse count was $-.67$. Multiple regression equations were derived for prediction of one test from the score of the other. These equations are:

$$x_0 = 276 - .09x_1 + .6x_2$$

where $x_0 = 5$ minute step test score

$x_1 = $ Work Capacity (PWC_{170})

$x_2 = $ Age

The equation for predicting work capacity from the five minute step test score is:

$$x_0 = 1482 - 5x_1 + 25x_2$$

where $x_0 = $ Work Capacity

$x_1 = 5$ minute step test score

$x_2 = $ Age

Multiple correlation coefficients for the two above equations were .72 and .70 respectively, indicating that only 50 percent of the total variance is explained.

Another method of relating the two tests presented itself in the use of oxygen intake values during both bicycle and step test. Nineteen subjects between the ages of 20 and 27 were tested on a constant load Lanooy bicycle ergometer. Oxygen uptake was monitored on a Dargatz closed system machine that is used extensively in German work physiology laboratories. The test consisted of four minute bouts of pedalling at 300, 600 and 900 kpm with a final bout at the load which would raise the heart rate over 180 beats per minute. Maximal oxygen intakes ranged from 2.00 to 3.85 l/min. Mean PWC_{170} was 1035 kpm.

The subjects also performed two progressive step tests — one in which the height increased every three minutes by three inches from a height of 6 inches to 18 inches and the second in which the height was a constant 12 inches and the speed of stepping increased by increments of 6 steps/minute from 12/minute to 36/minute.

The pulse rate of the final bout of work was divided by the oxygen intake during this period. Comparison of this index showed that the means were practically identical — bicycle, 67.8; speed step, 67.8; and height step, 68.6. The bicycle test correlated .80 with the speed step test and .83 with the height step test. The two step tests were highly related ($r = .88$).

The procedure followed allows for inter-test comparison which seems to be more valid than simply reporting oxygen intakes for any given exercise without reference to the intensity of the effort which produced it.

Measurement of Improvement — Improvements in work capacity and its physiological indicator, oxygen intake, can be measured in two ways. If we can increase the maximal oxygen intake capacity, we should naturally expect to make corresponding increases in working capacity. However, we can become more efficient by using less oxygen for the same amount of work, and thus, improve our capacity to work. The distinction between the ability to take in large amounts of oxygen and the ability to utilize less than maximal levels of oxygen efficiently should be clear. Proper training can improve the efficiency at submaximal levels and can increase the intake of oxygen at maximal levels.

It is generally accepted that maximal oxygen intake is the best measure of an individual's capacity to perform heavy work. However, few of these studies actually relate performance in work to performance in a laboratory (63). The assumption is made that if a subject can continue work for a long time on a laboratory instrument and reach a high level of oxygen intake, he will also be better equipped to perform heavy work for longer periods. The validity of this attractive assumption must be proved. In addition, the assumption that high oxygen intake equals high work capacity has led to another unproved assumption that high oxygen intake equals greater efficiency at submaximal work. Since most people work at submaximal levels for long periods of time, and since it is difficult to reach maximal levels of oxygen intake with many untrained subjects, submaximal tests have been devised and used to predict working capacity/maximal oxygen intake. In other words, a submaximal test is used to extrapolate to maximal work/oxygen capacity, in order to make a statement of a man's efficiency at submaximal working levels. It would be much simpler and probably much more accurate to use a standard submaximal test in standard conditions and use the results as a basis of inter- or intra-individual comparisons.

Fourth Problem

Six professional football players in various states of off-season condition were tested in May before spring training and again after one month of intensive pre-season training. Each subject was given a familiarization ride on the bicycle ergometer. The subject then rested until his heart rate returned to normal and was then tested on the bicycle at a submaximal work load. The bicycle used was an Elma-Schonander ergometer with constant working load at varying pedalling rate constructed according to Holmgren. It consists of a pedalling mechanism similar to that of an ordinary bicycle, the load being a normal separately magnetized d-c generator governed by an electronic regulator and connected to a loading resistance. Within the desired range, the electronic regulator maintains a constant output from the d-c generator irrespective of its speed. The system is dimensioned in such a way as to keep the load and friction losses nearly constant, though the number of revolutions may vary within prescribed limits. By keeping the total losses fairly constant, the mechanical effect delivered to the wheel by the subject also remains nearly constant and independent of the revolutions.

The bicycle test used was submaximal with resistance set at 450 kgm/min at 60 revolutions per minute. The subject was seated on the bicycle and necessary adjustments were made to assure comfort with the respiratory apparatus as well as with the pedalling mechanism. Heart rate was taken at the beginning of the test and each minute for six minutes. Gas samples of expired air were taken at the fifth and sixth minutes of steady state exercise. The O_2 and CO_2 content of the air specimen was determined by the Micro-Scholander technique.

The training methods used were those generally applied in pre-season training camps of professional football teams. One month in duration, the training consists of heavy doses of calisthenics, running and drills. Coupled with this strenuous regime is the high personal motivation of each player to "get into shape and make the team."

In five of the six subjects there was an efficient adjustment indicated by a lower heart rate after training for the same amount of work. The mean gain of 20 beats/min. ($t = 3.45$) is significant at the .01 level. The changes in energy expenditure are illustrated in Table 3. Less oxygen was consumed by each subject for the same amount of work in the post-training test. This difference was significant at the .01 level of significance.

TABLE 3
Oxygen Intake (L/Min./KG) Changes*

	Pre-training	Post-training	Difference T1-T2**
J.R.	.0173	.0116	.0057
G.B.	.0176	.0169	.0007
R.M.	.0160	.0159	.0007
G.D.	.0150	.0120	.0030
R.B.	.0151	.0136	.0015
J.A.	.0142	.0122	.0020
X (N = 6)	.0160	.0137	.0023

*Since there was some loss of weight during the training, efficiency improvements are expressed in terms of l/min./kg oxygen intake.
**S.D. of mean gain = .0014;
 S.E. of mean gain = .00056;
 t = 4.1; p < .01

REFERENCES

1. Aitkins, A. R. and Nicholson, J. D. *J. Appl. Physiol.,* 18: 205, 1963.
2. Anderson, K. Personal communication, Ottawa, 1963.
3. Åstrand, I., *et al. Acta. Med. Scand.* 173: 121 and 257, 1963.
4. Åstrand, P. O. *Acta. Physiol. Scand.,* 25: Suppl. 89, 1951.
5. _____. *Arbeits.,* 15: 21, 251, 1953.
6. _____. *Experimental studies of physical working capacity in relation to sex and age,* Copenhagen, 1952.
7. _____. *Experimental studies of working capacity in relation to sex and age,* Munksgaard, 1952.
8. _____. *Physiol. Rev.,* 36: 307, 1956.
9. _____, and Rhyming, I. *J. Appl. Physiol.,* 7: 218, 1954.
10. _____, and Saltin, B. *J. Appl. Physiol.,* 16: 971, 1961.

11. Balke, B. and Ware, R. W. *U. S. Armed Forces Med. J.*, 10: 675, 1959.
12. Benedict, F. G. Carnegie Inst. Washington, Pub. No. 167, 1912.
13. Bink, B. *Ergonomics,* 5: 25, 1962.
14. Binkhorts, R. and Leowven, P. *Arbeits.,* 19: 459, 1963.
15. Bonjer, F. H. *Ergonomics,* 2: 254, 1962.
16. _____. *Ergonomics,* 5: 29, 1962.
17. Buskirk, E. and Taylor, H. L. *J. Appl. Physiol.,* 11: 72, 1957.
18. _____. Standard Work Tests in Man, Performance Capacity—A Symposium, N. R. C. Washington, 1961.
19. Cureton, T. K. *Am. J. Physiol.,* 155: 431, 1948.
20. Dahlstrom, H. *Svenska läh - sällsk forhandl.,* 46: 944, 1949.
21. Erickson, L., *et al. Am. J. Physiol.,* 145: 391, 1946.
22. Gross-Lodermann, H. and Müller, E. A. *Arbeits.,* 9: 454, 1937.
23. Hettinger, T., *et al. J. Appl. Physiol.,* 16: 153, 1961.
24. Hill, A. V. and Lupton, J. *J. Physiol. Proceed.,* 56: 321, 1922.
25. _____. *Quart. J. Med.,* 16: 135, 1922-23.
26. _____, *et al. Proceedings of the Royal Society of London,* Series B., Parts I-VIII, 1924.
27. Holman, W. *Der Arbeits-und Trainingsernflus auf Kreislauf und Atmung,* Darmstadt, Steinkopff, 1959.
28. Holmgren, A., *et al. Acta. Medica. Scand.,* 162: 99, 1958.
29. _____. *Scand. J. Clin. Lab Invest. Suppl.,* 24. 1956.
30. _____, and Mattson, K. H. *Scand. J. Clin. Lab. Invest.,* 6: 137, 1954.
31. Karrasch, K. and Muller, E. A. *Arbeits.,* 14: 369, 1944.
32. Kelso, L. E. A. and Hellebrandt, F. A. *J. Lab and Clin. Med.,* 19: 1105, 1934.
33. Knipping, H. W. *Ztschs. ges. exper. Med.,* 66: 517, 1929.
34. Krogh, A. *Skandinav. Arch. f. Physiol.,* 30: 375, 1913.
35. Lanooy, C. and Bonjer, F. H. *J. Appl. Physiol.,* 9: 499, 1956.
36. Lehman, G. *Praktische Arbeits. Thieme,* Stuttgart, 1953.
37. _____, and Michailis, H. *Arbeits.,* 11: 376, 1941.
38. Linderholm, H. *Acta. Medica. Scand.,* 163: 61, 1959.
39. Long, C. N. H. *Proceedings of the Royal Society of London,* Series B, 99: 167, 1926.
40. Margaria, R., *et al. Am. J. Physiol.,* 106: 686, 1933.
41. Mitchell, J. H., *et al. J. Clin. Invest.,* 37: 538, 1958.
42. Müller, E. A. *Arbeits.,* 9: 62, 1935.
43. _____. *Arbeits.,* 10: 1, 1938.
44. _____. *Arbeits.,* 10: 67, 1938.
45. _____. *Arbeits.,* 11: 211, 1940.
46. _____. *Arbeits.,* 11: 732, 1941.
47. _____. *Arbeits.,* 14: 271, 1950.
48. _____, and Gross-Lordemann, H. *Arbeits.,* 9: 619, 1937.
49. Nöcker, J. and Bohlau, V. *Münch. med. Wschr.,* 97: 1517, 1955.
50. Robinson, S. *Arbeits.,* 10: 251, 1938.
51. _____, *et al. Science,* 85: 409, 1937.
52. Rutenfranz, J. *Entwichlung und Beurleitung der Körperlichen Leistungsfähigkeit bei Kindern und Jugendlichen,* Basel, New York, Karger, 1964.
53. _____, *et al. Arbeits.,* 20: 294, 1964.
54. Rhyming, I. *Arbeits.,* 15: 235, 1953.
55. Sjöstrand, T. *Acta Med. Scand. Suppl.* 196: 687, 1947.
56. Strandell, T. *Acta. Medica. Scand.,* 174: 479, 1963.
57. Taylor, C. *Am. J. Physiol.,* 142: 200, 1944.
58. Taylor, H. L., *et al. J. Appl. Physiol.,* 8: 73, 1955.
59. Tornvall, G. *Acta. Physiol. Scand.,* 58: Suppl. 201, 1963.
60. von Döbeln, W. *J. Appl. Physiol.,* 7: 222, 1954.
61. Wahlund, H. G. *Acta. Med. Scand.,* 132: Suppl. 215, 1948.

62. Wyndham, C. H., *et al. J. Appl. Physiol.*, 18: 361, 1963.
63. —————, *et al. Arbeits.*, 24 102. 1967.
64. Zuntz. *Arch. f. Anat. u. Physiol.*, Suppl. 1899.

In the Future

PROBLEMATOLOGY OF EXERCISE PRESCRIPTION*

BRUCE J. NOBLE
University of Pittsburgh

ABSTRACT

A conceptual model which offers a more rational approach to the generation and utilization of knowledge in physical education was presented. The
major components of the model were: a mechanism which facilitates the
flow of knowledge from basic research to practical application; a mechanism
for continuous interaction between the research process and the body of
knowledge; and, provision for study of the research process per se. Problematology, a branch of the science of Zetetics, was discussed as it relates to
the ordering of research behavior. Six categories and 22 items having relevance to exercise prescription were identified. A pattern sentence was designed and a computer program written so that each combination of items
could be structured in alphabetic form as a problem statement by the computer. Nine hundred seventy-two problems were generated in one problem
catalog. "Noise" contributed to the elimination of 648 problems. Of the remaining 324 problems, 64 were categorized as high priority. Using exact
duplication as the problem solution criterion none of 76 documents retrieved
and reprinted were found to be directly relevant.

INTRODUCTION

Knowledge is increasing exponentially. The knowledge curve not only
points to the "beauty" of modern technology and research interest but con-
comitantly to the "beast." On the one hand, vast resources provide man-
kind with great expectations for the solution of his problems. On the other
hand, the rapidity with which knowledge multiplies makes its retrieval and
utilization more difficult. Physical education, not unlike other fields, finds
itself at the banks of the knowledge Rubicon. To cross, that is to continue
to contribute to the generation of new knowledge, brings an irrevocable commitment to the solution of the knowledge problem. Not to cross predicts a
future of decline.

The purpose of this paper is not to discuss the knowledge problem and
its solution per se, but to present a conceptual model which offers a more
rational approach to the generation and utilization of knowledge in physical
education. In addition, and more specifically, this paper will describe and
demonstrate one technique for ordering research activity in physical education — Problematology.

*Special thanks is extended to: Chester Page and the University of Pittsburgh Com-
puter Center for assistance with computer operations (partial support from NSF
Grant G11309); Robert Robertson and Michael Goldberger for their diligence in
information retrieval; and Kathleen Zatko for her secretarial assistance.

The Need for New Approaches to Research Activity

The relevancy problem in educational research illustrates the paramount need for developing new approaches to research activity. Research output (knowledge input) in physical education which results in the production of end products utilizable in the gymnasium or on the playfield would be the exception rather than the rule. This laboratory-life gap requires an innovative bridge which coordinates the seeking skills of the research worker and the disseminating talents of the practitioner. Gilbert (2) stated "it is the neglect of systematic arrangement of the intermediate activities which is the major reason for the impotence of the research effort." Intermediate activities involve the development of basic research knowledge into educational packages which can be implemented within the school environment. This development will probably not be accomplished by either the research worker or the teacher but by a developmental specialist familiar with the problems and techniques of both. Similar job classifications have proven successful both in industry (2) and in agriculture (1). (The information explosion represents another problem which threatens the efficiency and productivity of physical education research and requires new approaches. Attempts to solve this problem will be discussed by Dr. Sherman in a subsequent paper.)

Problem selection is still another factor which affects the efficiency and productivity of research. Tykociner (3) lists five known methods of selecting research problems:

1. Individuals do what they feel inspired to do.
2. Individuals choose to do what they feel capable of doing.
3. Groups at various universities take up what appears to be the most promising problems in the most fertile fields.
4. Groups at existing research centers choose programs suitable for the manpower and equipment they have at their disposal or can muster.
5. Tasks are selected strictly for definite defense purposes, for economic advantages, or in line with governmental policies.

In each of these methods, and others that might be listed, subjectivity, rather than objectivity, dictates the selection. The ultimate value of knowledge generated by physical education requires more ordered behavior.

Problematology

Zetetics, the science of research, offers one approach to be taken by individuals, laboratories, or fields to systematize its research activity, i.e., the study of itself as it generates, develops and disseminates knowledge. Joseph T. Tykociner, the originator of Zetetics, has subdivided the science into eight categories. One of these categories is problematology. Its purpose is to study research problems with respect to their origin, systematization, delineation, and selection (3).

In 1931, Tykociner and Paine (4) developed an objective procedure for generating problems. First, a number of known entities in one problem area were identified. "One then groups the entities into categories, and, finally, sets up schemes called outlines for generating combinations of one entity from each category so that each combination produces a problem title. The totality of all such combinations then represents a series of interconnected problems" (3). The generated problem catalog is then examined to determine which problems have been solved and the remainder rated with regard to immediate and future interest.

Problem catalogs can benefit all research workers, but are of particular value to graduate students who sometimes find their lack of familiarity with the literature and inability to identify significant problems as a frustrating experience. Examination of problems, problem priority lists and compatible literature will be a stimulation to scholarship.

Storage of problem catalogs is probably a function of the library; however, until such time as this function is assumed individual investigators, laboratories, or departments must accept the responsibility. It is possible that, in the future, national research centers will generate and store problem catalogs for the entire field.

Violation of creative instincts and desire of individual expression is not thought to be a by-product of the order which problematology brings to research efforts. On the contrary, problematology is designed to stimulate creativity by pointing out previously undetected relationships between various parts of knowledge. Many argue that accidental decisions and/or some mysterious insight which causes a leap in the right direction, often proves to be the most fruitful problem selection technique. Tykociner states that "these leaps (sometimes called frog leaps) often prove to be just haphazard jumping from one possibility to another, without any guide whatsoever, and in most cases ends in frustration" (3).

FIGURE I
Model for Research in Physical Education

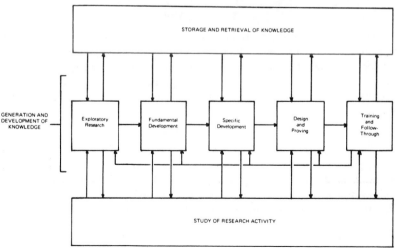

A Model for Research in Physical Education

An attempt has been made to incorporate the following components into a single model: a mechanism which facilitates the flow of knowledge from basic research to practical application; a mechanism for continuous interaction between the research process and the body of knowledge; and, provision for study of the research process per se. Figure 1 illustrates this model.

Parts of this model have been implemented in the organization of the Human Energy Research Laboratory at the University of Pittsburgh.

The central portion of the model pictures the flow of knowledge horizontally through various stages from initial exploration through training of personnel to implement it. Flow is probably not continuous, i.e., knowledge enters storage from any stage for later retrieval. One laboratory may not carry the knowledge through all the developmental steps, i.e., knowledge from one laboratory can be retrieved from storage by another and continued for one or more stages. Continuous communication between stages is essential for maximal development of knowledge. It should be noted that as many as five different research competencies are called for in this model. Gilbert (2) describes the exact nature of each stage and the corresponding research competencies which are necessary.

The upper portion of the model illustrates the storage and retrieval of knowledge. Such a system requires specialized library skills and equipment, but is inseparable from the research process itself. Fast and efficient access to documents or abstracts facilitates research output immeasurably. It should be noted that several levels of knowledge are represented in storage depending upon the research stage from which it is reported. The lower portion of the model illustrates the continuous study of the research process as it generates and develops knowledge. Study includes both the physical and psychological research environment. In addition, concentration is placed on the development of abilities required for research and the selection and formulation of problems.

THE PROBLEM

The main purpose of this investigation was to demonstrate the application of computer technology to the generation of a comprehensive problem catalog (i.e., collection of all possible problem titles) in one specialized area of physical fitness research. A secondary purpose involved a search of appropriate literature to determine the solution status of each problem generated.

METHODOLOGY

The general problem area to which this study was restricted was exercise prescription. Type of exercise was limited to continuous movement, e.g., walking, jogging, or running. All problems were to be experimental-longitudinal studies conducted over a six month period. Problems were also limited to normal, highly motivated, middle-aged men.

Utilization of problematology in the research process involves the following steps:

1. Examine indices, bibliographies, abstracts, tables of contents, etc. to identify the major categories and sub-categories (items) associated with the problem area of interest.
2. Organize the categories and items in outline form and assign each an appropriate symbol.
3. Use combinatorial algebra to determine the total number of problems to be generated.
4. Construct pattern sentence and use computer to generate the problem catalog.
5. Enter problems into information retrieval system to determine solution status.
6. Examine the problem catalog to determine priorities for future study.

Table 1 shows the categories selected for study along with associated sub-categories called items. Categories I, II, IV, V, and VI were independent

TABLE I

Problematology Categories and Items

	Category	Symbol	Item
I.	Exercise Intensity (distance/unit time)	a.	5 miles in 60 minutes
		b.	5 miles in 40 minutes
	$m = 9$	c.	5 miles in 20 minutes
		d.	3 miles in 60 minutes
		e.	3 miles in 40 minutes
		f.	3 miles in 20 minutes
		g.	1 mile in 60 minutes
		h.	1 mile in 40 minutes
		i.	1 mile in 20 minutes
II.	Exercise Frequency (days/week)	A.	5 days per week
		B.	3 days per week
	$n = 3$	C.	1 day per week
III.	Response Variables	1.	Electrocardiogram Response
	$0 = 2$	2.	Maximum Physical Working Capacity
IV.	Subject Somatotype	a.	Ectomorph
	$p = 3$	b.	Mesomorph
		c.	Endomorph
V.	Subject Age	A.	35-44
	$q = 2$	B.	45-55
VI.	Subject Physical Condition	1.	Average
	$r = 3$	2.	Poor
		3.	Good

variables while category III served as the dependent variable. As mentioned in the previous paragraph, categories and items are selected from known factors which have a bearing on the problem area of interest. Combinatorial algebra was utilized to determine the number of combined items and there-fore problems:

$$N = m \cdot n \cdot o \cdot p \cdot q \cdot r$$
$$= 9 \times 3 \times 2 \times 3 \times 2 \times 3$$
$$= 972.$$

Each combination was assigned a master symbol which designates the combination of items utilized (e.g., a A 1 *a A 1*, a A 1 *a A 2*, etc.).

The IBM system 360, model 20 was programmed, utilizing the linked list procedure, to systematically generate the 972 problem statements. A com-plete sentence was constructed in core by manipulating four lists. One list contained the basic pattern sentence. The second and third list contained the parameters and parameter values (words), respectively. The fourth list was an index which monitored position in the pattern sentence at any given moment.

The basic pattern sentence was constructed as shown below:

The objective of this study is to determine the effect of a continuous-movement prescription of (*Exercise Intensity*) on a (*Exercise Fre-quency*) basis, on the (*Response Variable*) of highly motivated male (*Subject Somatotype*) between (*Subject Age*) years of age in (*Subject Physical Condition*) physical condition.

Each problem statement was analyzed to determine "noise" and prob-lem priority. "Noise" constituted those problems which could be judged on their face value as unnecessary to study. The priority (high or low) of each study was determined on the basis of both empirical and experimental evidence.

Several information sources were utilized to determine the solution status of each problem. The documents located in the Physical Activity Research and Development Information System (PARADIS)* were searched. Also, *Index Medicus, Completed Research in Health, Physical Education, and Recreation,* and the *Research Quarterly Index* were examined to locate additional document titles. Problematology items were used as descriptor terms. Document titles, abstracts, or the first and/or last paragraph (extract) were examined to identify relevance. Documents with possible relevance were retrieved and reprinted. This investigation used a criterion of exact duplica-tion to identify solution status.

RESULTS AND DISCUSSION

It should be noted that the categories and items utilized in the develop-ment of the exercise prescription problem catalog were selected primarily for demonstration and secondarily for practical relevance. Focus was placed

---

*PARADIS is located in the Human Energy Research Laboratory, University of Pitts-burgh.

on technique, problems, and potential uses rather than direct application of the problem catalog.

Table 2 shows examples of the 972 problems generated by the computer. Of the 400 titles originally reviewed 76 were thought to have possible relevance and therefore were retrieved and reprinted. None of the 76 documents analyzed met the criterion of exact duplication.

The total number of problems was reduced to 324 because of "noise" or the discovery that some items could be combined. Item c was eliminated because it represented a work intensity too difficult for middle-aged men (5 miles in 20 minutes). Items g and h were eliminated because they were judged to be too easy (1 mile in 60 and 40 minutes, respectively). The response variables (1, 2) were combined since they both could be easily monitored in the same test.

TABLE 2
Examples from Total Problem Catalog (N = 972)

Symbol	Problem Statement
a A 1 a̲ A̲ 1̲	The objective of this study is to determine the effect of a continuous movement prescription of 5 miles in 60 minutes, on a 5 day per week basis, on the electrocardiogram response of highly motivated male ectomorphs between 35 and 44 years of age in average physical condition.
a B 2 a̲ A̲ 1̲	The objective of this study is to determine the effect of a continuous movement prescription of 5 miles in 60 minutes, on a 3 day per week basis, on the maximum physical work capacity of highly motivated male ectomorphs between 35 and 44 years of age in average physical condition.
e B 2 a̲ A̲ 2̲	The objective of this study is to determine the effect of a continuous movement prescription of 3 miles in 40 minutes, on a 3 day per week basis, on the maximum physical work capacity of highly motivated male ectomorphs between 35 and 44 years of age in poor physical condition.
e B 2 b̲ B̲ 2̲	The objective of this study is to determine the effect of a continuous movement prescription of 3 miles in 40 minutes, on a 3 day per week basis, on the maximum physical work capacity of highly motivated male mesomorphs between 45 and 55 years of age in poor physical condition.
i C 2 c̲ A̲ 1̲	The objective of this study is to determine the effect of a continuous movement prescription of 1 mile in 20 minutes, on a 1 day per week basis, on the maximum physical work capacity of highly motivated male endomorphs between 35 and 44 years of age in average physical condition.

High priority status was assigned to 64 studies while low priority was assigned to 260. Items given high priority were: a, b, e, f (offered a reasonable stress to a middle-aged man); A, B (one day per week frequency not validated in literature to offer sufficient stimulus); b, c (weight problem of mesomorph and endomorph more critical in middle age); 1, 2 (average and poor physical conditions were judged to be more critical problems than good condition). Items A and B remained unchanged. The high priority combinatorial equation is presented below:

$$N = m \cdot n \cdot o \cdot p \cdot q \cdot r$$
$$= 4 \times 2 \times 1 \times 2 \times 2 \times 2$$
$$= 64$$

Several information retrieval problems were encountered in this investigation which were not atypical of user-system interaction. First, the need for a thesaurus is apparent. Attempts to match the items (descriptor terms) used in the problematology with terms used in the literature were difficult because of the multiplicity of terms having similar meanings. Secondly, the need exists to transpose exercise intensity factors into equivalent form so results can be compared, i.e., foot pounds, watts, kpm, etc. Thirdly, parts of several articles were found to be relevant but none were exactly relevant. Extensive scientific experience is necessary to evaluate the solution status of problems from extracts of several documents. Lastly, document titles are often misleading. Scientists must be trained to provide titles which are compatible with the terminology of information retrieval and problematology.

Although this investigation used a criterion of exact duplication to identify the solution status of each problem, other criteria are possible. "The generalizations obtained by the solution of an important problem may reduce many others to obvious special cases whose solutions then become predictable" (3). Likewise the solution of one problem may be predictable on the basis of results of several other investigations.

REFERENCES

1. Clark, D. Phi Delta Kappa. *Third symposium on educational research.* Bloomington, Indiana, 1962.
2. Gilbert, T. F. A structure for a coordinated research and development laboratory. In Robert Glaser (Ed.), *Training research and education.* New York: John Wiley & Sons, Inc., 1965.
3. Tykociner, J. T. *Outline of zetetics.* Urbana, Illinois: Electrical Engineering Department, University of Illinois, 1966.
4. —————, and Paine, E. B. Classification of research problems on dielectrics. *Ill. State Acad. of Sci.* 24: 300-9, 1931.

DEVELOPMENT OF A MECHANIZED SYSTEM FOR RETRIEVING PHYSICAL ACTIVITY INFORMATION

MICHAEL A. SHERMAN
University of Pittsburgh

ABSTRACT

A tentative design was established for a mechanized (computer-operated) system for the storage and retrieval of information about selected aspects of human physical activity. Seven factors for consideration in system design were isolated from the literature of information science and technology. These factors were: (1) design objectives, (2) costs and expenditures, (3) information-processing operations, (4) performance requirements, (5) physical requirements, (6) compatibility with others systems, and (7) environmental properties. Procedures were developed for acquisition and analysis of source documents, control of terminology, recording results of analysis, storage of source documents, analysis of user questions, conducting searches for relevant documents to answer questions and delivery of search results. Eventual information services to local users in physical education, medicine (cardiology) and occupational and environmental health include Key-Word-In-Context index for current awareness, selective bibliographies, abstracts and interpretive summaries of research.

INTRODUCTION

In recent years, the scientific and technical literature in various fields has been flooded with information about human physical activity. This cascade of information comes from the expanding number of research centers concerned with understanding the process of man in motion as well as the human and environmental factors which affect and are affected by this process. Such productivity is valid evidence of the evolution of a physical activity science. Like his colleagues in other areas of science, the physical activity scientist is quickly learning that productivity has its price. That price is the information explosion which has made it increasingly difficult to exploit recorded knowledge. As stated by Kent (5), the publication of books, articles and documents is increasing at such a tremendous rate that no one individual can locate all that is published, read all that is located, recall all that is read or process for later recall all that is of potential interest.

Thus, the physical activity scientist has a real dilemma. On the one hand, he requires a constant stream of information to support his unique system of motivation, intelligence and creativity and to help him make critical decisions about the design, execution and evaluation of his research. On the other hand, he cannot afford the time, money and effort involved in a thorough search of the relevant literature. Some scientists have delegated literature-searching duties to their laboratory assistants and graduate students. Others have resorted to verbal communications with members of their work team and other formal and informal organizations. Surprising as it may seem, many scientists are beginning to show indifference toward the use of libraries and information centers.

A preliminary journey through the literature of information science and technology revealed three significant trends toward more "streamlined" information services. First, innovations in computer and communications technology have made it possible to automate many of the traditional library operations. Second, many professional societies have established specialized information centers, document depots, abstracting and extracting services and selective dissemination units. Third, the desire to share rather than duplicate information resources has given powerful impetus to the formation of national information communications networks. Which of these new developments, either singly or in combination, will be most beneficial to users of information about human physical activity?

PURPOSE

The purpose of the study was to design a mechanized physical activity information retrieval system at the Human Energy Research Laboratory, University of Pittsburgh. A mechanized information retrieval system is an organization of men, machines and other non-conventional tools which processes information in such a way that it will be conveniently accessible to future human users (6). The word "information" is used as a designation for printed documents such as books, journal articles and reports. The information-processing functions or units operations of the system are described in a subsequent section of the paper.

REVIEW OF LITERATURE

The concept of information retrieval was introduced in 1945 by Bush (2) who created a fictitious machine called MEMEX. It was a device in which an individual stored all his books, records and communications. By pressing out a code on a keyboard, desired information would be projected on a viewing screen. MEMEX had a tremendous capacity for information storage because of its ability to reduce printed material photographically. In a period of ten years after the "invention" of MEMEX several small-scale information retrieval systems were developed using relatively inexpensive tools such as the marginal-hole punch card and the electromagnetic card sorter (3). In 1955, a Russian scientist named Cherenin (6) predicted that a new revolution would soon occur in the storage and dissemination of data. He visualized an elaborate network of information storage and retrieval centers. At that time all of the technical components for such systems were available but no significant steps were taken immediately to implement them. But, the launching of Sputnik by the Russians (1955) stimulated generous federal support for the development of mechanized information storage and retrieval systems. In 1964, the National Library of Medicine began operating MEDLARS (Medical Literature Analysis and Retrieval System), a man-machine system that produces recurring bibliographies, demand bibliographies and the *Index Medicus* (4).

With support from the National Science Foundation, the Library of Congress established the National Referral Center for Science and Technology. This center has initiated a publications program that includes a Directory of Information Resources in the United States covering physical, biological and social sciences. Other government-related information centers are the Clearinghouse for Scientific and Technical Information (U.S. Department of Commerce), the NASA Scientific and Technical Information Facility and the NIH Child Health and Human Development Information Center. The Federal Government has already started a public information system for education (7) called ERIC (Education Resources Information Center) which continues to add educational subjects to its coverage of document collecting, indexing, announcement and distribution. In physical education, Michigan State University developed the Basic Information Retrieval System (BIRS) in support of a curriculum development project conducted with the cooperation of the Battle Creek Public Schools (8). The newest trend in information retrieval is the national network which interconnects individuals, systems and organizations engaged in a common pattern of information exchange over such communications media as telephones, teletype and television. In the Summer of 1966, 181 members of the Interuniversity Communications Council (EDUCOM) met to consider whether an advanced educational network using all media, from digital transmission to color television, would make American higher education more efficient and more economical and improve the quality of instruction and research (1).

METHODS OF RESEARCH

The design of the information retrieval system involved development of a plan for the arrangement of stored information, information-processing operations, personnel, machines and other non-conventional tools. The development of an acceptable plan proceeded according to the following steps:

1. Identification of factors considered in system design;
2. Identification of questions related to design factors;
3. Identification of alternative answers to questions related to design factors; and
4. Establishment of a tentative model for a mechanized information retrieval system.

The identification of design factors and related questions was accomplished by a review of the literature in information science and technology, participation in a graduate course in mechanized information retrieval, communication with information retrieval specialists (particularly, Professor Allen Kent, Director of the Knowledge Availability Systems Center at the University of Pittsburgh) and development of several marginal-hole punch card systems.

Alternative answers to design-related questions also came from the literature as well as from discussions with a restricted sample of local scientists, educators and students who represented potential users of physical activity information. Once the alternative answers were specified several decisions were made as to which were most suitable for the proposed system. These decisions were made using the "role playing" technique. With this method, the system designer assigns to himself the role of typical user and extrapolates from his own information requirements and experience in developing the system. This technique is not recommended for the designer of a larger system since, in most cases, the usual result is that the system suits the designer's needs but not those for whom it is designed.

RESULTS

Seven general factors for consideration in the design of a mechanized information retrieval system were discussed regularly in the literature. These factors and their related questions are presented below.

Factor I: Design Objectives

1. What motives underlie the design of the system?
2. What quality, scope, speed and economy of services are needed?
3. Who are the potential users of the system?
4. What are the subject-matter interests of potential users?

Factor II: Costs and Expenditures

1. What are the capital costs for acquisition and analysis of documents and purchase of a search medium?
2. What are the operational costs for conducting searches and for provision of services?
3. What are the costs involved in *not* providing suitable services?

Factor III: Unit Operations

1. What are the major classes of actions required to meet objectives?
2. What man-machine interactions are required to perform these actions?

Factor IV: Performance Requirements

1. What source documents should be included in the system?
2. What specific subject-matter should be covered in source documents?
3. What kind of training is essential to prepare personnel to perform unit operations?
4. What degree of detail is required in analysis of source documents?
5. What is acceptable precision of service (ratio of pertinent to non-pertinent documents) for the system?
6. What is acceptable speed with which unit operations are performed?
7. What is acceptable speed with which service is provided?

Factor V: Physical Requirements

1. What kind of equipment is needed?
2. What kind of equipment is available?
3. What form and type of information input is required?
4. What form and type of information output is desired?
5. How much space is available for the storage of documents and placement of equipment?

6. What provisions are necessary for security of stored information and equipment?

Factor VI: Compatibility

1. How will the system interconnect with other systems such as campus-based systems, specialized information centers, document depots, abstracting services and national communications networks?
2. How will the system support and be supported by similar systems being planned by other universities and professional organizations?

Factor VII: Environmental Properties

1. How will services be sold to potential users?
2. How will changes in user needs, subject-matter and available tools be determined?
3. How will increase in document file size be accommodated?
4. What funds will be required to support projected system growth?
5. How will information services to users be evaluated?

A tentative system model was developed. It consisted of eight information-

TABLE I

UNIT OPERATIONS OF AN INFORMATION RETRIEVAL SYSTEM	
Unit Operation	Definition of Unit Operation
1. ACQUISITION	Location, selection, ordering and receiving materials for a collection.
2. ANALYSIS	Perusal of materials and selection of analytic terms of probable importance for retrieval.
3. TERMINOLOGY CONTROL	Establishment of arbitrary relationships among analytic terms as revealed in dictionary definitions.
4. RECORDING RESULTS OF ANALYSIS	Transcription of analytic terms onto card, tape, film or other searchable medium.
5. STORAGE OF SOURCE MATERIALS	Physical placement of materials in some location, either in original form or copied onto a new medium.
6. QUESTION ANALYSIS AND SEARCH STRATEGY	Expression of question or problem, selection of analytics in terms of a particular search mechanism, and arrangement into a configuration that represents a probable link between the question as expressed and the materials on file as analyzed.
7. CONDUCTING SEARCH	Manipulation or operation of the search mechanism in order to identify materials in the file.
8. DELIVERY OF RESULTS	Physical removal or copying of the record from the file in order to provide it in response to a question.

processing or unit operations (see Table 1). The objective of the system is to provide articles from scientific journals, in response to requests, dealing with selected topics in the physiology of exercise and training. These topics are: (1) acute and chronic responses to physical activity, (2) evaluation of physical fitness and physical work capacity and (3) prescription of physical activity. Potential users of the system are scientists, educators and students in physical education, medicine (cardiology) and occupational and environmental health.

The acquisition policy requires regular location of relevant articles from about 150 journals, most of which are listed in the AAHPER's annual publication of *Completed Research in Health, Physical Education and Recreation.* The location operation is performed by eight members of the staff at the Human Energy Research Laboratory. Each relevant article is duplicated by Xerox process. The articles are read and points of view are selected which are considered to be of sufficient probable importance to the subsequent searching operation. These points of view are analytic or descriptor terms. The descriptor terms for each article are then compared with terms listed in an exercise physiology thesaurus. If a particular descriptor term appears in the thesaurus, it may be entered into the system. If it is not located in the thesaurus, it may be added or eliminated as a relevant analytic. The bibliographic information and key descriptor terms for each article are recorded on IBM punch cards. Each card is assigned an accession number which corresponds to the number assigned to the original article. The duplicated original articles are then placed in a central file. All of the above steps, from acquisition to storage of articles, are the input operations of the system.

The output operations start with the generation of a question or problem by a user. The question is examined by the system analyst, who is expert in exercise physiology, to ascertain whether it contains descriptor terms compatible with those already in the system. The next operation is to select a search strategy (or search prescription) which will maximize the chances of exploiting the contents of the central file. The IBM card deck is then manipulated by a card sorter to physically isolate cards containing each desired aspect requested via the search strategy. The accession numbers on the isolated cards are then listed and distributed to the user. Finally, the user goes to the central file, extracts the identified articles and reads them to determine their actual relevancy.

DISCUSSION

At the present time, the physical activity information retrieval system is in the primitive stage of development. The most advanced operation is the acquisition process which has already located and secured over 250 articles. Many of these have been analyzed and will be ready for entry into the system in the near future. An expansion of services to local users will include such features as a Key-Word-In-Context (KWIC) index for current awareness, selective bibliographies, abstracts of journal articles and interpretive summaries of research. A program to train graduate students to perform acquisition and analysis operations is also being planned. In order to answer several major questions related to the suitability of information services provided by the system, there is a need for continued study of the needs and interests of users and the relevancy of services.

The development of the physical activity system within the Human Energy Research Laboratory is running parallel to efforts of other mission-oriented groups at the University of Pittsburgh. A strong local movement is the development of a campus-based information system which would involve interaction among academic and professional school faculties, the Library, the Computer Center, the Knowledge Availability Systems Center and the Office of Communications Programs. The campus-based system represents an interdisciplinary approach to the provision of information services to universities, industrial organizations and other non-profit organizations in Western Pennsylvania.

From the developmental history of other specialized information systems, it is safe to predict the eventual formation of a national, computer-based network for improving services to users of information about human physical activity. Such a network might involve the exchange of graphic records, numerical data, films, cards and other magnetic media, all pertinent to the art and science of human movement. The birth of this network is dependent upon cooperation among several universities and professional organizations which desire to share information resources. The burden of responsibility for solving the information explosion problem lies squarely upon the shoulders of the scientist. It is now time for him to lead the fight for improved information services, not only for his own security, but for the benefit of his disciples.

REFERENCES

1. Brown, George W., and others (Eds.). *Interuniversity communication council (EDUCOM): report of the summer study on information networks.* New York: Wiley, 1967.
2. Bush, V. As we may think. *Atlantic Monthly* 176: 101-8, 1945.
3. Casey, R. S., and others. *Punched cards.* New York: Rhinehold, 1958.
4. Cuadra, Carlos A. (Ed.). *Annual review of information science and technology.* (volume 1). New York: Interscience Publishers, 1966.
5. Kent, Allen. *Specialized information centers.* Washington, D.C.: Spartan Books, 1965.
6. _____. *Textbook on mechanized information retrieval.* New York: Interscience Publishers, 1966.
7. Marron, H., and others. A novel concept in information management. *Proceedings of the 30th annual meeting of the American Documentation Institute.* New York: Thompson, 1967.
8. Van Huss, Wayne. The role of information retrieval in curriculum development. Paper presented at symposium on innovations in curriculum design for physical education. University of Pittsburgh. Pittsburgh, Pennsylvania, February 7, 1969.

FUTURE DIRECTIONS IN PHYSICAL EDUCATION RESEARCH

PAUL HUNSICKER
University of Michigan

ABSTRACT

The paper is concerned with an overview of research efforts in physical education over the past two decades and with selected suggestions for future avenues of research.

The first part of the report will be devoted to a brief coverage of the advances that have occurred in the period indicated with documentary data on the nature of the research efforts. Additional comments are directed at the methodology, instrumentation and sampling employed. A major emphasis is directed at a criticism of the research efforts during the past 20 years including statements as to where we have been remiss. As one form of yardstick, comparative statements are interspersed indicating rates of advance in other disciplines. The final portion of the report deals with areas of research which need exploration and which should prove fruitful.

INTRODUCTION

I recently read a statement attributed to another Michigan professor regarding future trends. This appeared around the turn of the century, "whereas the horseless carriage would probably someday be perfected, its means of power would definitely be steam because the internal combustion engine was entirely impractical." Fortunately, Henry Ford and General Motors didn't take the remark seriously; I hope my view of the future comes closer to the target.

The 20th century, and in particular, the last two decades have been marked with the greatest production of research and knowledge known to man. In a climate so favorable to the extension of scholarly frontiers practically all disciplines benefit. Let us examine briefly what has happened in physical education and make a few comparisons with other areas of investigation. This will be followed by some critical evaluations of our efforts, with suggestions for areas of future investigation.

In an analysis of the *Research Quarterly* over the last 20 years, one thing stands out; namely, that an overwhelming number of the papers are in physical education rather than health education or recreation. It can also be stated that statistical techniques including tests and measurements, physiological and motor performance research comprise roughly 70 percent of the contents. About another 17 percent are surveys, mechanical analyses or sociological investigations. The remaining 13 percent are distributed over 10 different areas with a mere handful in history or instrumentation. From this rough breakdown a few things are evident. If one uses the criterion of number of articles in the *Quarterly*, the tests and measurements teachers and the physiology of exercise people have been the most productive. While under-

273

graduate courses in the history of physical education, administration, methods and curriculum are usually required, the research production in these areas has been surprisingly sparse. To add to the disparity, one could examine the articles in the *Journal of Applied Physiology* and the *Journal of Sports Medicine and Physical Fitness*. Suffice it to say, the gap would widen!

Looking at research efforts from another viewpoint, there has been an increase in the number of departments offering graduate work and the number of schools with laboratory facilities. Unfortunately the two have not paralleled each other and some schools have entered the graduate field with courses that have the intellectual challenge of a cigarette commercial. Despite the inequities in graduate offerings, we do have better laboratory facilities available today than we did in 1949. Not only are there more laboratories in existence, but the hardware available in the laboratories has changed more in the last 20 years than in the previous history. Most of this can be traced to the growth of bioengineering, biomedicine or the space program. The fact that the federal government has been spending increasingly larger sums of money for research has also aided this development. As an example, the National Defense Education Act in its 10 years existence provided three billion dollars to buttress American education from kindergarten through graduate school. Additional funds from the National Institutes of Health have aided in laboratory development. While physical education might not have enjoyed its due share over the decade, we are beginning to make inroads into these sources.

Probably no area has advanced as fast as our ability to digest and analyze data. A little over 20 years ago I can recall Marie Boddy doing statistical work on a desk calculator for Professor Cureton's book, *Physical Fitness Appraisal and Guidance*. Today's computers would churn out the work in a fraction of the time. (Of course, I don't believe Marie, like any graduate student, would have any more free time. Tom would just expect more of her!)

While the hardware for handling data has improved drastically and there are studies using more sophisticated statistical techniques, there are still too many research papers employing incorrect analysis procedures. To compound the error, the sampling techniques have frequently been horrendous. I'm reminded of the admonition given early investigators doing animal research, "don't kill the second cat." No research worker should overlook his obligation to be in a position to generalize from his results. Isolated findings, like family motion pictures, attract a limited audience. You have to kill the second cat.

The advances in biochemistry, in communications media, in photographic and radiology techniques, in transportation, in computers, in medicine, in biology, and a host of other fields have outstripped the progress in physical education. It is not the main purpose of the paper to belabor our failures of the past, but to suggest possible avenues for future research.

In presenting topics for tomorrow's research no attempt was made at establishing a priority order although this is a consideration which most research workers face. As an aside, I should point out that one difference between a top-flight research worker and a run-of-the-mill drone stems from the ability to select significant topics. You can keep just as busy tracing the history of a garbage pail as you can running down material to evaluate the work of McKenzie. I don't believe the contributions would be comparable!

KINESIOLOGY

There have been texts and courses in this field since the last century, yet the research production has been virtually sterile. Too many teachers were satisfied with an oversimplified explanation of movement involving the name of the muscle, origin, insertion and muscle action of parts of the body and not enough viewed the action as the end result of a highly complex linkage system where forces had to be synchronized in a sequential order to produce maximum efficiency. Another aspect of movement which has escaped some kinesiologists is the explanation of differences between good and poor performance. After all, it is a basic function of a teacher to point out these differences. Add to this the obvious fact that one reason why a performer is a super star is because he comes through when he is at a mechanical disadvantage. As an example, think of the shortstop going in the hole and making the throw to first. He has to sacrifice mechanical position for time. For him to stand up and take a classical position for throwing the ball to first would be ludicrous. The world of sport is replete with similar situations. What is needed is investigators with the requisite mathematics, engineering mechanics and anatomy to use high speed photography, electromyography and whatever force indicators are necessary to do a thorough analysis of activities. The closest to what I am talking about is exemplified by the work of one of my former colleagues, the late Professor Dempster. One of our own Illini, Richard Ganslen has made a mark in this field. Another example in a popular vein is the book by Cochran and Stobbs, *The Search for the Perfect Swing*.

CURRICULUM

With all due respect to the American Association for Health, Physical Education and Recreation and their attempts to improve professional curriculum, we still need considerable work in this field. At the undergraduate level we point to zoology, anatomy, psychology, etc. when seeking academic respectability for our program. At the graduate level we need a counterpart to the Flexner Report in medicine which was completed shortly after the turn of the century. This represented a landmark in the field of medical education, and physical education could stand a similar study. Since changes seldom emanate from members of the fold, you can't expect to invite in representatives of every course currently extant and expect them to vote out their particular pet. The procedure is doomed to failure at the outset. Drastic revisions call for critical thinkers willing to use Draconian procedures. Don't expect the end product resulting from a convention to be the wellspring of frontier thinking.

PERSONNEL

One of the hallmarks of a profession is that it polices its own. There has been precious little done in establishing criteria for personnel selection. The men have usually been selected because of athletic prowess, and I would hazard a guess that most of the freshmen who have any kind of monetary assistance in our field have been selected because of their high school sports record. We need to develop criteria for attracting students who are interested in teaching physical education. In addition, we should develop indices for the early identification of potential leaders in the profession.

If we turn for a moment to the distaff members of the profession, I believe there have been some hopeful signs in terms of recruiting personnel. We have made progress in dispelling the image of female sports prowess being synonymous with physical unattractiveness. Last year the Miss America contest and the telecasting of the Olympics were giant strides in the right direction. Thinking again of the women, we need some information as to why so few are productive in research and how we can interest them in this area. They can't all be elementary specialists, and we are losing brain power by attracting so few.

HEALTH AND FITNESS

Despite the fact that there is a considerable volume of research currently available, much remains to be done.

Cooper's *Aerobics* was directed at quantifying exercise and more is needed in this field. It is my contention that one of the reasons doctors have been reluctant to prescribe exercise stems from their inability to quantify dosages. They don't have the same problem with pills. Energy cost information is needed along with desirable levels of dosage for different age and fitness levels.

The late President Eisenhower's initial heart attack did much to stimulate research in exercise and coronary heart disease, but the findings today are by no means definitive. At all meetings concerned with this topic the question of the risk factors involved in having a post-coronary exercise program is raised; however, I would also like to raise the question of how many people do we condemn to early cardiac episodes by not advocating exercise? The entire question of regular exercise as a preventive measure against disease needs exploration. The work that Montoye is doing in the Tecumseh Project is one example of this line of investigation.

While it is relatively simple to identify selected diseases, we need some indices of low grade misery or lack of social vitality. You know what I'm referring to — what the ad man calls the blahs! Let's face it. Millions of dollars are poured into pills to offset the condition. Can regular exercise contribute anything to alleviate the malady?

Remember, there is a quality factor to life. On a number of occasions I have facetiously remarked, "stay fit so you can dissipate."

There are other relationships between exercise and health which are more subtle to delineate. How does the fitness level affect decision making? Will the pilot of a supersonic plane be in a better position to react in an emergency if physically fit? How about the statesman's ability to make decisions at a summit meeting, or the surgeon at work? These are admittedly tough to isolate, but they are food for thought.

A closely related question comes to mind when one examines Eli Ginzberg's three volume work, *The Ineffective Soldier*. How many of the 2,500,000 "ineffectives" during World War II would have benefited from early physical education programs or special programs while in service? Conceived more broadly, what kind of an impact does the fitness level of the nation have on the effective manpower available? It seems like a legitimate avenue of research for those interested in health. Parenthetically, it is particularly disquieting to search the *American Journal of Public Health* in hopes of finding anything relating to exercise. For coverage in this area it stands out as a monumental Sahara.

There has been almost a continual procession of research studies telling us that regular exercise will increase strength or improve scores on physiological tests, but little, if any, light has been shed on how to motivate people to exercise. If I were to single out the problem whose solution would contribute the most to the fitness of the nation, it would have to be this one. And it is merely one example in the relatively virgin field of how do you affect human behavior. The possibilities are endless.

GROWTH AND DEVELOPMENT

There is a dearth of information based on national samples on the physical and motor skills of boys and girls through the growth years. We need guidelines in motor skills development comparable to the concept of reading age or carpal age in growth and development studies. We also need research indicating when a child is ready for certain activities. Curriculum committees are forced to do considerable "blind flying" without these data.

Closely allied is the problem of coping with individual differences. The prospect of even larger numbers of students in future classes makes it mandatory that research be directed at seeking answers to this challenge. I submit the thesis that the discipline which most effectively provides stimulating experiences to the entire spectrum of individual differences is the discipline doing the best job.

HISTORICAL AND SOCIOLOGICAL

There has been a recent awakening in the historical and sociological aspects of sports, and it is obvious that additional work is needed in these areas. Sports, like art and music, are a universal language and it should certainly prove fruitful to examine ways of unifying different cultures through this media.

RESEARCH COORDINATOR

To assist in the development of the interdisciplinary approach to research we need to train some professionals with a broad enough background to see the possibilities of various disciplines and be in a position to coordinate the efforts of research workers in different fields. Without this talent at the helm, interdisciplinary research results frequently resemble the proverbial camel, which surely must have been the work of a committee.

There is need for a National Institute of Sports Research to guarantee the accumulation of archives of research data and to develop long-range research studies that could conceivably be carried out over several lifetimes. Such an Institute could also serve as a clearing house for disseminating research findings. One of its functions could be to bridge the hiatus between research findings and the teacher and to continually work at informing the public and school administrators of the role of physical education. The future pressures for the educational dollar are going to increase and our profession has a long way to go to convince administrators that the money should be spent in this area in preference to other demands. Certainly at the university level the required service program faces a dubious future. Admittedly, part of this pressure is the result of the climate of the times. The students want a choice in selecting their programs. In the long run this could have a salutary effect on our offerings. We would at least be meeting what they perceive as their needs.

My thoughts have been entirely confined to the immediate future and I have purposely avoided reference to some of the more exotic possibilities connected with aerospace travel or underseas living. These are targets for a future date.

(I would be remiss if I did not make reference to Professor Cureton. A few of you may know him better than I do, but, none owe him more. I want to pay my respects and extend my thanks to Professor Cureton, whom I shall characterize as the "indefatigable international trail-blazer of Physical Education.")

REFERENCES

1. Dempster, Wilfrid T. The anthropometry of body action. *Annals of the New York Academy of Sciences* 63: 559-85, 1955.
2. Ewald, William R., Jr. *Environment and change.* Bloomington: Indiana University Press. 1968.
3. ————. (Ed.) *Environment and policy.* Bloomington: Indiana University Press, 1967. Press. 1967.
4. ————. (Ed.) *Environment for man.* Bloomington: Indiana University Press. 1967. Press. 1967.
5. Ginzberg, Eli, and others. *The lost divisions.* New York: Columbia University Press. 1959.
6. ————, and others. *Breakdown and recovery.* New York: Columbia University Press. 1959.
7. ————, and others. *Patterns of performance.* New York: Columbia University Press. 1959.
8. Kahn, Herman and Wiener, A. J. *The year 2000.* New York: Macmillan Co. 1967.
9. Machlup, Fritz. *The production and distribution of knowledge in the United States.* Princeton: Princeton University Press. 1962.

COMMENTS

Henry Montoye

Dr. Hunsicker has touched upon a number of interesting topics and has stimulated the thinking of all of us. I would like to comment on just a few points. I must agree with our speaker. We need a "Pharmacopeia of Physical Exercise." We know, for example, that if a limb is immobilized or if one lives under reduced gravity, the bones will lose calcium. Muscles surrounding or pulling on a bone are likely needed to maintain circulation to the bone. Some exercise is needed but how much?

Dr. Hunsicker spoke of the need for research in how to motivate people to exercise. As evidence continues to mount, showing the importance of regular exercise in preventing or delaying chronic degenerative disease, our medical colleagues will look to the physical educator for techniques of motivating people to be physically active. While serving on the Fox-Taylor Committee, to which I referred earlier in the symposium, some of the delegates in this room have shared with me the frustration of searching for criteria for selecting middle-aged men who likely would stay with an exercise program and of seeking ways to motivate men to continue a regular exercise regimen. It is not easy to change the living habits of middle-aged men and women; hence, most efforts are dismal failures. I'm sure we should not give up completely on the older generation, but I'm becoming more and more convinced we would be wise to concentrate on the new generation in our schools.

At this point I would like to mention some work which seems very exciting to me. It may be familiar to many of you as some of the data were published in the *Research Quarterly*. It will be "old hat" to Dr. Van Huss because one of his students, Dr. Dale Hansen, played a major role in the study. In this study when 45 rats reached the age of 33 days, they were divided into three groups. For the next 35 days (roughly equivalent to three years in the life span of a human being) the one group of 15 animals (the sedentary group) lived in small individual cages permitting a minimum of physical activity. The other two groups lived in similar cages but were free to run in the gymnasium (i.e. an exercise wheel) when so inclined. The animals in one of these last two groups were additionally forced to swim for 30 min. daily with a weight equivalent to two percent of their body weight attached. During this period, as one might expect, these last animals spent a little less time voluntarily running in the wheels. We also find this to be true with our human subjects in Tecumseh; the men who are active on their jobs spend a little less time in vigorous leisure activities. At the end of 35 days, animals in all three groups had free access to exercise wheels. The results that followed were dramatic. There was little difference in the amount of exercise taken by the first two groups: the sedentary controls and those who had access to the exercise wheels. However, the intensity and amount of spontaneous exercise was much greater in the animals that had been forced to swim. Furthermore, this continued for 180 days (about 15 years in human beings!). These animals had been changed fundamentally in some way — perhaps on the cellular level.

At the University of Michigan a well-respected scientist has trained worms to respond to stimuli. When these worms are cut in half, both halves retain their learning. What is more amazing — when these worms are eaten by worms which have not had this schooling, the unschooled worms learned several times more rapidly — further evidence of a change at the cellular level. (A suggestion frequently heard on the campus as a result of this work is the notion that the professor should be cut up and fed to the students.)

Dr. Hunsicker mentioned the need for research reviews. This is a part of a larger problem of communication among investigators and between the laboratory and the teacher in the schools — between the university and the local community. We are not alone in this problem. A few days ago the local paper in Ann Arbor quoted one of the country's leaders in medical education lamenting the fact that so little effort is being made to transmit medical research findings to the practitioner. I agree with our speaker that we need technical research reviews but we need something more. About one percent of physical educators in the schools are regularly exposed to the *Research Quarterly*. At one time I thought we could change this by training our teachers at the Master's level to read the research in our field. I no longer believe this. Then I thought providing them with abstracts of research might be the answer, but this results in a very biased impression from one or two abstracts in a particular area. Instead, I think we must learn from the agricultural workers. The farmer has applied research done at the university to increase his productivity manifold, and I'm sure he doesn't know a standard deviation from adenosinethriphosphate. This is possible for at least two reasons. He has a county agent close at hand who is a link with the university. Our physical education supervisors, if they were trained to read and interpret research rather than being trained almost exclusively in the mechanics of supervision and administration, could serve as this link in our field. The farmer also has available to him simply-written, non-technical publications based on solid research on almost every conceivable topic from growing beans to canning peaches. These are not technical research reviews. Agriculture has these too, but they are directed at a different audience. We need the non-technical summaries for our teachers.

I'm disappointed with developments at the undergraduate level in physical education in recent years. We've lost ground to "big-time" athletics; mainly, I think, because we've lacked courage. But I agree with our speaker, research progress in physical education is encouraging. When I came here to the University of Illinois a little more than twenty years ago to begin a program in graduate studies, there was almost no other place to go to obtain training in laboratory work related to physical fitness and exercise. To my knowledge, no other department of physical education had a motor-driven treadmill, for example. But today a student may select any one of many centers for research of this kind. Many of these laboratories are represented by investigators present at the symposium; for example, Dr. Balke and Dr. Stoedefalke and their large group at the University of Wisconsin, Dr. Guy Metivier at the University of Ottawa, Dr. Van Huss and Dr. Huesner at Michigan State University, Dr. Skinner and Dr. Buskirk at Pennsylvania State University. There are treadmills now from coast to coast and all of this has transpired in the last 20 years. Dr. Staley, one of the great leaders of my generation, had the vision to see the importance of laboratory work. Dr. Cureton, in turn, had the vision to see the importance of training future investigators besides carrying on his own research.

I wish to comment on one last point. I must disagree with one of the other symposium speakers who implied there is too much animal research in physical education. If it is good work related to exercise, why should a man so inclined not pursue these investigations? Whether animals or human beings are used as subjects, whether the number of subjects is large or small, if the work is carefully and honestly done, the results will fit somewhere into the mosaic of human knowledge.

Wayne D. Van Huss

My response is supplementary rather than critical and follows more specific lines. I mentioned earlier that the research on exercise effects is confusing because exercise is most frequently regarded as a single entity. Exercise programs either have not been precisely described in studies or the programs have been so general that the results have not contributed to knowledge concerning the effects of specific exercise regimens. The tolerance and response differences of the wide range of strains and species used for experimental study are difficult to equate. However, it is well known by individuals experienced in prescribing exercise programs that: (a) in terms of observable physical activity there are many kinds of fitness, and (b) a given fitness mechanism can be altered by specifically overloading mechanism. Thus, distinctly different training programs are designed empirically to develop specific capacities, i.e. oxygen debt tolerance, power or muscular endurance in defined movements, etc. The anatomical and physiological changes resulting from these various programs must be of considerable magnitude to make possible such marked improvements in the specific abilities. These changes, for the most part, remain to be identified. I am referring to the changes produced in the central nervous system, peripheral nerve fibers and endings, muscle fiber sizes, number of myofibrils, muscle fiber enzyme profiles, capillarization in muscles, heart, lungs and in the adrenals, etc., that result for example, from high-intensity short-duration training as contrasted with low-intensity long duration programs.

The relationships of the anatomical-physiological changes produced by the broad spectrum of exercise regimens to health range from speculative to scanty at this time, i.e. the differential effects of the various exercise programs early in life, late in life and continued throughout the life span; and the residual effects of such programs participated in during the pre-pubertal and adolescent years only. From such systematic research efforts on both animals and man a "pharmacopeia of exercise" should result. Negative as well as positive results must be reported if our understanding is to be complete.

Dr. Sherman mentioned information retrieval in his paper. Since we are in the midst of such an explosion of knowledge information retrieval procedures have become a necessity, if one hopes to keep abreast of the research even in a narrow area. Across an entire profession it is impossible. Hardware and functional retrieval programs have been developed. Input, identification of appropriate administrative structure and financing are the current obstacles. A major cooperative effort is needed to implement a quality system for the retrieval of research information for the profession of physical education.

My last two items both require improved information retrieval procedures if they are to be adequately implemented. With all due credit to individuals and various interpretive efforts more interpretive materials are desperately needed by practitioners. Methods of disseminating interpretive materials have lagged behind the acceleration in research. Solutions to closing the gap between research findings and curricular practices must assume high priorities.

Lastly, we need a structure or structures to guide the development of the research basis of this profession in a systematic manner. That is, the body of knowledge underlying physical education must be organized. Since the content of the body of knowledge is interdependent with one's philosophical position a number of such structures might be necessary. If one then takes the next step and determines the *status* of the body of knowledge, *a structure for the selection of applied research problems on a priority basis is in hand*. To determine status one must document and classify statements into proved, controversial, or speculative categories and the curriculum developer if he is to proceed must make judgments in the controversial and speculative areas. Wherever judgments are necessary in the absence of adequate data, areas needing applied research have been identified. With new evidence the body of knowledge should be revised, providing a plastic model which would mature systematically. Curricular changes should be based upon such changes in the body of knowledge.

Thanks to the efforts of Dr. Cureton and his contemporaries in training research personnel, with the second and third generation Ph.D. offspring we now have a fine body of sophisticated young research workers across the country. As a profession we have matured to the point that our underlying body of knowledge should be developed and maintained in a systematic manner.